M000119213

Other Books by Dusty Thompson

A Gone Pecan
(A Cady McIntyre Mystery)

Almost Odis

My Preppy Life with My Redneck Dad

Dusty Thompson

authorHOUSE

AuthorHouse™
1663 Liberty Drive
Bloomington, IN 47403
www.authorhouse.com
Phone: 1 (800) 839-8640

© 2018 Dusty Thompson. All rights reserved.

No part of this book may be reproduced, stored in a retrieval system, or transmitted by any means without the written permission of the author.

Published by AuthorHouse 12/21/2017

ISBN: 978-1-5462-1993-4 (sc)
ISBN: 978-1-5462-1992-7 (e)

Library of Congress Control Number: 2017918619

Print information available on the last page.

Any people depicted in stock imagery provided by Thinkstock are models, and such images are being used for illustrative purposes only. Certain stock imagery © Thinkstock.

This book is printed on acid-free paper.

Because of the dynamic nature of the Internet, any web addresses or links contained in this book may have changed since publication and may no longer be valid. The views expressed in this work are solely those of the author and do not necessarily reflect the views of the publisher, and the publisher hereby disclaims any responsibility for them.

To my father, Terryll Odis Thompson, Jr.
Whatever my level of Odis, I wouldn't be me
without you and I love you, Old Man

&

To my brother, SMSgt Ryan Thornton
Thompson (US Air Force)
It's not the only reason I wrote another book,
but I'm truly sorry I forgot you in the last one

Acknowledgements

First of all, thank you to **Liz Shellman**, for the idea to start a blog in the first place. Thank you to my sister, **Shontyl Thomas**, for reading this more than once, including while on vacation. You remain my sounding board and I love you. Thank you to my best friend, **Christopher Ramsey**, and my accountability partner, **Jamie Newman**, for your editing, advice, and encouragement. To my extra-sparkly unicorn of awesomeness who inspires me every day to believe in myself, achieve great things and fight the patriarchy, **Dr. Melissa Bird**, thank you for being in my life. And to the Master of All Things Fabulous and my fashion (and life) mentor, **Matthew 'LaDenckla' Denckla**, thank you for being so slow at getting ready for that gala, stranding me in your living room where I met Dr. Bird (and hubby **Jimbo,** the Army Vet/Marine Biologist) and for keeping me soaring by telling me continuously how amazing you think I am. A big rainbow hug to my best friend since 1986, **James Williamson** (and the esteemed **Mark Hertel**) for the support, encouragement, shameful remembrances of youth, and five-star hospitality in Palm Springs while I rested, shopped, ate, watched Netflix and also wrote a little. To my volunteer editor, **Bill Duch**, thank you for your thoughts on the difficulties in caring for an elderly parent; I had truly second-guessed myself until I talked to you. To the majestic **Countess of Long Beach** and her benevolent husband (otherwise known as **Gary Michovich and Henri Winters**) for the friendship, food, frivolity and general fanciness. I know you didn't read the book, and probably won't unless it's on tape, but whatever, I'm not mad. I just want to be in the will. Three Queens. Just saying.

And a very special shout out to the cast and crew of the **San Buenas Writer's Retreat** in San Buenaventura, Costa Rica. To my classmates and new friends (**Michelle Halverson (and husband Chris), Ray Aguilera, Tom Shaw, John Kapelos** and **Zach Roz**) thank you for your encouragement and feedback and laughter and great stories and not judging me for vomiting into a Wal-Mart bag on the very first day. *Pura Vida*, y'all! To my host with the most, the intrepid **Nick Halverson**, thank you for a level of hospitality, passable Spanish and machete-ownership unmatched in the US. To my teachers, the inspiring, supremely talented, ceviche-loving **Ezekiel Tyrus** and the gonzo disliker-of-all-things-tropical (except drinks) **Will Viharo**, I say, "*Salud!*"

To the group of wonderful women who have mentored, loved, supported and watched out for me throughout my life and career: **Wendy Thompson, Perrilyn Moore, Andra Thornton, Karen Everding, Arilla Boughton, Jeanne Johnson, Kendra Entrop, Payton Jackson, Hannah Thompson, Denise Wood Davenport, Juliann Wood, Emily Myers Garner, Paige Mills, Sharon Hillman, Terri Parker, Nita Gross, Elaine Cooper, Kathy Caldwell, Becky Gustin, Belinda Corley, Diane Sicuro, Jackie Collins, Marion Felix-Jenkins, Melissa McQuillen,**

Stevi Stevison, Ysok Schofield, Angie Harrington, Holly Hayes, Chandra Lake and **Deborah Windham** and my mentor/mama, **Dr. Billie Jane Randolph**. Words aren't enough.

Finally, a huge thank you and I love you to **Benjamin Nalzaro, Jr.** Your gentle prodding, editorial questioning and support have made this book, and my life, immeasurably better than I imagined. I've waited for you for twenty years and it was worth it. You make me happier than I thought was possible. I have all I ever wanted; this book is just icing on the cinnamon roll I'm not supposed to eat, but will enjoy, nonetheless.

My father has a peculiar habit when he answers the phone. He doesn't say "Ahoy" like Alexander Graham Bell preferred, "Hello" like the average American or even, "Ah-hello" like many from my childhood in the Deep South. Instead he repeats one of two phrases; either "Maggie's Mule Barn, Biggest Ass speaking" or "Joe's Pool Hall, Eight Ball speaking". I don't know why. Now that he is familiar enough with his Jitterbug cell phone to see that I am calling, he occasionally personalizes his greeting, with, "Hey, JD", his childhood nickname for me. It references Jefferson Davis Hogg, from the *Dukes of Hazzard* TV show in the 1980s as I was a chubby child, one of the things I have in common with The Dad. According to him, I also wanted a white suit like Mr. Hogg, which is not a taste The Dad and I share.

I call him The Dad as I often felt I was playing the part of The Son, when I was growing up. Like I had been cast in a play about a family with whom I felt some, but not complete, connection. Of course, that has changed since I'm an adult, but it kept The Dad, for many years, in the category of a character with the playbill descriptor, 'sharing DNA and the belief I am adopted', an oddly theatre-specific description for someone who graduated from a high school with no creative arts program outside of marching band.

1

Don't get me wrong, I enjoy theatrical productions as much as the next person; however, I am only theatrical in the sense that I am sometimes more dramatic than is necessary in everyday life.

I was born the middle child of nomadic Southern Baptists who left the wilds of Louisiana and traversed the rest of the geographical area known to TV weathermen as Ark-La-Tex. When I bemoaned my status as the middle child, my parents would remind me I was the oldest son, but I held onto my birthright as #2 of 3 like a raccoon with a shiny penny. I am named after my father. I am Dustin Terryll, he is Terryll Odis, Jr. I came perilously close to being Terryll Odis the third, God bless my sainted mother for standing her ground. Terryll, even with its constant mispronunciation as Tuh-rell instead of Teh-rull, I could deal with; Odis, I could not. The name Odis, for me, carries a connotation of a level of backwoods upbringing that you can never truly escape. My family is from the country, not the hills from where the 'billies' come. In my mind there is a vast difference. I'm okay with being from the country; I would never be okay with anyone thinking I had ever been a redneck.

When referring to my father I call him The Dad; when I talk directly to him it's Old Man or Pater. Of course, this is only as an adult. When I was growing up I referred to him as Sir, but not in the formal British way. It was more in the deferential way you speak to someone like an Army Drill Sergeant. The Dad is a former Army paratrooper and he can be a little intense, especially with his oldest son. I refer to my childhood as my military service.

Growing up you might not have imagined I would be who I am today, but I don't think you'd have been too surprised that I ended up somewhere outside of the south and in a profession where a suit is required. I've always been a bit different from those with whom I share DNA. I am an unabashed preppy raised among Wrangler-clad farmers and cowboys. Most of the men in my family have been farmers, carpenters or welders with the occasional preacher. Physically I am very much like my family. From my mother, I inherited small eyes which almost disappear when I smile and a love for Jesus. My father gave me short legs, a fiery temper and the ability to make people laugh. Both gave me a love of music and reading. When you put all the pieces together you should get a tried and true good ol' boy, an Odis, if you will. You're supposed to, but you don't. Instead you get me, an Almost Odis; a southerner to be sure, but one whose disdain for the outdoors and manual labor coupled with fashion-focused sensibilities stand in stark contrast to my people.

Other than a penchant for relocation, my family is in most ways typically Southern. We believe in faith, family and fried foods. We cherish Christmas, casseroles and (righteous) condemnation. You might think I am the black sheep in my family, but this would require you to believe I'm a sheep. What I am is more akin to a plaid koala bear somehow thrust into a family of, mostly, white sheep. Of course, we have our fair share of sheep who are both dark gray and black, but no matter how I tried and no matter what I did, I was never a sheep in any sense of the word.

Many people, when they meet me, imagine The Dad as an older version of me clad in seersucker or Brooks Brothers

3

pastel chinos with coordinated shoes and belts. Truth be told, The Dad looks like Uncle Jesse in the original *Dukes of Hazzard* TV show, if Uncle Jesse had red hair and didn't wear overalls. The Dad wears suspenders to hold up his everyday jeans; his dress jeans if he's going to church or out to a steak dinner.

I used to joke the only things The Dad and I have in common are anger management issues and the belief I am adopted, and our differences have been on display most of my life, long before I was even aware.

I have among my belongings a scrap book my mother and I put together many years ago. I looked at it recently when I moved and found a copy of my Kindergarten progress report. It wasn't a report card *per se*, as the nomenclature for grading was S (Satisfactory), I (Improving, but not yet Satisfactory) and N (Needs Improvement). I have always tried to excel, even as a child of four and I was proud to see I received an 'S' in 27 of 30 categories. Of the three categories where I received an 'I', two of them were my fault, the third was not. As we had moved three times by the age of four, I should have been given a free pass not knowing my correct address as we had only moved to Winnfield, Louisiana two months before school started. The other two categories where I was deficient were spot on: "Listens While Others Speak" and "Rests Quietly". Silence is not my strong suit.

Eastside Elementary had two reporting periods each school year and at the end of each period, the teacher had an option to write a narrative. Although I had a talking problem, my teacher left the narrative blank at the end of the first reporting period. At the end of the year, although I had improved to 29 of 30 categories with an 'S' and an

S- in "Rests Quietly", Ms. Brewer felt compelled to add the notes, "Needs More Male Influence" with the seeming afterthought "Performs Beautifully". I'm still not sure what she meant or what outcome she expected with those words, but the only change I can remember is I no longer took tap dance lessons or gymnastics classes. Of course, I don't remember being upset about these things. I was five and I had a brother, a sister, Legos, a dog and a tree house. I had no time to be sad; I had only time to play.

I don't remember how The Dad reacted to this information. He was a welder at the local sawmill, but he was home most every night to my memory. He attended church with us more often than in later years and was just a good ol' Southern Dad. True, when he taught me to ride a bike and I ran into a tree and started crying he told me to "Shut it up", but it's just how the men are in my family. The Thompson mantra is "Men don't cry, men don't hug, men provide."

Men also hunt, whether they want to or not. I don't remember The Dad taking me hunting at any time, but to be fair, most hunting was done while visiting my mother's family while The Dad stayed home to work. When we visited my relatives, I was included in all types of hunting (frog, raccoon, deer), due solely to the fact I was a male. I was never asked if I wanted to go, it was just something boys did. There was never an invitation. There was no, "Hey, buddy, want to go kill a raccoon in the dark for no reason?" It was more, "We're goin' coon huntin'. Get Jody (my cousin) to get you some coveralls; it's gonna be cold." They said it, I did it, end of story.

Once when we went deer hunting on Henderson Island in Louisiana and Jody and I were paired up to get into a deer stand and wait for the deer to walk by and then shoot them. You must understand I didn't find anything inherently wrong with killing these deer; it's what they were there for, I had been taught. I grew up in a carnivore's playground. If I was all about the eating, I had to be all about the killing.

While we were waiting in the stand, nature called as she does when you drink three glasses of milk with breakfast, and I found a way, I thought, to fit in with everyone. I decided I would pee in the woods, proudly. In my naivete I thought I was in the clear.

When my uncle walked by and saw me answering nature's call, he said, "What in the blue blazes are you doing, boy?"

"Tee-teeing," I said proudly.

He looked at me, shook his head and said, "C'mon y'all, we've got to find another stand. Dusty peed the deer away."

What? How could I have made a mistake? Isn't this what they wanted? And what did he mean 'peed the deer away'? Was my urine tainted? Did I need medical attention? I know I ate more than my fair share of Spam and crackers the night before, but I was hungry being out amongst all the flora and fauna. If the stench of seven men (well four men and three boys) didn't drive away the wildlife, how on earth could my bodily fluids send Bambi and his pals fleeing in fear?

I won't get into the details of what happened while hunting frogs and raccoons, but as I grew older, the invitations to hunt were reduced to the point where I assumed everyone had simply stopped hunting, which we both know wasn't true.

This was just during the fall and winter. My other-ness was on display in all seasons.

Darkness is how you tell time in the country. It's the dividing line between being able to see (working) and not being able to see (resting). It was just about dark thirty and the children, me included, were being rounded up for baths, supper and bed. While sitting on the back porch, waiting my turn, my uncle approached and instructed me to "go feed Misty (the Shetland pony)", proximity to the barn being the only logical explanation. I have never been a fan of horses, even on a merry-go-round. Carousel horses offered motion sickness; real horses offered a lack of control I found unacceptable.

I feel sure my initial internal response was, "Are you kidding?" My verbal response was, 'Yes, sir" due to the fact I was raised to never question those in authority and authority meant adults, anyone taller than me and my sister, regardless of her height. My second internal response was fear as I walked in the direction of the barn where there was only darkness, where evil resides waiting to attack children traveling alone, or so I had been told, by my sister.

I feel I need to clarify that while I did grow up on my grandparents' farm, it was mostly during summer breaks and all major holidays. Of course, this was back when we got three full months off for summer and a full month for Christmas. I had been around animals but at this point my only previous independent interactions had been making sure I didn't mix a monkey shirt with hippo pants in the Garanimals section of the JC Penney over the river at the mall in Vicksburg, Mississippi. My grandparents' farm was literally on the banks of the river, almost not in Louisiana.

I made my way across the yard with a gait that was an original choreography of actual trepidation mixed with attempted bravery through posture. I imagine I looked like I needed to use the bathroom. Upon my arrival at the pen, Misty paid no attention to me. I opened the gate, remembering to close it immediately behind me, like I had been taught, lest any animals escape. I walked to the little room where feed was housed and scooped a portion using an old coffee can as we are not a family who spends good money buying kitchen implements for animal husbandry purposes. I looked over my shoulder to assess Misty's location and saw her standing, seemingly glaring at me.

I turned to ensure I left no stray kernels of feed and in that instant, Misty turned around and readied her haunches so when I spun around to empty the can into the trough, she kicked me square in the stomach and seemed to laugh as I fell head over heels onto the dirt floor. While I tried to catch my breath, she stood calmly eating her feed beside me. Always one to go with my gut, now bruised, I fled the pen purposefully leaving the gate open in the hopes one of the monsters would come out of hiding and take her in the night.

Filled with the serendipitous athleticism often available to those in crisis, I raced towards the house holding my shirt up to show the now-purpling stomach wound, screaming I had been attacked.

Cut to various uncles, cousins and neighbors chasing a Shetland pony up and down the darkened road wondering, "what's wrong with that boy?"

"He's scared of horses" marked me in more ways than one.

There have been many times throughout my childhood where I was included in all manner of activities it was assumed I would enjoy based solely on my possession of testosterone. Case in point, I have ridden horses many times, never once voluntarily. The summer we moved to Texas, it was determined all the children in the extended family would ride in the Grand Entry of the Bogata (Texas) Rodeo.

For those of you who don't know, the Grand Entry is an opportunity for those who own horses and cowboy finery to non-competitively ride around the rodeo arena while smiling and waving to those who paid for said horses and finery. The horse selected for me was named Ginger and I sat atop her trying to pretend I wasn't scared or planning an escape. Truthfully, the only thing stopping me from fleeing was a fear of heights. What? You get on a horse when you're 4-foot nothing and tell me how far you think it is to the ground.

I sat astride this mare, swathed in ill-fitting denim, resigned to my fate, aglow with perspiration, looking like an overgrown Gerber baby in a cowboy hat and vest, waiting for the start of the procession toward what I assumed would be my death.

An upside for someone bereft of the instincts to control an animal is horses are communal by nature and will travel in herds given the opportunity. I found no major issues simply sitting in place, demonstrating how to wave with my eyes as I was not about to take either hand off the saddle horn, gripping it as tightly as the frog does the stork's neck in the "Never Give Up" cartoon. We made it around the one allotted loop with no issues and I was home free, or so I thought.

When we approached the exit, Ginger decided to turn and follow the horses just entering the arena. We made a second sweep in front of the crowd, then a third. By the fourth go-round, someone had apparently notified the people you notify in these situations and the esteemed Rodeo Queen, Darlene Brooks, wearing a white hat and tiara, appeared at my side, took the reins and led us out of the arena, to the cheers of the crowd. It could have been laughter. They sound the same, don't they?

I was hoping this embarrassment would quell any ideas for future equine events. However, as is the case with my people, getting back up on the horse is not just a phrase, it is a reality. I don't know if it was an alleged pursuit of fun or heat-induced insanity, but I found myself again astride Ginger, this time at home. However, I thought it might be okay as the last time we had simply walked in a circle too many times. I could handle this.

We were moseying along just fine when something happened. I later learned the cinch had broken and the belt had begun to slap her stomach. She took to running full tilt and I didn't know what to do except panic full tilt.

She suddenly stopped running and began bucking like the University of Wyoming mascot, causing me to grip the saddle as I was determined to stay atop my mount. I wasn't trying to be a proper cowboy, I had simply done a quick cost/benefit analysis and believed the possibility of flying with the saddle seemed a better option than certain death via trampling.

Never one to shy away from demonstrating my feelings, I proceeded to let loose a scream so loud, piercing and long the neighbors thought it was a test of the emergency broadcast system. After what seemed like an hour I and the saddle flew over her head and landed with a resounding thud on the parched, cracked summer soil. My scream transitioned immediately into silence as all the breath had been knocked from my Ocean-Pacific clad lungs.

The response from my uncle was, "Woah, Dusty, I think you rode her for more'n 8 seconds! We shoulda put you in the rodeo." Too bad this rodeo wasn't captured on film because I definitely deserved a giant belt buckle for the experience.

1982 was the year my family followed my mother's sister's and semi-permanently relocated into the Red River Valley in Texas and settled in a tiny hamlet, with a population of less than 500 unless you counted horses and crabapples. We didn't actually live in Bogata proper; we lived about seven miles northeast in a community called Fulbright, a misnomer to be sure. Fulbright wasn't full of anything except houses and barns and there was nothing big or bright about it other than the stars at night (clap, clap, clap, clap).

Moving here had been one of those moves common in my family and apparently no one else's; you know the ones where your parents say, "Get in the car we are moving"? I thought so. We became adept at packing an entire house quickly and into relatively small spaces. I promise you my mother could fit the contents of a 3-bedroom house in the back end of a Pontiac Bonneville station wagon, with room left for a cooler of fried chicken, a switch for when we 'smarted off' and my baby brother.

This move was the first one which caused me concern. I've never been one to get nervous around meeting new people and I have no issues with just sort of implanting myself in a new landscape and pretending I had been there for quite some time. And in Bogata, I wasted no time in acquiring a girlfriend (she was cool and played clarinet) and a best friend (he was also cool, and his Dad was the preacher). And it was a great summer, but fall arrived and brought a new activity into my life, football. Having never played before, I was uncertain what to expect but I knew The Dad wanted me to play, as he had throughout school. It was the subject of his fondest memories.

Up until this year, the only sport typically available to youth was baseball, and it was only during the summer. I had participated with a reasonable facsimile of athletic ability from t-ball up through sixth-grade. Full disclosure, I was known for striking out in t-ball and once, while playing left field, got so engrossed in a conversation with someone standing by the fence, I stayed in the outfield while my team batted, and no one seemed to notice, not even the umpire. I feel sure my coach noticed but very wisely alerted no one. The heart of the team I was not; the mouth of the team I was for certain.

I don't remember thinking sports were amazing, but I also don't remember disliking them to any degree. It's just what you did. But something had changed in sixth grade. I had realized I was much less like The Dad than I had previously thought, and I had a sudden need to improve as a son; to be more of who I thought he wanted me to be.

Having only played baseball until now, I had no frame of reference for football; I just knew I had to play. It's what The Son of The Dad was expected to do. In Texas, football is practically a religion. I pledged to be an ardent participant as my feelings were cemented by something The Dad had said on numerous occasions, "Any boy not playing football is a sissy." It would become my mantra and I repeated it several times on the junior high playground to, I feel pretty certain, utter confusion. Macho, I was not; determined, I was.

And I almost dodged the football bullet, but like any Secret Serviceman worth his Bass Weejuns, I leaped in front of it. One of the conversations my mother had with me was concerning our lack of resources. I knew we had suddenly found ourselves without many of the things we were used to and we had to sell our car and truck when we moved but I wasn't aware of the exact level of poverty until my mother said I couldn't play football because we couldn't afford to buy the football cleats. My reaction (tears) wasn't a proud moment for me but I didn't know what else to do. Ensuring The Dad still liked me hinged on the playing of the football with the appropriate *accoutrement*. Of course, not using words like *accoutrement* would probably have helped. Being in the band and an honor student hadn't seemed to work in my favor, at least to my 11-year-old mind.

My mother was never one to allow tears to sway her, but she apparently interpreted them to mean I was desperate to play ball and I was, but not for the love of the gridiron. I wasn't privy to the conversations behind closed doors but apparently due to my implied level of devotion to the game, it was decided my school shoes would be my football cleats and after a trip to The Wal-Mart, I became the proud owner and full-time wearer of athletic shoes. Of course, these were not regulation cleats. They were football shoes designed for short, portly youth to wear other places besides an athletic field; white with maroon stripes and a flap over the laces. If you were to look at my class officer photo from 7th grade (Class Reporter, thank you very much), you will see me wearing a short-sleeved button-down, overly-tight Wrangler jeans and my football cleats.

What could I do? When you are lacking in resources and you gain weight, you simply wear the clothes you have and lose either (1) weight or (2) concern over your appearance. Of course, I was hyper-aware of my appearance, but I was certainly not about to modify my eating habits. I had to play sports. Athletes need biscuits and gravy.

And I feel certain my mother was confused and disappointed as my passion for football was not evident in my performance or lack of restraint in complaining about two-a-day practices and football in general. You would imagine I would not cry out loud; I would keep it inside, like Melissa Manchester taught us, and learn how to hide my feelings. You would be wrong. For some reason my fear of ostracism never outweighed my desire for martyrdom. No, sir, I had a need to be as dramatic on the outside as I felt on the inside, which I'm sure only alarmed and/or annoyed those in my general vicinity, which included The Dad.

At the end of the season during eighth grade, I decided I had enough and did not want to play any longer. I mustered the courage to tell The Dad I wanted to quit, and his response upset me. He didn't get angry or yell or anything like I thought he would. He simply stopped talking to me and turned his attentions to my brother. I felt like a disappointment from that moment forward.

I remember on more than one occasion him asking my mother, "What's wrong with that boy?" It was a question I asked myself over and over and over again. Of course, I knew the answer, but I was too afraid to say it out loud. If I said it, then it was true. If I ignored it, maybe I could figure out how to change it.

In 1986, the summer between my sophomore and junior years, we moved to Tylertown, Mississippi. I graduated high school and started college drifting further and further from The Dad. Our relationship, admittedly weak, wasn't buoyed by his obvious (to me) favoritism of my siblings over me.

In Tylertown, I seemed to have found my place. I had plenty of friends and had as much fun as you can in a town with one red light and no Wal-Mart. Even here, there were a couple of times where I was called 'gay' and threatened physically. Outside of those few instances, self-esteem was tied more to anticipated, rather than actual, ostracism.

I graduated and started attending the local junior college as I was far too scared to attend any college with a population larger than Walthall County, of which Tylertown was the county seat. Walthall County boasted a population of only 17,000 people, in the entire county, at least in 1988.

I thought things might be different in college and I was actually very popular and well-liked, having been elected Freshman Class Vice President and Class Favorite; it's the South and we love our superlatives. But it only takes one person to try and make you unhappy. It's easy to say, "Don't let them get you down" or "They are just unhappy" or

"They are projecting". I would like to believe it but it's not necessarily true. Do I really think the guy calling me a faggot is himself gay and projecting? No, I do not. We'd graduated to different language by then as our vocabularies in high school and college are much more sophisticated. He is being mean because it's what he's been taught. Hatred is learned.

Was this verbal abuse constant? No, but it didn't soften the blows when it happened. Did The Dad still call me names? No, but it's hard for a kid to forget the bad stuff. You can get used to a certain level of self-hatred where it's almost impossible to recognize much less address. Don't get me wrong, I knew my Mother loved me and I had to believe deep down The Dad did; it's a rule when you are a parent. You have to love your kids. Of course, I figured, you didn't necessarily have to like them.

By my sophomore year in college, I had pushed myself to be anything and everything I could. At the time I was Student Body President, Co-Editor of the yearbook and had been elected Campus Favorite. I should have felt on top of the world, but I didn't because there were several guys on the football team who called me faggot and queer for reasons known only to them. It was not lost on me there was a pattern developing. It became such an issue, I moved out of the dorm and back home during my final semester. I don't remember what excuse I gave my parents.

Expecting a teenager to self-perform psychotherapy is ridiculous at best and dangerous at worst. However, as an adult I realized The Dad just doesn't know how to show affection other than through buying people things.

The summer after my freshman year in college, he and my Mother saved up and bought me a brand-new car. I had wrecked my first car driving to Vacation Bible School commencement at my church. (I feel the need to establish Jesus-adjacent context). My previous car was a '73 Mustang II; you know the one that looks like a Pinto? This car was a Nissan Sentra and I thought it was the most awesome gift in the history of gift giving. Growing up in various stages of lower and middle class, The Dad had gotten a job off shore and we were doing pretty well. I had always exaggerated our wealth as I was embarrassed to be poor. I know people saw right through me, but I was naïve enough to believe they believed me. And I was so proud of that car. I felt I was finally just like everybody else. The lies were becoming true, at least some of them.

One of the things my family does not discuss is my stent as a basketball cheerleader in college. I understand it was not something they considered manly, but they were more than the opposite of proud I chose to do this. By this time, I realized I was not the son they had necessarily wanted and felt lucky my brother had showed up four years after me with superb athletic skills and I could just go be my weird self. Being that person had its costs.

After a basketball tournament, I was about to leave campus when I stopped by the dorms to get an assignment from one of my friends as I had moved home. By the time I got back to my car, someone had carved the word FAG in the hood with a broken beer bottle. First of all, who would do something like that? Second of all, how could I let my parents see it?

I had to take the rest of the bottle and assist this bully in destroying the nicest thing I had ever owned. It remains one of the most difficult things I have ever had to do. Since we could barely afford the car, I had no insurance or money for a new paint job. I had to drive the car for another two years with the constant reminder there was apparently something wrong with me. Something so bad it drove others to vandalism.

And the curtain fell, and time passed.

I graduated from college, attended graduate school and started working for the Department of Veterans Affairs in Biloxi, Mississippi, at the age of 27. I got my first apartment and took my first steps to eke out a career in federal healthcare.

My mother had been sick for several years and when she died in March 2000, at the age of 55, it shook our family to the core. My brother and I were both living in Mississippi, he in the Air Force with a new family and me living in a small apartment on the beach. My sister lived in Austin, Texas with her husband and two children. My father and mother lived in an apartment in Brownsboro, Texas.

I've always lived in an apartment. Even when it was a 2,000 square-foot loft in Massachusetts, it was still an apartment. It never occurred to me I would have a house as no one in my immediate family had owned a home without financial difficulties. It was just something I wasn't willing to risk. When my mother died, The Dad began the geriatric equivalent of couch surfing even though his financial means had not changed. He had decided for some reason he could no longer afford the apartment he and my mother shared, and he stated he needed to move in with someone. When I questioned how he suddenly couldn't afford the apartment, he insisted. When I pointed out he had afforded it with two people living there with only one income, he told me to drop it; he was the father and I was to respect his decisions.

Not fully understanding the level of orneriness my mother managed to keep under control, he stayed with various siblings of his and my mother's until they either asked him to leave or he got mad/offended by something and left on his own. Most times he would arrive at the next home with no warning and simply state, "I'm moving in." This happened continuously for the next eight years.

Once my brother and his family had returned to the US from stints in Australia and the Azores (off the coast of Portugal) and settled in Colorado, The Dad called me one day and asked me to inform my brother he was moving in. I called and said, "Congratulations, it's a boy!"

He lived with them for almost 18 months until they were re-assigned to Hawaii. He left there and returned south to his sister Louise in Alabama.

Since my mother's death, I had called The Dad every Saturday to check in with him and he spent much of those conversations complaining about whoever he was living with at the time. He wasn't happy with anything.

When I was offered housing as part of my recruitment package for the position I had accepted at the VA Medical Center in Palo Alto, California, I was excited but hadn't given much thought to what I would do with all the extra space.

Once I arrived in the San Francisco Bay Area, in June 2011, I realized the house was far too large for one person. I briefly considered inviting The Dad to live with me, but I wasn't sure how to even broach the subject.

The Dad is a proud man. He would rather demand something than have you offer it. I discussed it with my sister who told me I would regret it. I held off for another month or so. Each time The Dad and I spoke, it made me a little sadder for his living situation. He was sharing a two-bedroom trailer with five other adults, sleeping in his recliner in the living room and I had sent money more than once to help spray for roaches.

In July, I prayed about it and before I could change my mind, I called and invited him.

My sister reiterated her assessment I would regret it and I admitted I would be thinking the same thing had she mentioned a similar plan, but I felt very strongly my mother would want me to do the right thing and honor my father.

Admittedly, I didn't really know The Dad and having experienced several episodes at different Christmases where we switched roles and I became the parent and he the child, I wasn't sure how we would be able to co-exist in one house. We are related, albeit different. Our similarities are physical, our differences philosophical. However, we are both adults and adults can be adults, right?

I have a wonderful friend from Texas named Liz Shellman. She is loud and funny, and we bonded over our own craziness as well as the craziness of our families. Once when she was visiting me, on a work-related trip, I took her and several friends to a fancy steakhouse in Palo Alto.

While we were eating, the singer Toni Braxton walked in and sat at the next table. Of course, I tried to play it cool and pretended I didn't see her. I am nothing if not completely at ease around famous folks. Liz looked and immediately starts to sing, *Unbreak my Heart* at top volume, with no shame.

When I mentioned my plans to invite The Dad to live with me she laughed and said, "Woo, Dusty Thompson! You're gonna live with your redneck Daddy! You have to write a blog about it!"

It never occurred to me to do something like that. As hip as I like to think I am, technologically I am more *Golden Girls* than *Girls*. A blog was an interesting idea. I enjoy telling stories and nothing makes people laugh more than stories about me growing up as the plaid koala bear in my family.

I asked her, "Do you really think people want to read about The Dad and me?"

She said, "Lord, yes, Dusty. It's like a redneck version of *Frasier*."

So here you go; *Frasier*, if they were from Mississippi but lived in California and Frasier wasn't rich and, well, just read it.

September 7, 2011

He has arrived with Recliner and Dog

The Dad is *en route* to my house today. He left his sister's in Alabama on Friday and I am not so much having second thoughts as simply running through scenarios in my head about how this will work exactly. I haven't lived with my family since I left for graduate school at the age of 23. It's not like I don't have anything in common with my father; we share oddly short legs, weird feet and the belief I am adopted. I am definitely more like my mother. The Dad is a good ol' boy in every sense of the word. There are many things on which our opinions and belief differ: money, religion, hygiene and style are just a few. Books, food and laughter are among the very few areas where we can find common ground, although as a diabetic you would think he would avoid sugar more than I, but you would be wrong.

He just arrived sipping a Mountain Dew because diet drinks "taste funny". I titled this blog 'Penny Loafers at the Rodeo' as it encapsulates the inherent differences between us. I have actually worn penny loafers to a rodeo. He hasn't worn penny loafers, ever I don't think.

When he arrived, his truck was completely packed like the Joad's escaping the Dust Bowl, y'all. He had purchased a tarp to protect his belongings including a power wheelchair, recliner, suitcases and a four-wheeled walker. It had seen better days weathering the rain and wind from Tropical Storm Lee as he drove from Alabama through Texas on his way here.

I almost laughed but then it hit me he has two different pieces of equipment to help him get around. I keep forgetting he's old y'all. Old like the Pope. He turned 70 in July and it's odd to see him in this light.

I remember him as the strong, loud, slightly scary man who I always viewed with a mixture of fear and respect. He wasn't a very loving man in the sense of those Dads from those 80s TV commercials; he wasn't and still isn't a hugger. But he did show love in the ways he knew. He would buy me things he thought I would like. He would have my Mother cook my favorite things when I visited home. He would make jokes, sometimes at my expense, just to make me laugh. He did love me, but I was much too dramatic (in an overblown 90210 way) to recognize he was doing the best he could with a son he truly didn't understand.

I guess it's come full circle. He didn't know what to do with me, but he let me stick around for as long as I needed and now it's my turn. I've just got be sure to have enough Febreze; he seems to smell like 'old man'.

Somebody throw up a prayer!

Saturday, September 10, 2011

More Funk than George Clinton

Other than an exponential increase in toilet paper usage that would indicate the arrival of a small family of refugees, the routine hasn't been a huge adjustment. I guess it's because we are in the vacation phase of any move. You know, the time when you don't actually feel like you've really moved; you just feel like you're on vacation? I mean, we've eaten out and shopped which is typical of the agenda when anyone visits me. We've been thrift store shopping and shoe shopping (it's been a long time since I ran across anyone not homeless who only had one pair of shoes) and grocery shopping.

One thing he has shared more than I would have liked is his, shall we say, aroma. The array and frequency of the discharge from his person is both frightening and awe-inspiring. Like if you saw Queen Elizabeth on the toilet. Now, I hoped I wouldn't have to devolve into so pedestrian

23

a topic so soon but as I write, my eyes are burning a bit and my trusty Febreze bottle is gently weeping next to me. We are working overtime and making little headway to curtail the fragrance in the room that has recently been designated a Hot Zone by the EPA.

I'm not trying to be mean; it's not like I am without sin in this arena, but this funk has grown like an over-caffeinated kudzu, people. And it's keeping me on my toes too. Each and every time he gets up from his chair, which is fairly often due to his water pills, I leap into action like those NASCAR crews. I jump up Febreze bottle in hand and spray like one of those aggressive perfume-tester girls who used to inhabit fine department stores nationwide. I try to ensure I finish the job before he comes back; I don't want to be rude. Of course, he has caught on as his chair is a bit moist when he sits again. I almost had him convinced the moisture was from him, but he very sagely concluded it had to have been "your little smell good squirty bottle" as he would "...never pee myself. I might dirty myself if I farted too hard..." I'll spare you the remainder of his musing.

We are having a good time, I must admit. It's been fun to show him "my world", as he calls it. I keep forgetting he hasn't seen any place I've ever lived since I moved from Biloxi in 2002. I always saw him at my sister's, my brother's or his sister's. We've shopped for a number of things from bath mats to ice trays because he has an issue with drinks that don't look cold enough. He makes his hems and haws about me not doing anything special for him, but I know he enjoys it and so do I. I love to find a bargain and that I can immediately brag about it is priceless. We both got shoes (tennis and house) yesterday and then I broiled pork chops and steamed some veggies for supper. I thought about trying to avoid obvious instigators like broccoli and onions but seeing as how oxygen and water apparently make the man gassy, it's a fight I shall lose dear friends. Like Custer at his last stand if the Native Americans smelled like feet and butt.

After supper we watched *Cops*, looking for relatives. I'm kidding, of course. But as the TV got louder, I took leave to my room to gather my thoughts. I never realized how quiet I actually am at home. I rarely make noise, and this is the first time I've had cable in more than 4 years, so I've never watched this much TV. I've survived with Netflix and I read a lot. He reads as well, but with the TV going in the background. He's like the teenager I once was without the aggressive derision, but definitely with the odd clothing choices.

He's decided he wants to find himself a fedora or a top hat.

When I asked why he said, "I want people to look at me when I walk by".

I asked, "Are you saying they aren't looking at you now? Because I assure you, they are."

He said, "Won't a fedora make me look cool?"

I replied, "No. Not even a little bit. Now pick up your teeth and put them in your pocket until supper."

I'm kidding of course, but only about the teeth.

Thursday, September 15, 2011

Suspenders and a Hospital Gown

Having an elderly parent move in with you is not like getting a roommate. It's like adopting a teenager with habits that reach back to the 1950s, y'all.

He did ask me to put him on a diet. I explained that losing weight is not a matter of dieting; it's a lifestyle change. He seemed nervous with that choice of phrase, but I have been able to show him, in just a few days, how to do portion control and stop eating once you are no longer hungry, not waiting until you feel full. I forgot how many of those rules I let slide because just monitoring my intake since last Tuesday, I've lost 2 pounds. Once he gets under 300, we can weigh him and see how much he's lost. I'm not being rude; my scale only goes up to 300 pounds.

And his requests for meals have been oddly specific with the expectation they will all be filled post haste or even sooner. Meatloaf and lima beans, which I found at a German place; catfish, hushpuppies and banana pudding, which I found across the street from my neighborhood no less. It's a good thing that I am the king of the culinary treasure hunt. He has requested hamburger steak and even though I found a place that has smothered steak with rice, he said it's not the same because he wants potatoes, not rice.

Considering he's living on the West Coast and not Alabama, you'd think he'd settle for a reasonable facsimile, but you'd be wrong. I mean I've had to adjust to the fact there is no cheese dip in California outside of a jar at the

Safeway and other than a couple of hissy fits and some pouting, I've been fine.

Speaking of bad diets, we went to the emergency room last night. It wasn't specifically related to his weight but the litany of woe that makes up his physical state. It was an interesting cap to an interesting day. He asked if I would drive him to the doctor. He said he was afraid he'd get lost on his way to the VA where I work, and his appointment would be. Fear from a man who just drove from Alabama to California in three and a half days with no map; who voluntarily jumped out of airplanes in the Army; who owned a hot pink welding truck; who got a perm on a dare when I was four; who went deer hunting armed with toenail clippers and self-confidence. I'm kidding (about the deer hunting) but you see how his request threw me for a loop.

However, the request to drive him was one I had no problem granting. I mean, his doctor's office was in the same building as my office so my time away from work would be minimal. I asked if he wanted to go with me in the morning (his appointment was at 1:30) and spend the day at the VA acclimating himself to the area and enjoying the farmer's market we have every Wednesday. Once I explained the cafeteria offered both biscuits AND gravy, no more convincing was needed.

So, I drove his pickup which smelled strongly of feet, dog food and contraband Cheetos because he needed to use his power wheelchair and my car is not properly equipped. Clad in my three-piece suit, I drove a pickup for the first time since I was forced to learn to drive a standard on the column when I was abandoned in a field by my feed store

27

co-workers the summer after my senior year in high school. I was country when country wasn't cool, y'all.

We got to the VA, headed to the cafeteria and met with our first roadblock of the day. No biscuits for the gravy. He was half-heartedly offered an English muffin with gravy but even the cafeteria lady who suggested it seemed to know it was an odd suggestion and our encounter became awkward until I blamed "California hippies" and we all laughed, and he ordered a quasi-Denver omelet with sausage instead of ham. I left him happily munching and reading his book about the FBI's plot to bring down Al Capone; your typical light breakfast reading. He would then entertain himself at the Farmer's Market.

After lunch, he went to the doctor and after about an hour, they called me and said they are taking him to the emergency room due to labored breathing and I rushed to meet them there. He's sitting in his wheelchair, slightly stooped due to a bad back and somewhat irritated due to Irish heritage.

We sat there while they performed a battery of tests and took a rather large sampling of fluids. They forced him to take off his shirt and put on a hospital gown, but he insisted on wearing his suspenders over the gown. When they protested I explained, it's either that or the full moon, as it were.

Those wide pieces of forest green elastic are the only thing between a reasonably amicable but oddly dressed patient and a naked and irritated redneck. I told them if it was all the same to them, I'd prefer to keep at least a layer of denim between his flatulence and my immediate air space. And seeing as how the face masks didn't seem to be distributed based on who was best dressed, I needed some assistance.

However, the oddest moment came when they wanted to perform a blood gas test and he winced at the needle, an odd reaction for a diabetic who self-injects insulin four times a day. He likened the pain to being shot in the butt, which he consequently admitted had happened to him on more than one vaguely felonious occasion before my mother agreed to marry and remove him from the mean streets of Epps, LA, population 250, if you count cows, dogs and slow-moving squirrels.

With his admission, the "real pretty Indian doctor lady" asked if I were his attorney. I was confused until I looked down and realized I was still in my three-piece suit and he was outfitted in what I've come to describe as "slightly medicated, topless *Hee Haw* extra". I laughed and said, "No, I'm his son. Thank goodness I didn't inherit the 'heathen' gene." I mean, the only 'shot' I've ever been is through the heart by someone who gave love a bad name. He laughed and said, "Yeah, his Mama is what made him turn out so good. You know he runs a department here? He's real smart."

In that moment I realized while he is very vocal about his pride in my accomplishments, I don't think I have ever reciprocated. I thought about how he came from nothing and worked his fingers to the bone, literally up to the point where he hurt his back off-shore, just to make sure his family had what we needed. I thought about how he scrimped and saved to buy me a new car in college and how hurt he must've been when it was repossessed after his accident and his workman's comp check was much less than his normal pay. All I could think about at the time was how embarrassed I was; I didn't stop to think how it affected him. He has his faults to be sure but for someone who got his GED in the Army, it was never a question of if I were going to college, it was when and where. It was practically pre-determined I would be successful. He never wanted me to follow in his footsteps; he wanted better for me. He told me he knew I was going to "be somebody" when I was in elementary school. All I remember is I never wanted to be him.

And I felt ashamed for thinking being him wouldn't be good enough; for always making sure everyone knew how different we were, when in actuality we aren't so different. We both want to make people laugh and to take care of those we love, and we'd give our last dime to help somebody. I'm not sure why I never saw it.

Wearing Calvin Klein suits and having a color-coordinated life doesn't make me better than anyone. And although I'd like to think if God were to choose a "look" it'd be from the Brooks Brothers Black Fleece collection, I have a sneaking (Baptist) suspicion he might be wearing a John Deere hat or, at the very least, jeans. Maybe I'll start borrowing The Dad's boots every once in a while. You know, just in case.

Thursday, September 22, 2011

Soup Nazi?

It happened. We had our first tiff. It was over a request for hamburger soup, if you can believe it. As someone who until recently, rarely cooked, I have more than my share of top-shelf kitchen *accoutrement* courtesy of my best friend Christopher's culinary prowess and former position as manager of a Sur La Table. For those not in the know, SLT is like Williams-Sonoma. For those readers who are still in the dark, I always referred to SLT as a hooty-tooty Wal-Mart for kitchen crap. Maybe I am more country than I thought.

Even though I am not a gourmand by anyone's definition, I felt I was reasonably equipped to take on most cooking requests, this side of risotto. I mean, I have a small copper pot solely to melt butter.

Anyway, The Dad was visiting me at my office, waiting for his doctor's appointment and stated, out of the blue, he wanted to make hamburger soup. When I asked what day he planned for this event, he said, "Tonight." I asked what he needed to make this soup and he rattled off a list of ingredients were familiar enough to me to know I had exactly none of them in my home.

So, I pulled out my trusty list making tools and began quizzing him on what he needed and informing him if he wanted to make this soup tonight we would be eating later than usual as the most important ingredient for soup was a "soup pot", which I do not possess. The only person who would have one the size he described would be a witch doctor from *Scooby-Doo*; it sounded as if he wanted a stainless steel 1977 Caprice Classic station wagon with "hannels on the side so I don't burn muh-self".

I also informed him that I did not own a ladle, slotted spoon, four cans of Veg-All or a container of salt. After he stared at me with a mixture of condescension and pity, I made another error. When I attempted to sway him to use ground turkey instead of ground beef, as it would be better for him, he looked at me with a look of horror that can only be described as akin to a Republican who just realized poor people and minorities vote.

He said, savoring each word like the contraband M&Ms I found in his bedroom last week. "I. WILL. NOT. PUT. TURKEY. IN. MY. HAMBURGER. SOUP!" Then hamburger it shall be. He has made several dietary changes since he's been here. We've cut out most sugar and salt and almost all fried foods. We have also eliminated soda and he's lost 11 pounds in 2 weeks! I should have my own show, people. Start the on-line campaign.

I know I should have left well enough alone, but I'm not afraid to nudge a little further if it's for the greater good. I'll re-create the conversation *ver batim*, which is Latin for "only a twerp would remember every word somebody said".

"If you want to use hamburger, then you at least need to reduce the number of crackers you eat with it."

"Why?"

"Your doctor said to reduce your carbs."

"What's carbs?"

"Well, bread for one."

"Crackers aren't bread."

"Yes, they are."

"How?"

"What do you mean how? What do you think crackers are?"

"Crackers are crackers. They're not bread."

"Are you kidding?"

"Well, I guess you learned that in college?"

"What are you talking about? Everybody knows crackers are bread."

"I don't."

"That may be, but they are, and you eat too many of them."

"How many is too many?"

"You should have like 6 or 7 with your soup. The saltines you like are about 10 calories each."

"6 or 7!?! I eat that many putting the soup in my bowl."

"I know. It's why you've got this right here," I said poking his belly, which he hates because he is hyper-ticklish.

"Just forget it. I don't even want soup anymore." And then he made as dramatic an exit as you can make while riding in an electric wheelchair with the speed set on "turtle".

Cut to me buying the above-mentioned items. He's making the soup tonight.

Sunday, September 25, 2011

Me, you and the Boob Tube

For those who asked, the soup was pretty good. I tried a little the day he cooked it and it's a good thing I did as he finished off the entire pot by the next evening. I've never seen so much food eaten so quickly since the last time I watched *Man vs. Food*. And he wasn't even trying to win a t-shirt or to get his picture on a wall.

He has been trying to get me to buy a painting of a cowboy for my living room. When I questioned which particular painting, he said "Oh, just any of 'em. Everybody needs a cowboy picture". Untrue. I do not need a cowboy picture, not even if it was an original Andy Warhol of Elvis as a gunslinger. The decorating scheme of my living room is a modified art deco meets thrift store chic. It's quirky. Cowboy *anything* is not quirky. Cowboys wouldn't call me quirky, even at church. That's just not how they talk. What some of them called me behind my back and even to my face occasionally, is better left to history.

I can't really blame them; after all I did dye my top-siders aqua blue and use Madonna in my successful campaign for Sophomore Class Reporter. Apparently "Desperately Seeking Dusty" resonated with somebody besides me. And this was at a consolidated high school with around 250 students in Northeast Texas. I must have been insane. Most of the people who knew me must have thought I was some sort of social experiment. I wonder if they wondered if they were all on *Candid Camera*. My sister used to tell everyone I was adopted. I used to joke the only thing The Dad and I had in common is the belief I am adopted. And it's become more apparent as we enter our third week as roommates.

I knew there would be a learning curve living with someone in their 70s. And while he and I have never really been on the same page, I thought I had a reasonable idea of who he was based on the fact I have visited with him several times a year since my mother died in 2000. Truth be told, we've never been in the same section of the library, y'all. I tried to combine the new him of the visits with my memories of who he was when I was growing up and the reports from my brother and sister-in-law with whom he shared a home for the immediately preceding two years. None of this prepared me for the reality show that is my father.

He is an enigma, wrapped in bacon, swathed in big'n' tall denim. The overbearing, judgmental and downright scary father of my childhood has somehow morphed into an aged, slightly depressed version of Dan Conner from *Roseanne*; all bathroom humor and false bravado.

His complaints are both understandable and irritating. He wants to be in Alabama without being in Alabama. I just want him to assimilate as quickly as I do. He wants me to be a housewife from the 50s armed with a war chest of carb-heavy comfort food recipes and slotted spoons. I just want him to change 70 years of eating habits overnight. I want a roommate; he wants a Southern June Cleaver. Other than a tendency to be over-dressed while cleaning, June Cleaver I shall never be. Although if you read my book (*A Gone Pecan*) you might think I certainly sound like a middle-aged woman. Quacking like a duck doesn't make me a duck, dear friends; it simply makes me duck-esque; duck-onic, if you will.

You must forgive this digression. I am trying to collect my thoughts while the entire nation of Guatemala is celebrating something in the parking lot of the *El Rancho Supermercado y Tacqueria* across the street from my neighborhood. *Supermercado* is Spanish for Supermarket. As far as I can tell, *Tacqueria* is Spanish for "add cheese". And you know I'm on board for that. If you put a boot in a casserole dish, topped it with cheese and set it out at a Fifth Sunday Dinner on the Grounds, I'd at least take a bite.

TV seems to be the one area where we're willing to compromise. I have been subjected to boxing, football and re-runs of *America's Funniest Home Videos*. He's been subjected to *Project Runway*, *Dr. Who* and *Drop Dead Diva*.

We both like *Big Bang Theory, NCIS* and *Bait Car*. The Judds may think love can build a bridge, but so can TV, y'all. And any chasm can be bridged with a shared enemy. I have never agreed with him more than just now when he said, "Them people need to turn that mess down."

Amen, Old Man. I mean, we're trying to watch funny videos over here.

Friday, September 30, 2011

Onomatopoeia

It's almost funny the number of noises emanating from the general area of my father, up to and including his dog, Lulu. Not only are there the previously mentioned toxic fumes but there are also random bursts of what I can only describe as auditory clatter. For example, he has recently begun singing, apropos of nothing, the 1960s song *Brand New Key*. You know, the "I've got a brand-new pair of roller skates; you've got a brand new key…" song? I don't know why either. Of course, it's preferable to his usual song of choice which starts with the timeless phrase, "I don't know but I've been told, a green grasshopper has a red…" I'll leave the last word to the mysteries parked in his noggin, y'all.

There are also the staccato bursts of whistling which, although impressive, occur at random times and tend to startle one who is used to a quiet little abode. I didn't realize old people are such loud people. Not only with the level of sound needed for them to enjoy the TV, but the loudness of the talking, the coughing, and the wheezing. Hold on a minute, I think he needs his inhaler.

Sometimes I can't tell if he's having a bronchial incident, as the ER docs call it, or if he's just practicing his pre-pout huffing. And he is an Olympic level pouter. It's truly astonishing. The fact he's lost 12 pounds in three weeks is purposefully ignored by him. His only focus is he has only been allowed one soda since he arrived. I explained to him that diabetics can't have regular soda. Since he refuses to drink diet soda because of the aftertaste, he can't have any at all. What aftertaste he's referring to is beyond me, since he is a big fan of Sweet and Low and everybody knows that tastes like an old lady smells; White Shoulders and baby powder.

Anyway, the noise level doesn't abate even when he begins to slumber, which occurs at any given time of the day or night. He sleeps in bursts, like an overworked programmer for some Silicon Valley company. Every couple of hours he'll nod off and then suddenly wake up like the girl in *Pulp Fiction* when John Travolta gave her the adrenaline shot. You know, when she jumped and gasped? Although he adds a look of accusatory confusion that says, "where am I and what happened to my sandwich?"

I already discussed our TV tastes and the fact we have agreed to "play nice" and allow each other to watch our favorite shows from time to time. Being a non-regular viewer of TV, but a hard-core user of Netflix, I am usually exceedingly generous with the remote. However, I have grown used to the habit of enjoying my DVDs on Tuesdays and Saturdays and watching each one the day it comes in and returning it the next day. Obviously, all the selections in my queue were chosen long before this co-habitation was even a glimmer of an idea in the back of my mind. And even though he enjoyed the *Burn Notice* Season 4 marathon, he does not care for multiple episodes of *The New Sherlock Holmes*.

He decided to be polite and said, "This show is not in'tresting me at all, so I'm gonna take a nap 'til you get your fill." That seemed awfully benevolent; until the snoring began. Both he and Lulu are mouth breathers in the literal sense. She because of her Boston Terrier heritage (short snout) and he because of the numerous nose breakings throughout his life, from incidents and allegations the likes of which even he will not disclose. And this reticence is from a man who had a conversation that veered from flatulence to the Playboy channel in his initial conversation with one of my employees.

And the snoring not only began in earnest, it crescendoed to the point I had to leave the room as I couldn't turn up the volume enough to hear it without waking the slumbering duo and I just flat out refuse to use closed captioning on any program spoken in English. I'll gladly read a foreign film, but my "fanciness" has boundaries, y'all.

I was forced from the room like a despot from his third world throne although the noise from those unhappy mobs is no match for the chaotic symphony of numerous sleep-interrupting horks, the loud, metallic pwangs and wooden plomps of his recliner being declined (is that the opposite of recline?) and the random snorffs (that's a snort and sniff combo) of both father and dog. At least I'm used to them now. The first night he lived here and got up to use the bathroom at around 2:00 am, I thought somebody was trying to break in the house and "git" me and I near about wet myself before remembering he was here and a successful burglar/serial killer wouldn't make that kind of racket.

Throughout the evening, I've been trying to think of a way to bring this whole thought home and maybe make some sense of the situation, but I've come to realize, it's not really that simple. There's not always a *Family Ties*-esque synopsis that both educates and entertains. Truth is, he's old and loud and set in his ways. I can be downright persnickety and am more set in my ways than I ever imagined or admitted. But we're family and you make do with the cards you're dealt. At least that's what Kenny Rogers taught us and although some days I may feel ready to run, I'm not ready to fold 'em just yet.

Friday, October 7, 2011

Redneck is the new Black

It's the end of the first month and we've settled into somewhat of a routine. I accuse him of being the source of all odd smells and he accuses me of "forgetting where you come from". Now, I have been accused of many things in my day, some nefarious, some untrue and others quite on the mark. But as someone who is able to recognize a Jim Ed Brown and Helen Cornelius duet within the first four notes, I take exception to this.

I may want to forget some of the more redneck aspects of my heritage, like peeing in the yard without the cover of darkness, but as someone who once dressed as Buck Owens for Halloween, I feel I am sufficiently country as to be welcomed at a 4-H meeting, y'all. I mean, I am the former owner/caretaker of a cow, sheep and horse; not necessarily in that order. I have worn Wrangler jeans and cowboy boots, albeit under duress, but I actually bought chukka boots last year, people. The fact they are navy and come with a matching suede belt shouldn't take any of the shine of my spurs, if you know what I mean.

After being confronted with this information, my father's terse reply was, "Well, pardon me, Conway Twitty. Did you get your pink pants at the feed store?" *Touché,* Old Man. *Touché,* indeed.

And so, it goes. I have cooked boiled okra, but I made him watch *Project Runway,* which he says he doesn't like but still manages to vocalize his opinions on which dress looks most "like a hooker". Oddly enough, we usually have similar tastes although I am able to guess which weird-shouldered Barbarella dress the judges will pick, whether I actually like it or not.

I think this sudden interest in fashion stems from his purchase, upon arrival, of a black bowler. He has now decided that he wants to collect hats and has since purchased a gray bowler and a brown fedora. He asked me what I thought about his hats. I said I liked them just fine, but if he insisted on wearing them he needed to start dressing in more fashionable attire. As it is he looks like a hillbilly who mugged a British banker in the 1870s. And he agreed! I was rendered speechless and fled to Marshall's before he could rescind his comment.

Why not TJ Maxx, you ask? Well, I'll tell you. TJ Maxx and Marshall's (and Homegoods) are owned by the same company (TJX) but there are distinct differences. TJ Maxx has jewelry, only women's shoes and more designer labels. Marshall's has shoes for the entire family, no jewelry department and Big & Tall Menswear.

In my frenzy, I purchased an additional pair of khakis (he now has two) and a blue plaid button-down. Gingham is the new black. You heard it here first. Of course, he hasn't actually worn the shirt yet, but I'm holding out hope, y'all. I have made it my duty to make the world a better-dressed place one person at a time. I guess I should have picked a less complex pupil for my latest project. But fear not. Those huge, yeti-like feet will be encased in coordinated socks by the end of the year. I mean, he can't see his feet, so he wouldn't know anyway, right?

Stealth fashion seems to be the best bet for this redneck redo. I'll be like a Navy Seal of fashion, without the guns or camouflage make-up or the combat. Okay, maybe not a Navy Seal. Maybe just a navy-jacketed style coach for those who wear overalls. I'll do whatever I need to do, as long as I'm cute, not sweaty and get a free pass for being judgmental. You pickin' up what I'm throwin' down?

Saturday, October 15, 2011

Change ain't just a jingle in your pocket

Since we last spoke, I had an interaction with The Dad which aired out some laundry so to speak. One of the items on the agenda was, in fact, the laundry or lack thereof. I was concerned when I washed his clothes on Saturday, I found a lone pair of underwear, pants and socks. For the entire week. Now I am not one to go searching for household chores. Truth be told, if it weren't for this Southern Baptist guilt related to the cleanliness/Godliness connection, I'd have those Merry Maids, making merry all up and through here.

However, when the stench can rouse you from sleep like the most unpleasant of alarm clocks, something must be done. "Old Man Butt with Feet" would be the worst Yankee Candle scent ever. As I have previously mentioned, but feel compelled to repeat, this odor proves to be more than these new Febreze canisters (that supposedly can cover the smell of a room full of rotting meat) can take. The funk has got to go, do you hear me?

During the ensuing discourse on habits that are just flat out wrong, I spoke so eloquently of the need for portion control when eating, better aim when peeing and the actual definition of a clean dish, grown men wept and Mary Lou Retton flipped through the living room in her American flag unitard, a sparkler in each hand.

And I think I got my point across. Now, you have to realize portion control for him is the most quixotic of pipe dreams. Giving him free reign of the kitchen and expecting him to control himself is like giving the most felonious of carnival workers full access to the funnel cake/corn dog cart. It's just too much temptation not to end in gastrointestinal distress. And he seems oblivious to the connection. When I explained the average person does not use a double roll of toilet paper every two days unless they are decorating someone's lawn, he seemed genuinely shocked.

I recently attended a retreat with my church choir and he was left to his own devices for exactly 46 hours. When I returned, the level of carnage in the kitchen simply defied logic. Had he been my teenage child, I would have immediately accused him of having either a party with 80 of his closest personal friends or having offered housing to a small family of refugees. Either way, more food than could have been safely consumed by one person had disappeared.

You have to understand my father views eating as a competition. It isn't an activity to enjoy so much as it's a means to an end. And it doesn't matter if it's good; as long as it's a lot. This intake of food is Olympic level. That chubby little dude on *Food Nation* is an amateur, people, compared to *mi Padre* (that's Spanish). His need for crackers is nothing short of an addiction. I fixed him BBQ pork roast, macaroni and cheese and broccoli for dinner the other night. And he asked for crackers to go with it. When I asked why on earth he needed crackers, he insisted if he didn't have "bread" he didn't think he could enjoy himself. I told him I felt pretty certain he'd survive. If one of the tenets of parenting is a mastery of sarcasm, I may be parent material after all.

I tried to explain that if he insisted on getting full every meal, he would never lose another pound. And since his only exercise is walking to the toilet to relieve himself, his food consumption should have a commensurate decrease. He accused me of speaking French and went in search of a sugar free Popsicle.

I don't know what he's doing in the bathroom, but there is pee EVERYwhere. It's as if he were a urinating Willy Waterbug. You remember those water toys from the 70s that had little tubes that sprayed water every which way? Imagine this, but with pee. I mean, how else do you explain urine on the rug in front of the sink and on top of the toilet tank? Try to un-picture that, dear friends, I dare you.

I realize I should have left well enough alone, but I just had to slip the last topic into the *conversacion* (also Spanish). Now I am fully aware that you can't un-poke a bear, but I just had to ensure that he understood the real definition of washing dishes. See, he has decided his "chore" is washing the dishes after I cook. And as a harried homemaker, I appreciate the effort. However, washing dishes is not his forte. Mind you, there are both dishes and water involved but oftentimes they do not meet. I have witnessed him wetting the silverware, with cold water and then wiping it with his fingers and placing it ever so gently onto the towel to dry.

At first, I tried to give subtle hints by placing still-dirty dishes back in the sink to be washed again, but it was to no avail. Now I don't know if his eyesight is such that he truly can't see the food remaining. However, a good rule of thumb for cleaning should definitely be "if you can still smell the chicken, the casserole dish might not be clean."

Apparently our "talk" worked. He has been toeing the proverbial line for the past week. I washed four, count them, four pair of underwear today. And he even ate the pre-portioned meals I cooked with very little pouting and protestations of hunger. Have we reached a middle ground? Or is he just trying to lull me into a false sense of security? Surely, he hasn't matured that quickly. He couldn't possibly have grown as a person in a week, could he?

I should have known he'd do something so nefarious, so diabolical. I mean, how dare he become a better person, just when I've begun documenting this social experiment. Selfish!

Sunday, October 23, 2011

You can't pop your collar without a good breakfast

Apropos of nothing, The Dad enters the room and says, in a pained voice, "So if I grew a ponytail, you'd just cut it off?"

"Yes. Lopped. Immediately." To catch you up, we had recently had a conversation about things I loathe; men with ponytails being one of them. Al Franken, Dick Cheney and people who think 'irregardless' is a word are three others.

"Lopped?" he asked, with the same look on his face that Lulu (his dog) had the first time she saw herself in a mirror.

"Yes. Lopped. Maybe even with pinking shears."

"Just like that?"

"Just like that."

"But it's my hair."

"Obviously if you are so inclined to grow a ponytail, you have taken leave of your faculties and someone needs to intervene. That someone is me."

"Ok, but what if I wanted a mullet?"

"A mullet is simply a ponytail having a party. It would be lopped as well."

"Without any warning."

"This counts as the warning, just so you know."

"Who made you the hair police?"

"It's not just hair; clothes too. And I was elected."

"I don't remember voting."

"It was secret ballot. But I assure you, you voted for me. Twice."

"Why are you so aggressive about this?"

"Ponytails on men are aggressive. So are popped collars on old people, so don't get any ideas."

"What's a popped collar?"

"You'll never need to know. See how I protect you?"

Dear readers, I feel I must take a minute and apologize if anyone reading this has been offended. Of course, I'm not apologizing for my opinion; I feel confident I am right. But if you have a ponytail, feel a kindred spirit for those who do or are at present wearing a popped collar (and you're over 21), I apologize for the fact I am judging you so hard right now, I think I may have just pulled a muscle. And for this I am truly sorry.

After the hair discussion, The Dad decided to "git inside that head 'a yours" and asked me for my opinions on any number of topics. I would like to think it was to truly gain insight into what makes his eldest son tick. I suspect, however, that is was simply a ruse to distract me while he foraged for illegal items that he doesn't know I know he hides in the deep recesses of his bedside table. What sort of caretaker would I be if I didn't spy, people? Don't be so naïve. I have to save him from himself. This is a diabetic who fixates on sugar to the point it's almost funny. In the middle of a meal that he has personally requested and is eating with as much as haste as a Minuteman waiting for Paul Revere to ride by screaming about lanterns and boats and British dudes, he will state, "Boy this sure is good, but not as good as chocolate ice cream. I'd love a gallon (!) right now."

So, I am forced, FORCED do you hear me, to sneak and spy, peek and pry. I have, however, found very little in the way of evidence of contraband snacks. I have, so far, simply found more empty wrappers of his approved snacks than is typically allotted. Even if they are sugar free, eating seven popsicles in a day is not good. Anyone who has gone on a sugar free diet can tell you what sugar alcohol does to you.

I started to think I was making headway. Maybe he is listening to me and not eating foods that are bad for him although he has stopped losing weight after the initial 20 pounds. And I was about to get all proud of him (and myself) when my network of accidental spies began reporting.

Before you get all judgmental, let me say it all started innocently enough. My assistant Marie casually mentioned that she saw The Dad at the snack machine (on the hospital campus where I work), buying a soda one afternoon after his doctor appointment. Another time she made him some coffee and when she asked how much sugar he took, he told her two spoonsful, never mentioning that he is supposed to use Equal or Splenda or Old Lady (Sweet n Low) since he is diabetic. Later her daughter, Dawnyielle mentioned she had seen The Dad on the other hospital campus (where we live) reading a book outside the convenience store, soda in hand. When I casually mentioned this chance sighting, The Dad had the nerve to say that she must have mistaken him for someone else. As if there are two redheaded rednecks with a grey bowler and green paratrooper suspenders, riding a red scooter. Really? That's your defense? It wasn't me. Are you suddenly an R&B singer? If you're going to make a concerted effort for people to notice you, which was his goal with the hats, then you must deal with the consequences of being noticed. Wearing colored pants (pink, kelly green, aqua) keeps me honest, y'all. You can't perform any activity that requires stealth or secrecy if people can see your pants from outer space.

I decided not to press the issue as I was secretly proud of him for actually leaving the house without me, even if it was to cheat on his diet and move ever closer to the reality of "the sugar taking his feet", which is his favorite lament.

At least he's doing something. The fact these activities are simply sketchy as opposed to openly larcenous is a workable paradigm. This coupled with the fact he's started to cook for himself in the mornings is progress. I'm looking past the fact there's not much else to do once you're awake at 4:30 AM. Apparently, he feels God has tasked him with ensuring the sun rises on time because he wakes at the same time each day and he has no chickens to feed or cow to milk. The only downside is he is not one to cook breakfast foods on a consistent basis. I have attempted to grow accustomed to being awakened to a variety of smells. Some are awesome (bacon); some are subtle (grilled cheese) and some are downright odd (shrimp and okra?!).

The fact he is up makes me happy. I worry about his health being negatively impacted by his lack of activity on a daily basis. So even when I would prefer not to be roused from slumber with an offer of stewed tomatoes, or tommy-toes, as he calls them, I am happy I am offered something other than silence. I know that day is coming, and I can't bear to think about it.

Tuesday, November 1, 2011

Bumpkins are people too?

I'm starting to feel like the title character in Cal Smith's 1974 hit, "Country Bumpkin" and not just because I know the words. The song greeted me this morning as The Dad had awakened earlier than normal due to his appointment at the hospital and apparently couldn't start the day without a little country music. See, his doctor wanted to see him at 1:30 pm, so naturally he felt the need to arise at 5:00 am, cook himself, but not me, breakfast and ensure we arrived at the hospital by 7:00 am, just in case. Thank goodness, I work there. Heaven forbid he not drive himself to the hospital and stay at home sleeping his day away. He'd rather come to the hospital and alternate sleeping in the lobby, cafeteria or my office. Imagine trying to conduct a conference call with a sleep apnea-riddled yeti leaning precariously close to the edge of your desk who snorts himself awake and demands peanut butter crackers.

And that's not even the reason I'm feeling all bumpkinish. No, the main reason I am feeling "fresh as frost out on the pumpkins" is yesterday, The Dad called me at work and asked me to find him a container to store used cooking oil with which to prepare the animals he isn't supposed to eat in a manner which isn't conducive to achieving his goal of outliving me. Of course, those are my words. What he said was, "Git me a grease can so I can fry me some chicken." As if he had not already fried chicken, which is not allowed, filling my house with a scent that, while wonderfully nostalgic, was so thick you could "sop it up with a biscuit".

Upon opening the front door, I took a deep breath, immediately gained three pounds, and said, "Did you rob a 'tucky Fried Chicken?" Tell me I'm not as country as the Mandrell Sisters. Okay, I'm probably more Arlene than Barbara, but whatever. The point being, he asked me to help him fry chicken which he had already done, but tried to hide. I know his eyesight is less than it used to be, but I find it hard to believe he didn't think I saw the flour, pepper and salt covering almost every surface in the kitchen up to and including his hat and the dog. Not to worry, it was one of his six identical Tractor Supply hats. Apparently stealth-cooking requires something less formal than a fedora or bowler.

My point, besides the sinking feeling I am being forced to acknowledge my roots more than I would like, is The Dad is incapable of hiding anything; feelings, prejudices, candy wrappers. Nothing is hidden; nothing held back. He has taken to telling all sorts of tales to my staff and I don't know what stories he shared with my administrative resident, but trying to explain *Hee Haw* to a 23-year-old master's candidate from Chicago while keeping one's cosmopolitan façade intact is difficult. Thank goodness, I have been able to keep the "I reckons" and "fixin tos" to a minimum. I have had to resort to becoming an interpreter of sorts for those who come in contact with him.

There is a certain code to know when talking with my father. A unique language, if you will, although I don't believe Rosetta Stone offers training in his dialects which include Basic Southern, Judgmental Redneck, Big Honkin' White Trash and even Mumbling Cajun, although I secretly think the last one is due more to a lack of denture adhesive than anything else. And as much as I go on, I sometimes find myself using his phrases to confuse and intimidate my staff. That's leadership, people.

The reason I bring this up is to know my father is to listen for the clues in what he says to give you the realities of what he's done. It's a matter of gleaning the trace amount of truth out of his statements. For example, when he entered my office this afternoon, after his doctor's appointment, he stated, "I sure did want a Mountain Dew today, but I didn't have one." To the uninitiated, he is following his diet. To those in the know, he in fact just finished a Mountain Dew. As I am attempting to keep "the sugar" from taking his feet, as you know, I have taken it upon myself to micro-manage his diet. When his blood sugar goes up he gets very sleepy. This leads to moments when he will nod off in mid-sentence and has on more than one occasion caused alarm with visitors who ask about "the homeless man asleep in (my) office". Just today he fell asleep sitting across from me at my desk and I had to complete an employee's performance appraisal in the conference room as there is no method to wake a sleeping bear without causing some sort of unpleasant interaction with either gas or curse words, both of which he lets fly with alarming speed and frequency. Even with more combat experience than is expected in a childhood this side of Chechnya, I am sometimes caught in the crossfire.

And I am not exactly thrilled with the turning tides at home, so to speak. I can't pinpoint exactly when the power shifted. All I know is there is a skillet full of grease on my stove, a belt sander in my foyer with an orange extension cord trailing through the front window and a 15-pound sack of potatoes in my pantry. There is some nefarious scheming afoot and I think the end goal is to create some hybrid country caretaker/cook. All I can say is if I wanted to be a Southern woman, I assure you I'd choose Julia Sugarbaker instead of Aunt Bea. I will fight this tooth and nail. I will keep my zebra-striped occasional chairs, mirrored furniture and pastel chinos. I will continue to eat at the dinner table with no dog and a balanced meal. As God as my witness I WILL NOT make biscuits from scratch. I feel like Scarlett O'Hara but without the turnips and drama. Okay maybe some of the drama, but definitely not the turnips, unless there's cornbread.

To be honest, I don't remember where I was headed with this thought, but I do need to go. My favorite Lacy J. Dalton song just came on the radio and I've got a roast in the crock pot.

Thursday, November 10, 2011

Is one day enough?

Today is Veteran's Day. The Dad is an Army Veteran, my brother is Active Duty Air Force and I have countless uncles and cousins who have worn the uniform of our nation's armed forces.

As an employee of the Department of Veterans Affairs, I am in a unique position to thank our Nation's Veterans every day for their service. My department is Prosthetic and Sensory Aids. We provide any item or service a Veteran uses in their home, including but not limited to artificial limbs, power and manual wheelchairs and lifts, glasses and hearing aids, pacemakers, artificial hips and knees, computers, ramps, home remodeling, automobile adaptive equipment, shoes, walkers, canes, crutches, blood pressure monitors, home tele-health equipment, home oxygen, hospital beds, blind aids and items of daily living.

All these devices and services are free of charge to Veterans, regardless of their status or medical condition. This care is available at 153 VA medical centers at a cost of around $2 billion for 2012. I say this only to educate everyone about the exceptional care offered to our Nation's heroes.

I don't know why The Dad joined the Army at the age of 16. What inspired him to serve his country? Did he want to escape the desperate poverty of his home? Was he tired of the endless days of working and the endless meals of beans and potatoes and the occasional biscuit? Was he leaving behind a mean-spirited and selfish father who was in actuality, and not for dramatic effect, a sharecropper? I also wonder why my brother joined the Air Force? Was he escaping a life which was not exactly one of poverty, wasn't so far removed as to be comfortable? Why didn't I join the military? My aversion to authority aside, wouldn't it have given me an escape?

Regardless of the whys, both they and others like their service to keep this country great. This reason alone is enough to honor them today and every day. I take pride in the fact I help Veterans like The Dad. This is what gets me up every morning and gets me to work. I love the energy of a hospital. We help people. Many have questioned my decision to leave a very cushy job in Washington, DC to return to the "front lines" to run a hospital department, but as I've grown older I've realized what's important to me in my career and it's a sense of pride in helping people. I'm not driven by a title; I'm driven by a sense of obligation to give back to those who gave so much, where I can see them and talk to them and, selfishly, receive their gratitude.

Regardless of a Veteran's length of service or position in the military, the fact they offered everything they had, up to and including, their life if necessary is something which compels us to honor them. It's not just another day off for federal employees or another inconvenient day when the banks close. It's a way for us to honor those who honored us by offering their all. It's not often I quote Billy Ray Cyrus, but his song sums it up best: All gave some; some gave all.

I capitalize Veteran as I'm used to doing so at work. VA Secretary Eric Shinseki started this several years ago as a sign of respect and I like it. It's one small way to remind ourselves, as VA employees, why we come to work every day - to serve those who serve(d).

So, tell a Veteran thank you. If you're traveling, thank the soldier you see in uniform at the airport. Buy him, or her, a drink or a meal. Let them know how much you appreciate their service. We can go to church, protest anything we want and blog about our crazy redneck Dads, but only because the members of our armed forces willingly sacrificed for our freedoms.

Just because "Freedom isn't Free" is a cliché, doesn't mean it's not true.

Saturday, November 12, 2011

If Wal-Mart can rush the season, so can I

All I want for Christmas is a butt. It's a lot to ask I know but it's something I have wanted ever since I was old enough to notice the extra "seat" in my trousers. I am, of course, referring to the excess material which bunches as you walk when you have nothing to fill the back of your pants but hope, dear friends. If I have ever had a conversation with anyone, I have invariably discussed the complexities of trying to be fabulous while wearing husky-sized Tuffskins. That statement encapsulates my childhood. I feel sure many other episodes and character traits were in play during my formative years, but I remember feeling somehow, I had been switched at birth and there was a sad preppy family in the North (I was always hot natured as a child) who was stuck with a red-headed redneck and they spent their days doing extraordinary things, pining away for their long-lost son.

Chad Wolf was a boy who was born on the same day in the same hospital as I (Lake Providence, LA for those who don't know). For many years I felt perhaps the parents of the Wolf family were really mine. That is until we met them unexpectedly at a basketball game in Texas when I was in the seventh grade. I was very unhappy to find they were more like us than we were. The only difference between Chad and I was *his* Buster Brown haircut did not have a cowlick.

Don't get me wrong, my childhood was not unhappy, my Mother was an exceptionally fabulous person; it was more I felt out of place. It's not even like I was the black sheep of the family. I would have traded my fake Members Only jacket to be a sheep of any color. As I've said before, I felt more like the plaid koala bear.

What happens to plaid koala bears in a herd of sheep? They feel a never-ending weirdness. At least that stupid Ugly Duckling was a bird. Where's my image-affirming children's book?

I've grown up, so everything should be okay, right? Well, I can tell you the only difference between a baby plaid koala bear and an adult plaid koala bear is the financial means to buy more plaid and the limited ability to not seem uncomfortable should sheep-like behavior and/or sheep-adjacent activities become necessary.

Back to my butt, or lack thereof. I inherited this lovely physical trait from The Dad. I guess it could be worse. My butt is teeny-tiny, but it has many butt-like qualities. It is, in fact, butt-esque. His butt on the other hand doesn't even contain the essence of a butt. It's the mere memory of a butt which may have been. It's not even flat, it's actually concave. It's less than a butt. It's an anti-butt. There's more meat on a chicken neck, people.

On his 70-year-old self, it's not a bad as it could be I suppose. However, on my 41-year-old-thinking-I'm-cute self, it looks as if I have been wearing my pants for three weeks the minute I put them on freshly pressed from the dry cleaners. I age 30 years from front to back. I could get a senior citizen's discount at Denny's if I were to walk into the restaurant backwards.

My assistant told me about a product which will give you a fanny, so to speak. She had noticed my lack of derriere and, like me, has no filter. Apparently, there is underwear that has fake butt cheeks built in. What a technological marvel. She suggested I buy one. I informed her I felt enough shame purchasing my Spanx t-shirts at Nordstrom's and tried to do so only late in the evening while wearing a ball cap and jeans just in case someone recognizes me. I would NEVER buy fake-butt panties or whatever you call them. I just want a normal butt.

I feel compelled to tell you I only buy those over-priced spandex t-shirts because they are a medical necessity. They keep all the excess skin from my significant post-surgery weight loss under control and in a shape that is a reasonable facsimile of a normal body. Without them, I am unpretty, dear readers. Unclothed, I look like an uncooked turkey after a steam. Consequently, the only time I am unclothed is in the shower, due to the knowledge that showering in your underwear is stupid. A fact I wish I had known at the age of 12.

This bit of childhood trauma is etched in my memory as it was the only time I showered in the locker room after a football game in junior high. Most of the time I just went home sweaty and stinky. Well, as sweaty and stinky as you get standing on the sidelines talking to the cheerleaders. I was short, chubby and had a bad self-image which was not helped by the fact my locker mate had a visible moustache, in the 7th grade. I called him Burt Reynolds behind his back due to that and his thinning hair. Now that I think of it, how old was this guy? For several years after the incident (which he not only pointed out to everyone in the locker room but also recounted the next week for all who would listen), I suffered panic attacks anytime I heard running water or saw a black Trans Am.

Also like The Dad, I also have oddly short legs. At 6', my inseam is 29". It could be worse, I suppose, his inseam is 27". From the waist down, we could have our own reality show on TLC. To give the illusion of normal length legs, I wear my pants so high my belt buckle is at my belly button. But it looks normal. No one would ever know. Until now, I suppose. Hmm. I didn't think this through. Can you just un-read the last sentence? Then we could go back to where I imagined we were which was where you felt I was fabulous and I agreed wholeheartedly. Buying into someone's delusion is an inexpensive gift, folks.

Which brings me back to Christmas gifts. The Dad recently gave me insight into what he wanted this season. We were returning from dinner when we passed a Harley Davidson motorcycle and he said, "I wish I had that fella's hog (motorcycle enthusiast vernacular for, well, a motorcycle) and he had a feather up his butt. Then we'd both be tickled."

I don't think I can get him either of those things, seeing as how I am not about to buy a Harley or a feather. But I do think I can find him something he'll like. He has mentioned on more than one occasion he feels I am "mean" in my oversight of his diet. How dare I try to keep candy and soda from a diabetic? At this point, I think he'd be thrilled on Christmas morning to be allowed to drink an entire Mountain Dew in one sitting (FYI: serving size is 2. Check the bottle) without my signature look which is a mixture of condescension and pity. When you set the bar low, you're pretty sure to exceed it, right?

Anyway, Happy Holidays!

Wednesday, November 16, 2011

Between me and paradise

My holiday plans have taken a turn. My brother is Active Duty Air Force and was transferred to Hawaii with his family this summer. I know, right? Out of his 13 years in the military, he has been stationed in Biloxi (MS), Australia, the Azores and Colorado Springs. The only glitch in this almost perfect list was the bustling metropolis of Enid, Oklahoma. Their time in Enid is referenced somewhat like that random cousin in jail. We agree it is unpleasant and only refer to it when pressed and even then, in code. For people who have often lived on the edge of poverty, we've had a number of relatives on extended "vacations".

Anyway, my sister and I had discussed going to my brother's house for Christmas this year. However, two things put a crimp in those plans. The first was the cost of the tickets. Now, last year I took my sister and niece to Hawaii with me when I had to visit Honolulu for work. The trip was their Christmas/Birthday/Valentine's/Easter present for the next six years. My previous job afforded many opportunities to travel. Your tax dollars at work and I thank you. *Traveler's tip: the week after Thanksgiving is the best time to go to Hawaii. Ticket prices are reasonable, and the island is practically empty of tourists so no waiting in lines for the exciting performances and crappy food at the luaus and no need for reservations at the overpriced restaurants. Also, if you're ever in Cheyenne, Wyoming I can recommend an excellent Cajun restaurant.*

The second, and main, reason is the disaster that would befall my family should The Dad ever come into contact with airport security.

I have never traveled with The Dad outside of a multi-state car ride as a child with my mother driving and my father riding shotgun, parrot on shoulder. We have had our share of unique pets who have left our home is various ways, mostly through death. This particular parrot, Seymour, took his leave in the avian equivalent of a teenage girl eloping with a biker. He flew away one day when the door was accidentally left open and we saw him a few weeks later, circling the house with a hawk in tow. I guess he came back to rub it in our face? Can a bird flip 'the bird', I wonder?

In his defense, The Dad has traveled by train successfully. But if you've ever taken an Amtrak ride you know you can walk onboard the train with a see-through box of Ebola-riddled gibbon monkeys holding placards that say "Death to America" and as long as you have your ticket punched at some point on the ride and don't talk in the quiet car, you will be left to your own devices.

When I close my eyes and imagine The Dad attempting to travel by plane, this is the scene that unfolds: *Not wanting to tip a porter to curb-check his luggage, he walks inside thinking he can just get on the plane and immediately becomes distracted by the smell of bacon wafting from the concourses.*

Not having the patience to stand in line to check in for his flight ("I bought my ticket, what else do they need?") he will loudly disparage the moral fiber of not only the airline employees but various members of their family tree. He will also demand to know the source of the bacon and an ETA on when that bacon will become his.

Since I have to check my luggage (the wardrobe for a week's vacation, for me, consists of more than 2 pair of underwear, a Costco sized bottle of antacids and a bag of insulin needles), I ask for his ID, so I can get his boarding pass as well. The thought of him trying to manipulate the self-check kiosk without setting something on fire or accidentally launching the space shuttle is hilarious. The man has never purchased, or even touched a computer; much less learned how to use one.

Once I get him to understand it is a law they must see his ID to get his boarding pass, I will then have to threaten him with a bacon-less future in order to keep him from openly maligning the character of every member of Congress and the airport police force as we head toward yet another line to get to security.

Entering security, he would have to remove his shoes, which is possible. However, putting them on again would require a series of ropes and pulleys I feel sure would not make it past the screeners.

Hopefully they won't ask him to remove his suspenders because they have metal parts. They are only semi-successful in keeping his pants in the general vicinity of where they need to be to keep a public indecency charge off his record. One of the reasons his previously mentioned tiny almost-butt is so readily available for photo ops is in order to get underwear which fits him at the waist, we must battle so much superfluous fabric we could incorporate knife pleats and still have enough left over for a matching poncho.

You would think with all the extra material and the lack of buttock, there would be little chance of a viewing, so to speak, but these cheeks act like an overachieving middle child, desperate to be center stage.

I wish I could come up with a strategy to combat this issue. However, as I am not comfortable discussing this predicament with my local seamstress, we simply accept this as a reality and take our chances with the possibility of an eclipse. I am not referring to the vampire movie, although the skin tone is roughly the same. Well, if I'm being honest, that vampire dude has a rich cocoa tan compared to mi padre. *If he only moons me, I can take it. As I am 1/16 Native American, stoicism runs in my blood.*

Even if we successfully navigate the previous procedures, I can assure you at some point before we board the plane, he will tire of the entire process and loudly proclaim, "What do they think I am a terrorist?" At this point the FBI will arrive and I will have to forgo my traditional pre-flight beverage from Starbucks (Venti Black Iced Tea, 3 Splenda, No Water) to accompany him to the airport "jail" to assure the authorities that he is (1) not crazy enough to be locked away and (2) not a real threat to anyone unless they have a sense of smell and/or are offended by racial epithets involving turbans. Of course, I could always deny I know him and due to my East Coast travel wardrobe of jeans, loafers, button down and sport coat with pocket square, I think they would believe me. What's the point of overdressing if it can't get you (1) a free upgrade or (2) a place above suspicion?

Of course, if he did land in jail, his "vacation" if you will, I would need to get refund for his ticket. Is having a crazy father covered as an "Act of God" in most travel insurance policy?

Sunday, December 11, 2011

Sweeter than a turkey?

I was in Maine a few weeks ago, lunching at a cute little overpriced bistro called "The Salt Lick", which sounds more country than I would have imagined in Southern Maine. Although, if I were being honest, I always felt Maine was like Mississippi with snow when I lived in nearby Massachusetts several years ago.

Normally I don't answer the phone when it rings as it is rude, in my opinion, to do so while dining. However, seeing as how The Dad had been left to his own devices in California while I was gone, I immediately answered hoping the query would be mundane and not involve anyone who had taken an oath, either Hippocratic or "to Serve and Protect".

"Where's your stool softener?" he bellowed into the phone loud enough that my table mates could hear him without the utilization of the speakerphone option.

"I don't have...*that*," I said, at once disgusted and desperate to erase the picture forming in my mind. "What is the problem?"

"I haven't dirtied in about 6 days," he yelled. Deciding I wanted this conversation to end post haste or even faster I took the bull by the horns and proceeded to say in one breath, "That's not true I haven't been gone for 6 days and I can assure you you've never missed a day I don't use it I don't need it I'm just lucky that's rude you need to go across the street to the grocery store yes the Mexican one and buy that product if you are in that great of a need yes they speak

English no I don't know how to say softener in Spanish that's almost racist why are you talking so loud unless you or the house are on fire I have to go because I'm eating remember I'm 3 hours ahead of you, no, you shouldn't eat lunch yet it's not noon where you are yes it's good but you wouldn't like it because its sorta fancy yes I'll probably have lobster tonight I know you could eat one the size of small dog and I promise I'll talk to you later tonight love you, bye." Good thing I played trumpet in band all through school. Circle-breathing does wonders in all sorts of situations.

This is just another example of my father's inability to do anything quietly or discreetly. He has no issue discussing his many bodily functions regardless of our location or relationship with those within earshot. And if you know The Dad, everyone is within earshot. And I mean *every*one. His hearing has gotten worse over the years and now he feels sure you can only hear him if he can hear himself. And don't bother asking him to whisper as he doesn't understand the concept. His version of whispering is him lowering his speaking voice an octave but with no discernible change in volume.

This poses no issue at home but becomes somewhat nerve-wracking when we are out and about like this morning. We were eating at our favorite brunch spot and as he had decimated his eggs and sausage with biscuits and gravy, much more quickly than I was eating my food, he became bored and began to comment on everyone around us. Under normal circumstances, this is normally what we do, but then he started to say things like, "That old man with the jigglin' legs and the shaky arms sure is eatin' a bunch. I wonder how much longer he's gonna live? He looks old as Methusaleh."

Or "That Messican (redneck for Hispanic) lady sure is being a turd. She's arguing with that waiter about the table. She ought to sit her bubble-butt down somewhere."

And it wasn't so much I disagreed with what he said, that old man was 130 if he was a day; he looked like he had done his student teaching when Adam and Eve were in Pre-K. And the woman, whose butt did in fact resemble a large bubble, was being extremely rude, but it's just not polite to say these things out loud. A good Baptist does it in the confines of their house or at least in the fellowship hall at church. He may have been confused because of the food. You know the rule, if gossip is shared over breakfast items or a cheese-covered casserole, it's called fellowship. For those Southern Baptists who are offended by what I just said, please refrain from talking about me until you can do it in a group, with food, and have a proper prayer circle about the condition of my soul now that I live in the land of the heathen.

My father is still in denial about where he now lives. He realizes California is not Alabama but doesn't understand why it can't be. *Por ejemplo* (which is Spanish) we went in search of meatloaf yesterday and when I found it plus lemon icebox pie, he didn't seem surprised although I was; he seemed only to be concerned about the lack of available sweet tea. I informed him outside of the South you can't get sweet tea unless it's fruit-flavored. Even in the South sometimes you can't get sweet tea. Of course, what do I know seeing as I have only lived outside of the South since 2002 and he hasn't? Every time we go to a restaurant, he orders sweet tea and has one of two reactions. If they say they don't have it, he questions their right to live in America

Dusty Thompson

and breathe the same free air. If they say they have it and
he orders it and it is fruit flavored, he seems surprised and
loudly questions the American-ness of the entire dining
establishment and adjacent stores in the strip mall.

Prior to leaving for my trip I cooked up a storm to
ensure he had enough pre-made meals to get him through
a nuclear winter, or at least the 8 days I would be gone. If
I give him enough meatloaf, taters and greens he seems to
not notice there is no sweet tea and he feels more at home.

When I returned I found that he had not eaten all the
food I made. Apparently, he had grown tired of eating the
fried turkey dinners I had also made from Thanksgiving and
I noticed several contraband Chinese take-out containers
and a fortune cookie in the garbage can when I emptied
it into the bin. Apparently, he had ventured out from the
house. When I questioned the containers, he insisted that
he had only gone to the "messican" grocery store and had
ventured no further. He said he guessed the containers were
left over from the previous tenants although I have lived here
since June and he since September.

So, the battle continues in our fight for his health.
He swears I'm trying to starve him. Today we ate brunch
around 9:30. At 11:00 a.m. he said, "It's time for dinner."
My response was it might in fact be 11:00 but he had only
recently eaten and there was no way he was actually hungry,
adding, "You haven't truly been hungry since sometime
around 1957."

He said, "The way you starve me, people'll be able to
count my ribs pretty soon." I replied it would only be at a
BBQ joint as his body's ribs were firmly encased in several

layers of pudge and then I poked his belly which makes him giggle uncontrollably.

After he made a strange announcement at brunch, I began to wonder if he had frequented the donut shop across the street. As you know, when The Dad has done something he shouldn't he makes a random statement to the effect he has, in fact, NOT done something. When he announced, apropos of nothing, he had NOT eaten any donuts while I was gone, I immediately became suspicious and skimmed his diabetic diary entries he keeps for his doctor. I noticed several spikes in several days. When I questioned one particular spike from 130 to 253 over the course of four hours one day, he spent considerable time trying to convince me the turkey had caused the increase, and this was the reason he didn't eat the rest of it.

Silly me, how did I not know turkey was a dessert?

Friday, December 30, 2011

Is this what that Scorpions' song was about?

It's been an exhausting Christmas season. First, I got sick, then The Dad got sick, then he got me sick again. It's the first time we've shared something since the opinion I was adopted became our unspoken agreement sometime during my Duran Duran haircut phase. Since September, we've realized that although we still don't have a whole lot in common, we have both made efforts to get along and have been doing a pretty darn good job of it until last night.

I witnessed an incident so hypocritical it was absolutely breathtaking in more ways than one. Now as I have been, at various times in my life, a Southern Baptist and an Art major, I am more than familiar with those who are both self-righteous and hypocritical. Truth be told, I can lay down some judgment both hypocritical and hypercritical myself, so I am not casting any stones from my glass abode, mind you. But this particular situation was, I believe, the single most ridiculous reaction to an event I may have ever witnessed and I'm including that boy from my hometown who ran his truck into the tree in front of his house to demonstrate to his mother he was mad at her for something pork chop related. I'm not sure if he was pro or con, but he was fired up do you hear me?

The Dad banished Lulu, his faithful Boston terrier, to her bed at 8 pm for the sin of...farting! Can you believe it? Is he kidding me? The Department of Energy has designated his bedroom as a possible alternative fuel source. Ed Begley, Jr. texts me daily, urging me to "do my part" by procuring mass quantities of legumes, both Pinto and Great Northern.

When I questioned the banishment he said, with no sense of irony, "She needs to stop farting. It's starting to smell in here." *Starting* to smell? It has smelled since he wheeled into my life in September. I have single handedly rescued the Febreze people from the throes of this recession in my vigilant fight against the stench that has invaded my home. The walls in his bedroom have turned a lovely shade of yellow I call "Unbrushed Tooth".

When I laughed with my signature blend of condescension and pity, he seemed truly surprised. When I scoffed and pointedly told him anyone who passes gas as often as he should be the LAST person in the Americas, both North and South, to place sanctions on someone else's *faux pas*, he not only pleaded confusion over my use of a French term but wanted to know when farting had become so political.

On that note, I offer my assistance to the public. For 2012, let's "air" our opinions, shall we? I say we take each of the candidates for President, regardless of their party affiliation or level of delusion concerning their electability and force them to sit in a room with The Dad. Any time one of them says something stupid, hateful, racist, xenophobic or simply untrue, The Dad would get to fart on or near them.

In order for this to be fair, he would need an interpreter as his definition of xenophobia would probably be "fear of xenos". And as you know, the only people who could survive this apocalyptic situation would be a cockroach, Gary Busey or Cher, so the fate of these candidates lies in the hands of those who have a somewhat limited worldview. But I say we give it a try. The worst thing would be no one in the aforementioned paragraph would survive except The Dad and Cher and, truth be told, we might be better off.

Gives a whole new meaning to the winds of change, doesn't it?

Like any proper Presidential historian, I wanted to take stock of the first 100 days of The Dad's residency. To ruminate over the successes, failures and omens both good and bad. It was mere coincidence the New Year was upon us and with my sister visiting, gave me time to reflect on how we had evolved, this family of mine. My sister, Shontyl, is unafraid to state her opinion on any topic at any time.

She had warned me I would regret this decision and I was interested in whether or not she maintained this stance.

Also, there were times when I did wonder if I had made a mistake as I was unaware of his depression. When I was too tired to cater to his every whim, he became moody and isolated. He didn't understand I needed time by myself when I came home from work as I am an extroverted introvert who needs time to recharge. After eight to nine hours of dealing with people all day, I just wanted to relax, rest and read to decompress. He wanted to visit as he had done nothing all day other than listen to music or TV, eat and crochet and wait for me to get home. No matter how much you love someone, there are times when you wish they simply were elsewhere. I resorted to hiding with a book and, usually, Lulu, who always seemed to find me.

I am also not a big fan of TV so when I had more than I could take within the first couple of months, the main thing we enjoyed together was gone. He watches TV from 5 am until 10 pm. Or rather he will tell you he isn't watching it, but it is on throughout the day. I never had cable in my home in my adult life until he moved in with me. When I pulled away from TV viewing with him, I pretty much pulled away from him and he was very unhappy. Of course, The Dad in his passive aggressive way, didn't directly address his unhappiness, he simply took every opportunity to ruin any other pleasant time by pouting. It's somewhat unnerving to watch a grown man sigh dramatically and repeatedly until I ask, "What's wrong" to which he will reply initially, "Huh?" Then, sigh, "Oh, nothing."

How do you interact with a 70-year-old angst-riddled teenager, filled to the brim with coffee, Spam and ennui?

I'm sure I wasn't always patient, but I had no children by choice. The Dad Gene isn't in me; the Uncle Gene I have in spades. I am great in short bursts and from a distance, but I do not have the patience to deal with a child and while The Dad didn't always act like a child, he could sometimes seem extremely childish and I had to assume the adult role, which was just odd to me and appeared condescending to him. He most common lament was, "You think you're better than me" or "You talk to me like I'm some kid".

The one time I responded, "Then don't act like a kid" caused us both so much discomfort we simply backed away into our separate bedrooms without further discussion, neither of us quite sure how to make the next move. We silently agreed to simply pretend it never happened. The next morning, in a typical Thompson Man response, I offered to cook his favorite meal for dinner and he told me he liked my tie.

All in all, it was working fairly well; I had no expectations of a house unfettered with random problems; we are human and therefore imperfect. With this in mind, I started the New Year with, if not a new outlook, at least an idea of the need for a new outlook.

Sunday, January 1, 2012

Grace Under Fire?

While visiting for the holidays, my sister Shontyl asked, while reading my niece's *Vogue*, "Did you know that Coco Chanel was a real person?"

Me: "Yes. Didn't you?"

71

The Dad: "Isn't that Ice-T's wife?"

Me: "Who? Chanel?"

The Dad: "Yeah. His wife's name's Coco."

Shontyl: "Mr. T's wife is Coco Chanel?"

Me: "What? No! He said Ice-T and that's wrong. She may be named Coco and she may be female but those are the only things she has in common with Chanel you can be sure." *I would have said more but I'm afraid of Ice-T and what may happen if he ever reads this blog. Excited about the visibility of my blog, but very, very afraid.*

Shontyl: "Who's Ice-T?"

The Dad: "He's on one of them shows with all the letters. You know, CSI? NCIS?"

Me: "Law and Order SVU." (In my head: Who are these people?)

To understand my frustration, you have to know I am downright persnickety about my trivia. I know scads of things which matter not to most people. I am a trivia nut and there are numerous tomes and board games in my home sitting unused as my family has tired of my triumphs. It couldn't have been my victory dance and chant (all five verses), could it? Surely not.

I know a mastery of trivial facts does not make me smarter than anyone, but I do enjoy being informed on a number of subjects both intellectual and pedestrian. Full disclosure, it's mostly pedestrian. I have read Foucault's *Madness and Civilization* but only the first 32 pages.

My trivial knowledge does make me a great Six Degrees of Kevin Bacon-er. I realize this game is considered *passé*, but I like it and will revel in my un-coolness. My sister, in her attempt to malign my trivial character, double-dog dared me to link the most obscure movie star she could think of (Tyra Banks) to Kevin Bacon through six movies or less. Challenge accepted dear sibling. Tyra Banks was in *Life Size* with Lindsay Lohan who was in *Mean Girls* with Tina Fey who was in *Date Night* with Mark Wahlberg who was in *Boogie Nights* with Philip Seymour Hoffman who was in *State and Main* with Sarah Jessica Parker who was in *Footloose* with Kevin Bacon. And that's without using my old standby of Dan Ackroyd-was-in-*Blue Brothers*-with-John-Belushi-who-was-in-*Animal House*-with-Kevin-Bacon-link. Dan Ackroyd has been in a bunch of movies, y'all.

The reason I bring this up is I have a great memory and quick recall and I know many in my immediate family do not. For example, my sister gets Chevy Chase and Bill Murray confused. Yes, you read it correctly. And The Dad's frames of reference are boxing, football, *Barney Miller* and *Hee Haw*. But my conundrum is I just don't know what I'm supposed to do when The Dad gets dates and facts wrong when he tells a story. Now, those who know me know part of my charm is I am honest to a fault. I don't know how to be anything but, so I am very direct in my conversations with The Dad and all those in my circle, be it work or play. But I don't know if he's misremembering due to his age (he's only 70) or his need to re-interpret the past. And it's constant, like he works for Fox News or something.

And I find myself trying to catch his mistakes, like some intrepid reporter. It's almost become a contest for how many times I can correct him. Is this some latent rage at our past relationship or lack thereof? Or am I just being tooky, which is a word my family apparently coined because any time I use it people question what it means. Tooky is, well, tooky. You know, persnickety.

What if I'm just a run of the mill butthole? And if I am, is it hereditary and can I blame him? And if it's not my being obnoxious, do I just let the inaccuracies slide? Even if he's using them to malign someone's character or call into question someone's motives?

I just don't know what to do. The only thing I know is whenever I correct him he gets his feelings hurt and withdraws physically from me unless we are eating. Nothing will keep him from his "grosh-ries". I have taken the tack of saying, "Are you sure that's right? I remember…" and then I tell either the version of the story I have heard my entire life or I re-state the facts as I remember them if I bore witness or participated, willingly or otherwise.

Sometimes it's harmless, like the year he had his picture taken on the bike from *E.T.* at a mall somewhere. It's the most hilarious picture. He swears it happened in 1977 in Louisiana. *E.T.* wasn't released until 1982 so I know his version is not true. Other times he talks about car wrecks I supposedly had which never took place, in locations I have never been, in vehicles I have never owned or driven, doing all manner of things my little Southern Baptist mama's boy heart just couldn't have done out of the all-consuming fear of being cast into the Lake of Fire.

So, I sit here unsure of what to do. Do I let the lies fly, or do I swat them all down, like so many poorly designed paper airplanes? Do I conduct a brief cost-benefit analysis before I speak, or do I just do damage control after the fact? Since we're expected to do New Year's resolutions, should I just take the high road and let him tell his version of the story?

Even if he skews everything negatively and uses these re-tellings to cast dispersions on loved ones' characters? What if I agree with his take on their character but for reasons other than those misrepresented? Do I agree to keep the peace or just say "oh" or "uh-huh" and hurt his feelings because he thinks I'm belittling him? Mind you, he didn't quite say those words. What he actually said was, "Oh, am I not important enough for you to talk to me? Would it help if I used bigger words? I've got four hours of college, you know."

Also, should I refrain from comments about his hygiene and general demeanor? Should I have not said, "We could grow corn in your underwear" when he asked if I wanted a garden in the backyard? Am I hateful? Is the latent aggression not so latent? I went to six months of anger management therapy two years ago to find the root of my hostility and it a seemed to boil down to *mi padre*. And even if he didn't treat me very well growing up shouldn't I just get over it already? Shouldn't I just put on my Incredible Hulk Underoos and deal with it? You know it's bad when you get on your own nerves.

So, there you have it. I resolve to be a better person in 2012. To be more graceful, in the Biblical sense of grace as I am fleet of foot per the witnesses to my dancing skills last night at the Presbyterian Singles Dance. I don't think God was mad at me for (1) dancing or (2) with Presbyterians. I'm sure he didn't like it when I silently judged the one girl who was wearing mis-matched animal prints and whipping her hair with more dedication than was warranted at a church function during Bon Jovi's *Living on a Prayer*, but I have asked forgiveness and have resolved to be less judgmental this year. Amen!

January 8, 2012

Como se dice, "Who ate my sandwich?"

I should have known turning into the drive thru of the Jack-in-the-Box would lead to ruin. I fastidiously avoid fast food as it is (1) not very tasty and (2) egregiously fattening and I would like to retain my newly trim "figger" as The Dad would say. But the greasy siren beckoned me and as I am embarrassingly susceptible to advertising I had decided that I *needed* one of their value menu chicken sandwiches with bacon.

As I was turning into the parking lot I noticed a small gathering of Hispanic men. Now, I know most of you are familiar with the undocumented workers who congregate at busy intersections waiting to be offered money to do all sorts of manual labor somewhat like a prostitute, if Home Depot was involved in that sort of thing.

Never having engaged one of these workers lest I ruin any future chances of becoming a Supreme Court Justice, I usually pay them no heed and go about my merry way doing all manner of glamorous activities like buying potatoes and sugar-free popsicles in bulk. As I turned into the lot, one of the men signaled me with his finger and greeted me with a questioning eye and hopeful look on his face. Although I was flattered he thought I might be of the stature to procure his services (I'm not wealthy but I have more money than him) I was immediately caught off guard wondering how to respond.

I didn't want to ignore him; it's not his fault he's an undocumented worker in our country. Well, I suppose it is his fault, seeing as how he came here illegally. But are we to assess fault for someone trying to make a better life? I don't want to get all liberal sounding, but, are they all here illegally or is the economy so bad even legitimate immigrants are out of work and desperate to provide for their families? Even if I didn't have any work for him could I just hand him money? Would it be offensive? Would he care? Do I?

You must understand I pride myself in being a very compassionate and generous person, unless I am behind you in traffic or the express lane at Target. *No, old man in front of me last Tuesday, 27 cans of tuna do not count as 1 item just because they are identical. On the other hand, if it were an old lady, I'd think, "Bless her heart" and simply wait my turn. A gentleman is always a gentleman after all, when it comes to a lady. Other dudes, regardless of their age, are on their own.*

Unsure of how to respond without giving him any reason to think I needed his services, regardless of what they were, I tried to smile without any erroneous signaling lest I inadvertently request something through an incorrect nod of the head or too lengthy eye contact and end up with an unwanted employee, bag of drugs or live chicken.

Is there some sort of code? Shouldn't there be an information sheet? Where do I get one? I felt a little like a spy; like Jason Bourne from all those books and movies. I feel sure I could be mistaken for a suave, intelligent CIA agent. At the very least I feel I could be mistaken for someone named Jason.

I guess it's a good thing I'm not in the CIA. For one, the CIA has secrets, people. And if you know me, you know I can't hold water. I'd be on the phone with my sister saying, "Ooh, let me tell you who we tried to assassinate today.

You will never guess, but his name rhymes with 'Dennis Quaid's brother'." Plus, I can't beat up an assassin with a rolled-up newspaper. I can barely kill a bug with a rolled-up newspaper. I usually resort to stomping it with my shoe and that doesn't seem to be an effective method for saving America from the terrorists, I think we can all agree.

In my zeal to non-offensively, non-signal this man who may have simply been trying to scratch his nose as far as I know, I somehow ended up leaving the parking lot through the 'enter only' lane and almost turned the wrong way down a one-way street. Trying to maneuver my car in the right direction while hiding my shame and ignoring the honking from the other customers who were in fact not attempting to scratch their noses (I am quite familiar with that particular gesture), I was able to head back down the road to the Target from whence I came, as I had forgotten to purchase breath spray for our dog Lulu.

I'm not sure exactly when she began dining on dirty diapers filled with athlete's-foot-flavored bilge water, but something's making her breath reek. How am I supposed to convincingly say, "Who's a good girl, yes you are" if I'm trying to breathe through my mouth?

I'm not quite sure where I was going with this entry, but suffice it to say, I made it home in one-piece sans illegal alien but with some basics for the pantry, you know stuff like a $5 DVD of *Fletch*, an awesome movie starring the guy my sister thinks is Bill Murray, a Big Grab® of Doritos®, two 9-volt batteries and 3 packs of spearmint Extra. I told you I was susceptible to advertisement. Once I got home I immediately regretted not stopping to get a worker or two, undocumented or not. You see, today was housecleaning day and I was not in the mood, do you hear me? I have no problem with cleaning up after myself and when I lived alone my house looked like it was unoccupied most of the time as I am very particular and very neat. Living in a house with multiple bedrooms means you can have houseguests and roommates, but it also means you have to clean, even the rooms you don't ever use. Yes, sun porch, I'm talking to you.

The maid duties have increased far more than the occupants as there is a swirling vortex of disorganization that is The Dad residing with me. Things on shelves move out of their proper alignment simply by him walking through the living room. When he sits at the dining table, food leaps from his plate onto the placemat and table. And don't even get me started on the delicate maneuvering required to sweep around more yarn than a nursing home craft room or a Brownie troop trying to earn their "Knitting" badge.

Although, now that I think about it, how would I have communicated with this gentleman of the parking lot what I needed from him anyway? Do the men from Mexico clean, seeing as how Mexico doesn't seem to be a hot bed of women's lib, based on what I read on the news? And how do you say clean in Spanish? I only know how to say, "Where's the party?" (*Donde esta la fiesta*), "I want two chickens" (*Yo quiero dos pollos*) and "that statue is Greek" (*esa estatua es Griega*). This, I feel sure, is not going to get me clean bathrooms or a fully dusted living room, although it might get me a cooked meal, an invitation to a party or a look of confusion as to the statue in question.

Ah, well, at least I have my chicken sandwich from Jack-in-the-Box to sustain me through this cleaning binge. But now I can't find it. I'll bet The Dad ate it.

Tuesday, January 10, 2012

Does preppy come in pill form?

Anyone who knows me knows I have one cowlick in the front of my hair and two in the back. Why my parents left me in the care of bovines in my formative years is anybody's guess. The cowlick in front is a nuisance to someone as particular about my appearance as I am. For the remainder of this entry, I will refer to my cowlick as the swoop as shortening it to, 'the lick' makes me as uncomfortable as I was accompanying my niece to the premiere of *Eclipse*, one of those horrifying Twilight movies. Since when did pasty become the new chic? If I were in high school now, I would be *muy popular*, as I am so pale, I'm almost translucent. And I have been known to sparkle in the sunlight. Well actually I freckle, but they both end in 'kle' so I'm still in the game, right?

When the swoop is parted on the left, it causes my hair to swagger into a formation not unlike Conway Twitty. For those who aren't familiar with Mr. Twitty (may he rest in peace) you can reference John Travolta in *Grease* or Johnny Depp in *Cry Baby*. If you're younger than that, you shouldn't be reading this and need to go to bed. I feel quite sure it's past your bedtime.

However, if I part my hair to the right, the swoop leaps into a formation resembling Superman, from the movies starring Christopher Reeve, not the TV show where Bo Duke was the Dad.

The point I am trying to make is why do we call it a cowlick? Why this particular animal? Why this particular gesture? Did it actually happen to someone back in 16whatever? I have researched the history of the swoop and here is what I found.

Cowlicks are also referred to as hair whorls and trichoglyphs. It was started in the 16th century and referred to the way a mother cow licks her young's head causing a swirling pattern in the hair. While those are interesting facts, the name needs work, doesn't it?

Trichoglyphs could be useful in my quest to use as many obscure references as possible in casual conversation. Telling someone I have multiple trichoglyphs could elicit all manner of responses depending on whether they thought this was a medical condition, weird animal or tattoo. Hair whorl could be interesting although it would be consistently misspelled by a citizenry who for some reason can't seem to master the proper use of your and you're.

I realize the word cowlick is not something to which most people pay much attention; however, it is the one thing I feel is keeping me from becoming completely amazing. I think we can all agree with fantastic hair I could take over the world. Well, hair and a family fortune. And considering The Dad lives with me, I'm thinking the family fortune is nowhere to be found. When he asks me why he couldn't have been born rich instead of good looking, I wonder myself. About the money, that is. I have grown accustomed to ignoring The Dad's rants about his awesomeness at anything other than reality show competition-level eating, Olympic caliber flatulence and, oddly enough, crocheting.

Yes, my redneck, macho father crochets. It's an interesting dichotomy to reside in someone who retains no semblance of the couth he apparently faked throughout my childhood. Don't even start with me, the man leaves his (sugar-free) Popsicle sticks stuck to the placemats on my dining room table along with used blood sugar test strips, crumbs of indeterminate origin, his electronic solitaire game and whichever paperback western he is enjoying at the moment. It looks like he robbed a Walgreen's. And he never says, "Excuse me," when he passes gas from either end. He ignores it, guffaws or begins to look for the frog he assures me he just stepped on.

Back to the crochet, which is French for "hook". He is pretty adept at a skill he obtained while being jailed for some random fight on some random weekend in the bustling metropolis of Lake Providence, LA when he was younger. I'm not sure if it was one of those times where he got in a fight because he was bored or simply doing any manner of things that were illegal in that era. I can never depend on him to stick with the same lie twice; much less tell the truth once. But whatever the situation he is a skilled crochet artist. And he produces them at a rate you can only compare to southeast Asians sewing hidden buttons for Alan Flusser. He crocheted eight afghans and four scarves between Thanksgiving and Christmas. He's already finished a gift for someone who is retiring from the hospital in June.

I have made more runs to the craft section of Wal-Mart for thread than an ill-prepared Vacation Bible School teacher. And if I have to lie to the woman at the check-out line about my daughter Kinley's last-minute school project one more time, she's going to get suspicious. Apparently, I *do* care what Esperanza thinks of me.

Oh, did I tell you that I now have a daughter named Kinley? She's ever so sweet. She is a carbon copy of my niece Payton. So much so I could use Payton's photos and say she was Kinley if push came to shove. Not that I would do it. Well, at least not more than once. Okay, once at Wal-Mart and once at Target. Lydia, my Target cashier, seemed curious as to why I had so many boxes of popsicles, Uncrustables and Kool-Aid. "That darn Kinley," I laughed and gave her my "parent shrug". "What can you do with a teenager?"

What am I supposed to do, admit the Uncrustables are for me? That'd be like admitting I like the song by the boy who used to have that haircut and I stood in line to see *Toy Story 3* and that's a bit more mature than I care to be at this juncture.

And I fully intend on blaming The Dad. Apparently lying is contagious. I knew catching "country" was just a gateway, y'all. I'm slowly becoming a redneck again. But I'm going to do everything in my power to fight it. In fact, tonight I'm wearing a tie and matching pocket square to bed.

Tuesday, January 17, 2012

Out of left field

If you've ever read *Vanity Fair* magazine, you know they end each edition with a Proust Questionnaire. This is where they ask someone of note a series of questions such as "What trait do you despise about yourself?", "Who are your heroes?", "What is your definition of happiness?", etc. As I was reading the latest edition, I decided to ask The Dad some of these same questions, just to see what he would say.

His answers were not really surprising (marrying my Mother was his proudest moment, having a Harley is his definition of happiness) until I got to the one where I asked, "Who are your heroes?" When he said, "You and your brother", I was caught off guard, but I continued with the questions as I had already added this activity to the running list in my head and I needed to cross it off.

When we got to the end, I re-visited his answer and asked him, "Why did you say Thornton (my brother) and I were your heroes?"

"Why?" he asked.

"I was surprised."

"Surprised? You're my heroes because you both have good jobs that you like and that you're good at."

"Really? I never knew."

"I'm prouder of you than anything. You knew *that* didn't you?"

"Of course, I knew," I said, thinking I *so* did not know.

I now have a new definition of happiness.

Saturday, January 21, 2012

Give me a D, give me an O, give me a NUT...

This morning I was awakened by an unnervingly peppy gentleman who looked disturbingly like The Dad. This man came into my bedroom and practically sang me awake, wanting to know if I wanted coffee. My mother did this most of my life, and while my teenage response was usually one of internalized annoyance, I really appreciated her sunny disposition. The Dad (he had admitted his identity under rapid-fire questioning), on the other hand, has never been called vivacious by anyone other than some random cousin mispronouncing the word 'vicious'. I kid, but The Dad typically moves very slowly and is often less than peppy due to a lot of pain from his back and shoulder surgeries.

When I asked to what I owed this new Mary Poppins-esque temperament, he said he wasn't "hurtin' too bad" due to his new pain medication, but I suspected it was also due to his happiness over my allowing him two Krispy Kreme donuts for dessert last night. Who knew a sugar high could last until the next day. If he weren't diabetic, I'd give him donuts every day.

While I enjoyed my coffee, and he sat grinning and chatting, I had a bit of déjà vu due to his maniacal smile and chirpy disposition. It reminded me of the time I got stranded in San Antonio due to a snowstorm in the DC area. It's a long story, but the reason I was in San Antonio to begin with was at the invitation of my sister who was attending, along with my Aunt, cousin and cousin's daughter, the Mid-South Cheer Finals.

I was aware of competition cheer squads being as involved in my niece Payton's activities as I can be from a distance of half a country. But prior to Payton joining a competition cheer squad, I was confused about private cheerleading teams. Who did they cheer for I wondered? Did they have private football teams? Maybe they rented themselves out to schools with no coordinated girls or something. I don't know. But you can get money for cheerleading in college. I should know. I, your humble chronicler, was a cheerleader for one semester in college. Two of my aunts, two of my cousins and one of their daughters and now my niece Payton have led the cheers at various sporting contests. This is a phenomenal level of school spirit to come off one Louisiana turn-row, do you hear me?

Let me tell you these Mid-South Cheer Finals were an experience I'll never forget. As a side note, if you've ever lost a polka dot, well, buddy, I found it. EVERYTHING there was polka-dotted, zebra-striped or bedazzled; sometimes all three. Red glitter eye shadow, pink glitter lip gloss, and rhinestone studded hair bows which could've topped the Christmas Tree in Rockefeller Plaza. And that's just the "Cheer Moms" and "Cheer Meemaws".

We make it to the Alamodome and stand in line to buy a ticket; $30 per person. Ouch! However, as I was dressed for the occasion in red chinos, white button down and navy blazer, I was mistaken for a coach and let in for free, given a commemorative backpack and a free bottle of "Spirit Water". Well, not really, but I was thanked for my spirit on more than one occasion. Well, not thanked *per se*, but people said "whooo!" a lot and pointed at me. It's nice to see others supportive of my fashion choices.

As far as this competition, let me tell you nothing could have prepared me for this. 3600 hyperactive tots, tweens and teens being herded onto a stage to perform gravity-defying stunts with a disturbing amount of sass and spunk and even more disturbing amount of eye makeup. Those contortionists in Cirque du Soleil couldn't have pulled off what some of these little Hunters and Fallons and Dakotas did, without losing their hostile smiles. The coaches called it "projection". I called it maniacal. Of course, I said this to myself. Hell hath no fury like a "Cheer Mom" with her own bejeweled spirit stick accompanied by her "I Pay, She Cheers" t-shirt clad spouse.

And you would not believe what these children are asked to do. There is a move called a scorpion. They take their foot and pull it in a circle behind them until their toes touch the backs of their heads. Standing up. Six feet or more, in the air. In someone else's hands. While "projecting".

It's almost more than you can bear to watch. But we did, from 9 am until 6 pm, without a break. After so many groups, it's funny how commonplace something unbelievable can become. No wonder this generation isn't impressed as they are going through regimented exercises which would've put Mary Lou Retton into traction during her heyday. After several hours of similar routines, with varying degrees of success including lost bows, which is a deduction (in points), and somehow a lost shoe, which is another deduction, I almost couldn't take it anymore. I don't know if there are points deducted for making overweight performers wear belly-shirts that Heidi Klum couldn't pull off without some degree of embarrassment, but there should be. Those poor babies.

Prior to this experience I had never witnessed a scorpion other than in my sister's yard in Texas. After a while I began to get bored with the whole thing. The same snippets of songs, with similar routines. It blurred together. By the end of the day after I had ingested more overpriced water and foot long corndogs than a felonious carnival worker, I began to view those amazing feats with bored derision like, "Is that all you've got Amberly? A scorpion? How about when you're fully extended, you ring a bell with your feet or spell out Cheer Nation in sign language with your toes? Maybe then I'll be impressed." Knowing full well I could not contort my body into those shapes with the assistance of a mechanical taffy puller and an overzealous chiropractor. Some things aren't meant to move in those ways, least of all while wearing clearance –priced Brooks Brothers.

When I saw the first team complete a scorpion, I felt compelled to give them a standing ovation. I stood and clapped but noticed the only people standing were the parents of the performers. My sister just shook her head and laughed. By the end, I was done. I was so weak from the overwhelming too-much-ness of it all I would have agreed to chips and queso with Charles Manson to get back to the hotel.

Speaking of queso, I just remembered I have a leftover quesadilla in the refrigerator and I feel compelled to attend to this matter right now. I'll leave you with this, I salute all those who cheer, those who clap along in the stands (psychotically or not), and most importantly, those who make Krispy Kreme donuts. Seriously, they're doing the Lord's work, y'all.

Wednesday, February 15, 2012

English as a Second Language?

I was reminded again just the other day how my family has a folksy vernacular; an odd combination of country, redneck and Southern that is peppered with words I believe we may have invented. I was sitting at the dining table talking to my friend Adam and The Dad was looking at my magazine. It was the latest edition of *Vanity Fair* and it was, unfortunately, turned to the page which features photos of some of the contributors. As a rule, writers are not an overly attractive subset of humanity. There are exceptions, of course. John Grisham and I are among those who are considered attractive. Well, more attractive than, say, J.R.R. Tolkien (I imagine) or Truman Capote (I am certain).

When he saw the photo of one particularly unfortunate-looking individual he said, "Woo, she's so ugly, she'd make a haint take a thorn thicket!" I'm not sure if he has regressed since my Mother's passing or if he always talked this way and I chose to ignore it, but sadly I knew exactly what he meant.

Adam, who is a graduate of Northwestern (in Chicago) seemed confused and very quietly asked if The Dad were having a stroke. I laughed and explained the definitions of both haint (ghost) and thorn thicket (something akin to a flowerless rose garden, all thorns). While I am not certain of the accuracy of his statement (why would it concern a ghost to run into the brambles seeing as how they really aren't wearing sheets?) I found it interesting I knew exactly what he was talking about.

Once The Dad retired to his room to sleep, Adam asked me why he used such odd phrases but I didn't. Well, I could fill up a book about the inherent differences between my father and me (you are reading it right now, congratulations!)

This question caused me to review words and phrases my family uses fairly regularly, some of which may be familiar.

Jouvous – Nervous.

Tooky – Persnickety.

Rernt – Ruined. Could be in reference to a person, place or thing.

I swonny – An exclamation like "My goodness!" or "I swear!" or in the case of Jane Strawn of Bogata, Texas, "My lands!"

Wompy-jawed – Askew. See also catty-wampus.

Chicken Doody – Any unidentifiable spot on your dress, car, shoe, sidewalk, etc. Does not refer to actual poultry excrement.

"Fine as frog hair" – Said in response to "How are you?" The joke being frog hair is so fine you can't even see it. It's not as funny as The Dad thinks it is.

"Ain't fit to shoot" – Not even good enough to bother with wasting bullets. See also triflin', low-down, no-good.

"In a toot" – In a bad mood.

"Going to town" – leaving your home in search of something to purchase and/or eat, regardless of whether you reside within the city limits or not; stemming from a youth spent in the boonies.

Boonies – Living so far outside of the city limits, wild animals question your presence.

Coke – any flavor of carbonated beverage. Yankees refer to it as soda or pop. We mock those Yankees, sometimes to their faces.

Beautimous – Very attractive. Examples include Linda Evangelista, Jaclyn Smith or my niece Payton.

Hooty-tooty – Extra fancy. See also hoity-toity or foo-foo.

Uppity – Extra fancy but in a condescending manner.

Lawd! – A version of 'Lord', which is a version of 'My, Lord!' or 'My, God!', sometimes shortened to 'Law!" out of sheer laziness I suppose.

Feel free to use these words and phrases in casual conversation to confuse or intimidate frenemies, future in-laws or people eavesdropping at Starbucks. I would caution against using in the workplace as you may be demoted. I'm not ashamed of my upbringing, but I know enough not to say, "I reckon" beyond the comfort of a Tractor Supply store or a conversation with someone named Herschel or Oda Lee. How else do you think I got to be so hooty-tooty?

The Dad accuses me on a continuous basis of forgetting where I'm from and often tells me I'm rude when I call him a redneck. However, I explain to him that he is indeed a redneck by anyone's definition, so I'm just being honest; judgmental, but honest.

As much as I put on, I am glad I grew up in the South and I am, in the deepest recesses of my heart, a good ol' boy. I just prefer to show my Southern pride through the wearing of seersucker. Can I get an Amen?

Tuesday, February 28, 2012

I don't care if Casper IS friendly...

When last, we spoke, we had discussed language, stemming from The Dad's use of the term "haint". This led to a conversation with my sister where she reminded me another word we pronounce incorrectly was "mont-ner", meaning monster.

Being a naturally nervous person, I normally make an effort to avoid all mention of scary things lest I conjure up some creature in my head which will cause me to lose precious sleep. I don't know what happened to me during childhood, but I have been afraid of the dark since somewhere in the neighborhood of birth and lasting up to and including last night. I don't know what makes me skittish in the darkness but if someone were to scare me with, say, a chainsaw, I could outrun any Olympic sprinter regardless if they used steroids or not.

Once, as a teen, I just about outran a car when I thought the Blue Lady of Humble Lake (in Texas) was trying to "git" me. The unfortunate situation occurred when I attended my first teen bonfire, wearing my best corduroy pants. I mention the wardrobe choice simply because, during my flight, said *pantalones* eventually started to smoke from the friction of my chubby legs pistoning me toward safety. Now where I thought I was going to find safety in the boonies of East Texas with 'Flock of Seagulls' bangs and 3 Swatches was beyond me. All I knew was I wanted to be elsewhere.

And elsewhere was where I wanted to be recently when The Dad told me he had seen a ghost in my house.

Now, I realize I am a big strong man (well, a *man* anyway) but I did not need to hear this. Before he could describe this recently sighted apparition, he turned to me and said, "All this talkin' 'bout spirits 'n' stuff put to mind the stories my mama told me."

While he reminisced, and I pretended to listen, I thought of several occasions of my own where I lost any shred of coolness I, or my friends, imagined I had by possessing a lack of bravery which would have gotten me banished from most any Disney movie. While my friends never abandoned me, *per se*, most certainly my date to the Junior Prom was less than thrilled when I abandoned her, faster than a celebrity breaks their wedding vows, at the breakfast afterwards. The brother of the hostess (I won't tell you his name, but it rhymes with Scott Holliday) decided to dress as Freddy Krueger and casually tap-tap-tap, on the French doors to my immediate right in the den while I was actively pretending to watch "A Nightmare on Elm Street, Part XVXVIII" along with seven to eight of my closest personal friends and their dates.

When I ever so nervously turned my head toward the doors and saw this particular face, I screamed like a peacock set on fire, shoved past my date (I apologize again, Denise) and ran down the hall to the bedroom of the slumbering parents due, I can only imagine, to the overwhelming belief Mr. and/or Mrs. Holliday would save me through the use of gunfire or fisticuffs. I don't believe either of them were the same after experiencing the invasion of their inner sanctum by a chubby tuxedoed youth and a full 1/3 of the remaining guests alert enough to have noticed my flight and quickly followed suit.

I may be exaggerating these points; this was, after all, 1987 and it's a bit hazy, but not due to alcohol or drugs, mind you. I was a good Baptist youth, although I will cop to an addiction to Aqua Net; something had to keep all my hair in place. All I know is the following year, the Prom breakfast was held in a well-lit hotel suite with suitable chaperones and, for me, a mild sedative, which may or may not have been chicken strips and Dr. Pepper.

The most recent event I will share happened in Alaska, while camping. Anyone who knows me is aware while I am not an ardent fan of the outdoors at night, I can be shamed into complying with the requests of the nature loving pseudo-hippies I have collected as friends.

This particular outing was Memorial Day weekend in 2003 and, being Alaska, it was a balmy 40 degrees. As I was much larger then, the lack of heat was a plus. Underarm sweat stains large enough to effect local weather patterns are not a good look for anyone.

I had watched the horror movie *The Ring* just prior to this trip. Suffice it to say it was not a romantic comedy about a wedding. Yes, I know, why on earth do I watch scary movies when they actually scare me? I have no answer other than peer pressure. What? I have peers. In theory.

We get to the campground and as there were six of us, I felt my odds of surviving the weekend without being murdered were fair to middlin'. I wasn't the slowest, did not have the largest breasts and am absolutely incurious concerning the source of random snapping twigs. I felt pretty sure I wouldn't be one of the first to die, per the typical plots of axe-murderer movies.

Once we scouted out the restrooms, however, I discovered the source of my pain for the weekend. Even though they advertised toilets, they were actually toilet seats attached to the top of very deep wells. Like *Journey to the Center of the Earth* deep. And if you've seen *The Ring* you know the girl monster, at one point, climbs out of a deep well and comes to *git* the people. Well, I can assure you I don't need someone to *git* me whilst I am conducting my business; the psychological repercussions I don't want to imagine. Needless to say, I spent the weekend avoiding the bathroom which became increasingly difficult while trying to digest elk cooked in a skillet over an open fire.

I had yet to feel uncomfortable in my new home even when living alone for almost four months, but when The Dad told me he had seen a ghost, my first instinct was to flee. The high cost of real estate in the Bay area held me in place, however, and I asked him to describe this ghost. When he stated it was a woman with a large hat and veil and a parasol, I was both delighted she seemed fashionable and suspicious of the accuracy of the fashion as my house was built in 1929 and parasols haven't been used in any manner since *My Fair Lady*.

As I left to walk around and cleanse the house of evil through the recitation of any song I could remember with the most Jesuses in it, I noticed a figure alarmingly like the woman he described! Right in my face! It was the lovely lady in the painting I have over the buffet in my dining room; my first real piece of art. The Dad was either all out of conversational topics not involving bodily functions or he was trying to scare me. Rude.

I told him if the phantom was well-dressed, then we could co-exist quite happily, and I strode off to bed with the full knowledge he had simply fabricated the story and I had nothing to worry about. Dustin does mean "strong hearted leader" according to the book of baby names. My parents chose well.

Monday, March 12, 2012

I only hunt bargains, y'all

Even a life spent on a path which allows you to remain true to your value system, can be de-railed by the simplest of suggestions. The Dad had ever so innocently asked if he could choose the meal for our Friday night dinner. As I have certain activities on my schedule throughout the week (Dinner/Trivia on Tuesdays, Choir Practice on Wednesdays, Single's Bible Study on Thursdays) I have designated Friday as The Day of The Dad and he gets to choose the meal and/ or activity due to his continual lament he feels like he lives by himself.

He suggested he cook pork chops and home fries. I immediately began to formulate the many reasons why he should not when my stomach took over and I was downright shocked to hear myself say, "How much bacon do you need?" He adds bacon, onions and peppers to his potatoes and cooks them to absolute pieces and they are some of the best things I've ever eaten. If God is actually Southern, and I've been assured by a number of Baptists He is, we're having home fries in heaven, y'all. To this coma-inducing meal we added turnip greens, so I could at least pretend it was reasonably well-balanced.

I woke up the next morning moving slowly from the grease and carbs running through my veins and discovered he had taken the leftovers and made omelets. Not wanting to be rude but not really happy with another 'cheat' meal so quickly, I ate the food and thought about the activities to which I was often an unwilling participant throughout my formative years. Besides coon huntin' and frog giggin', I have hauled more hay than an extra on *Hee-Haw,* rounded up horses and hoed cotton. To be honest, the last one was probably only two of three weeks of my life, but whenever it gets hot outside I find myself needing to sing spirituals bent over in a field, y'all.

And while I embraced these activities with all the joy of a Republican acknowledging a poor person, I did try ever so hard to fit in and be "one of the guys", with varying degrees of success.

I won't get into the details of the hunt for frogs and raccoons. Suffice it to say raccoon hunting is like deer hunting but at night. Frog gigging is like raccoon hunting but in water. And hauling hay is indentured servitude, people.

Again, I am navigating a landscape that is unfamiliar and again without a map, but I think I can do better this time. We are intrepid explorers. Well, at least one of us is. We don't need Sacajawea to make it to the Pacific. His Lewis and my Clark can get there just fine as I am the only one who can actually get us anywhere out here in the land of the hippies with my buddy Siri. And we can take those first steps as soon as we can get up from the table. Those taters have weighed us down, y'all.

Thursday, March 15, 2012

Surely that Bible verse wasn't referring to beauty pageants

Having recently judged the 2012 Miss Seattle (WA) Pageant, I am amused/amazed someone from my background is considered an authority in selecting the ideal young woman to represent a city or state in the Miss America system.

Now that we're talking about Miss America, I have to take a minute to educate and inform you on the positive points of the Miss America system. First of all, you have to understand this is not the toddlers and tiaras kind of pageant. A full 75% of the scoring in Miss America is talent and interview (including on-stage question). There are no fake teeth, here, people. This is glamour on an academic scale. There are those who get Miss USA and Miss America confused. Let me explain once and for all the differences between the two.

Number one, I would NEVER be involved with something Donald Trump had his name stamped all over. And all those YouTube videos with confusing answers to on-stage questions are part of the Miss USA competition, people. I assure you those baffled beauty queens are *not* competing for Miss America.

A quick history: There was no Miss America 1950. This was the year they started postdating the titles. Miss America had added a talent component in 1935 and the new winner (Miss America 1951) was Yolanda Betbeze, an accomplished opera singer from Alabama. At the time Catalina Swimwear was the major sponsor of the pageant and the winner was expected to serve as a swimsuit model for a year. Miss Betbeze refused stating she was an opera singer, not a swimsuit model. Lenora Slaughter, then Executive Director, agreed and told Catalina Swimwear as much. When they threatened to withdraw their support, Miss Slaughter said she would find other sponsors. Allegedly, at a press conference, Miss America 1949, Jacquie Mercer (from Arizona) remarked, "You should start your own pageant." They did, and it was the birth of the Miss USA pageant, which, purposefully, has no talent category.

As a side note, I must say I love me some Miss Arizona. I had the privilege of judging their pageant in 2009 and met some amazing and fabulous women, including Misses Arizona 1984 (Rhonda White Pawlak) and 1986 (Terri Kettuenen Muschott). Ms. Pawlak took me to Sonic and then bargain shopping after the pageant. You know I just adore her, right?

I am not saying that former Miss USA's have no talent and aren't intelligent. What I am saying is if you aren't talented, intelligent and well-spoken you WILL NOT become Miss America. I don't care how pretty you may be.

However, let us not forget there is a beauty component. If you are ugly, it doesn't matter if you cure cancer on stage, you will not be crowned Miss America. Ugly will just not win. Odd looking or vaguely horse-faced but still not unattractive, sure; there have been those years, but I shall not repeat them for you here. I don't want to be impolite.

I should know about beauty, as I *was* 1st runner-up in the Little Mr. Dixieland pageant in 1975. The fact there were only 3 contestants is a not germane to this discussion. It could have been worse. I once showed my calf in the 4-H County Fair in Clarksville, TX and being the only entrant in my class I felt I would easily win Grand Champion. To my dismay, I was summarily awarded a white ribbon, which is the equivalent of third place. Yes, third place.

A little pageant birdie told me Miss America might be moving to Mississippi this year; Biloxi to be exact. I am pleased and not surprised. As one of the premiere pageant states, Mississippi is a logical choice. As Suzanne Sugarbaker once said, "You will never see an ugly Miss Mississippi." No truer statement has ever been spoken. Mississippi has had 4 Miss Americas, which places us right behind California and Oklahoma with 6 each and Ohio, Pennsylvania, Illinois and Michigan with 5 each (Mary Catherine Campbell from Ohio won two years in a row in 1922-23, but I count her as one Miss America). Plus, we're the only state on the list with casinos and superior food. It just makes sense, doesn't it? As a side note, three of the four Miss Americas from Mississippi were from Ole Miss. Do what you want with the information Mississippi State fans.

I love the Miss America system. I love the opportunities this program gives to young women. Interview skills to give them an edge over their competition in the job market are invaluable. And, of course, I love the excitement and the dresses and being surrounded by beauty. I get all bumfuzzled thinking about the glamour and the glitz, as long as it doesn't involve children with those fake flipper teeth. My family would say that is *rernt*. And as someone who has judged the Vernon Alabama Street Fair Queen pageant, I know from *rernt*, do you hear me?

I have gone and forgotten the point of this missive, so I'll just say see y'all in September at Miss America. I'll be the perky gentleman near the front wearing my fantastic $6 vintage thrift store tuxedo. If you come early enough, we can count the number of pitiful Yankees wearing white shoes after Labor Day. This being a casino, it could take a while. I hope you bring snacks. Tater tots from Sonic should do the trick.

Sunday, April 1, 2012

Cornbread and Public Indecency

The inherent differences between my father and I have never been quite as obvious as they were this weekend. I arrived at the San Jose airport returning from a week-long project management certification for the government and I was wearing a basic travel outfit of colored chinos, white oxford, white Jack Purcell lace-ups and a grey cardigan. For this trip, my chinos were fuchsia. Fuchsia is the physical manifestation of the word awesome, in case you didn't know.

Now, you don't have to dress like me in order for me to refrain from judgment but when The Dad rolled out of his truck to let me drive home, he was wearing his redneck uniform (jeans with suspenders, pocket t-shirt and Tractor Supply hat). And this, I truly don't mind. However, the addition of house shoes with no socks was a bit much as was the fact his pants were not buttoned or zipped because, I assume, he couldn't be bothered after his pre-airport toileting. I'm not sure I even want to know the reasons why.

After we got home, and I unpacked, he reminded me that since I was away for his "day to pick the groceries" he wanted to choose where we ate dinner. I was too tired to cook so I heartily agreed and left to get the BBQ pizza and wings he had seen on a commercial. I guess he is also susceptible to suggestion. Maybe that's where I get it.

On the way back from Round Table Pizza, I stopped to get our drinks (Coke Zero for him, Snapple Diet Peach Iced Tea for me) at the quickie mart down the street. When I pulled into the parking lot, I noticed a woman with her pants completely pulled down; all the way down. I saw more of her butt cheeks than I have of my own. And she was urinating. Squatting beside a gas pump. Visible from the street. Without shame. I thought, at first, I must be hallucinating as this is not something I expect to see even in California, land of the heathen. And then we locked eyes. The amount of confidence she exuded could have gotten her a career in politics had her lot in life been a different one.

I parked and walked inside and said to the cashier, "You know the woman by the gray pickup is urinating in your parking lot?"

The cashier said, "Dang, man, I told her our bathroom was 'Employees Only' but she could ignore the sign and use it anyway."

After I paid, I left still not believing I had seen what I had seen. I couldn't wait to get home to tell The Dad and then we could laugh about how gross people are and maybe he'd remember some misbegotten adventure with some heinously white trash cousin and we'd be set for dinner time conversation if I included my extensive knowledge of the behavior of sketchy folks. Sometimes at dinner, we read because there's just not a whole lot to say between two people who have nothing in common but their lack of commonalities.

After I told the story, he just looked at me. I said, "I still can't believe it."

He replied, "There oughta be a law."

I said, "I think there has to be."

He said, "I hope so. I mean, businesses shouldn't be allowed to have an 'Employees Only' bathroom."

I stared and said, "THAT's what you got out of my story?"

He looked confused and said, "What?"

"You think the weird thing was the bathroom rules and not the woman who stripped half-naked and tee-teed on the side of a gas pump facing the street?"

"What's the big deal about that?"

"You've done it before, haven't you?"

"I see what you think about me."

"Answer the question please. Have you or have you not urinated in public?"

"I won't dignify that with an answer," he said with more disdain than is warranted from a person who considers potted meat an *amuse bouche*. My assumption was based on the fact he was eating it when I got home knowing full well I was *en route* with dinner.

I wasn't sure what else to say so I just stopped talking while he pouted. Then we shared our pizza and wings and the ensuing indigestion. Nothing says uncomfortable like two people attempting to burp in silence.

I felt kind of bad so this afternoon I made cornbread, in a cast iron skillet, just like a Southern woman, which is fine except I am not a woman and do not remember purchasing said skillet. Where would one obtain this item, anyway? Aren't they just always *there* in a southern family, like grits for breakfast or crazy relatives? I try to tell him love isn't buying things but apparently, I think love is cooking things. Otherwise I have no explanation for my behavior.

These latent abilities in the kitchen are a little closer to my roots than I am comfortable admitting at this juncture. I need to go put on a smoking jacket and cravat and read something really pretentious, just to be on the safe side. Full disclosure, I would need to buy a smoking jacket and cravat, but I *could* just go sit on my sun porch and silently judge people while pretending to read French deconstructionist philosophy or, at the very least, the *Andy Warhol Diaries*.

He really enjoyed the cornbread.

He never did answer my question.

Wednesday, April 4, 2012

Every trail ends at Wal-Mart doesn't it?

Like other storybook children, my father can usually be found by following a trail he's left behind. While Hansel and Gretel dropped breadcrumbs to ensure they would not be lost, my father's trail is both colorful, due to the bits of thread from his crochet projects, and inadvertent due to his seeming disinterest or inability to pick up his feet as he walks. I think it's because he just likes to shuffle about. Maybe the clip-clopping of his rubber-soled house shoes reminds him of the horses of his youth, I don't know.

At first, I thought it was because he was getting older and was losing his ability to walk with a steady gait. However, one mention of going for ice cream or a steak dinner and the spring in his step magically re-appears leaving a swirl of colored bits of yarn in his wake, like a ticker tape parade sponsored by Joann's Fabrics. It's become a part of my daily routine, running across a veritable rainbow in the oddest of places throughout the house.

I understand in order for the yarn to find its way to the nether regions of my home, The Dad's feet have to be the vehicle by which they travel, but how on earth did he get variegated thread behind the toilet in my (not his) bathroom or inside my messenger bag in the hall closet by the back door? What exactly is he doing while I am at work? Seriously, this man can't even put on his socks without my help, but he can move all around to the classic country he blasts throughout the day? How does one combine interpretive dance and Johnny Paycheck?

As I mentioned in the last post, he had been left unchaperoned due to my travel for work and he was living the life of a wild and crazy bachelor. Well, as wild and crazy as you can be with $20, a Jitterbug phone and a scooter with a basket too small to carry your dog.

Typically, on these trips I will call him when I arrive at the hotel to let him know I was not killed in some grisly airline crash. However, we don't check in every day, so it was odd he would call while I was having dinner with some colleagues at Romano's Macaroni Grill. There is some deep emotional connection between government workers and chain restaurants I truly do not understand. Utilizing the lessons learned in our Negotiations class, ½ price wine with mediocre Italian food won out due to my withdrawal and surrender. Hell hath no fury like a federal employee who has exceeded their allotted per diem, y'all. *Per diem* is Latin for "you better eat cheap".

Since I feel talking on the phone at dinner and in the presence of others is rude, I decided I would call him when I got back to my hotel room. When he answered, he seemed very excited. He said, "You're gonna be happy. I did something you've been after me to do since I got here."

"Really?" I said, wondering which suggestion he had taken. Had he cut his toenails, using clippers and a trash can and not wire cutters and the floor? Had he voluntarily sprayed his own recliner to combat the "old man smell"? Had he finally thrown away that horrifyingly ugly brown striped shirt? Had he actually used a paper towel to cover his food in the microwave, so it didn't look like a crime scene? Had he started wringing the water from the sponge before placing it in its cozy? Had he finally given up sardines and pork skins for Lent?

He answered my silent query saying, "I rode over to the nursing home today." This was as unexpected as if he had declared his love for Carmelita, the omelet chef at the hospital cafeteria. Seriously, I have been trying to figure out ways to get him out of the house during the day since he moved in last September. I told him he is simply existing and not really living and he needed to go interact with the veterans in the nursing home on the same campus where we live. I thought he'd enjoy it. It'd give him something to do, get him out of the house where he overeats from boredom and he'd have somebody to swap lies with as, in my experience, it's what old men do.

"Yep," he said. "I went to the nursing home and took them some of the afghans I made and asked them if I could give them to the people who lived there."

"Well, whodathought," I said, so surprised I started talking like my grandmother.

"Yep, they were amazed that I crocheted 'em."

"I'll bet! What made you finally decide to go?"

"I thought it'd be good to see who was there and give me something to do. I do listen to what you say, even if you think I don't."

"Well, look at you." I wanted to say I was proud of him, but can you say something like that to your Dad?

"Yep. The nurses thought it was pretty cool and asked me if I'd make some shawls and scarves for the lady vets. Did you know there were lady vets there?"

"I assumed there were." The VA has greatly expanded its services for female veterans in the last few years.

"And they want me to come teach a crochet class."

"Aren't you something, professor? I am very proud of you." I had decided that it didn't matter I was proud and wanted to say it.

"I know," he laughed. "I'm gonna have to get myself a yellow bow tie. Ain't that what professors wear?"

"It's awfully specific. A *yellow* bow tie. I'm not sure society is quite ready for that."

He was not to be deterred. "They laughed when I told 'em I learned how to crochet in jail."

"I would imagine. I feel quite sure a felonious redneck wearing a bowler riding on a scooter was not what they had in mind when they imagined the answer to their need for an arts and crafts instructor."

"With a yellow bow tie," he laughed. I hadn't seen him this excited in, well, ever, I don't think.

I hope these nurses realize what they've done. He is intense under normal circumstances. Now he has a purpose, he will become a crocheting fiend. He will produce these items at a rate that can only be equated with Toyota. It's impressive to say the least.

Knowing him as I do, I predicted the ensuing request for a thread run to the Wal-Mart once I got home. We piled in this truck and headed toward discount utopia, hoping against hope Esmerelda was on her day off. I didn't need her to ask about Kinley and I couldn't admit I had fabricated a child; I have my pride, y'all. I didn't want this innocent, sweet cashier to know I had lied. The last thing any American needs is another white guy in a suit telling lies in the presence of off-brand cigarettes and clearance priced undergarments.

Plus, I didn't need The Dad thinking he had a grandchild he couldn't remember. We already joke about his memory. When he asked if I was going to hide eggs for him to hunt at Easter, I said I hadn't planned on it. I did casually mention maybe I would just wait until the Monday after and tell him he hunted eggs. He did not find any humor in my remark.

In the spirit of the occasion, I decided I needed to be more involved in his projects. I even offered to help him choose the colors of his thread. I mean, if it's going to be strewn around my home, I want it to color coordinate with the décor. We are not savages.

Saturday, April 14, 2012

Is a Clown at a Conference Really Kidding?

Due to the recent debacle with GSA, I feel, as a government employee, I must speak to this matter. First of all, you have to realize not all government workers are this insane. Apparently, GSA should stand for 'Guess you Should've Asked'.

I have attended many federal conferences in my day; mostly in obscure and/or boring places like Oklahoma City; Omaha or that part of Chicago out by the airport where the closest restaurant was a Dunkin' Donuts at the gas station a half mile away, to which I walked in the sleet because I will brave inclement weather and possible run-ins with gang members to get me some good iced tea, y'all. Addictions are only called that when you're trying to stop.

In my career I have planned and coordinated a large number of meetings, trainings and educational opportunities, all successful, all within the bounds of policy, regulations and, of course, good taste. For those who attended my conference in Chicago last year, I can't help the fact the hotel dressers didn't have any drawers. I have to believe it was in keeping with the style of the area in which the hotel sat. Truck stop chic is a real decorating scheme, I suppose. If you don't think it is, then I suggest you tell all those people who hold it near and dear to their burlap-covered, wagon-wheeled hearts. I wish you luck in that endeavor.

I attended a two-day conference in Oklahoma City this week, just one block from the new American Banjo

Museum. During one of our allotted 15 minutes breaks, we discussed the circumstances of the GSA's various sins and poor judgments. We just could not believe what those people thought they could get away with. I'm so flustered I'm ending sentences with prepositions.

Hiring a mind reader? Really? You want to read a federal employee's mind during a conference? I can do it for free. The women are thinking (1) why is the food so expensive and (2) where is my sweater, its cold in here. The men are thinking (1) why are all these women wearing sweaters and (2) where is the nearest Hooters. The only difference between the married and unmarried men is the added thought, "Hey, my wife has that same sweater."

The coordinator of my conference (this past week) is like me in that she'd rather just provide the snacks herself than lose her good government job over something as silly as food. And I was happy with that. I mean, where else would you be able to get good sheet cake and fruit salad?

And the gifts they supposedly gave away. iPads? Really? I have never gotten a freebie more exciting or costly than a "Leverage the Passion" keychain.

I realize how fortunate I am to have my good 'guv'ment' job seeing as how, as The Dad puts it, I "git to sit on (my) butt and talk all day and get paid to boot." And I couldn't agree more. I thank the good Lord and my boss for a career I love and a nice pay check. I guess I should thank you too, taxpayers.

The silliest thing in this whole mess is they thought they could spend thousands of dollars on t-shirts and ridiculous entertainment and someone wouldn't tell on them. Are you kidding? Anytime you are a supervisor and have the authority to hire someone, there will always be one person who feels you have made a grave error in your decision to not hire them and you must be punished, so they lie in wait for you to make an error in judgment they can use against you the first chance they get.

I kid, but there are some very sad, vindictive people on the federal payroll. Of course, I'm not talking about the good people over here at the Department of Veterans Affairs where I work. No, sir. They are the salt of the earth. I am of course referring to sketchy people from other federal agencies like Fox News.

I think those GSA people should have been fired for the simple fact they hired clowns. I hate clowns. Truly, in my heart, I hate them. I know it's not Christian, but I think I should be given a pass on this one. Clowns think they are so funny and they are NOT. They are evil, and I loathe them, and they can just keep away from my conferences and my house. Great, now I'm thinking about that stupid movie, *Killer Clowns from Outer Space*. Lovely. Now I've gone and scared myself.

I'm scared because if those creepy clowns wanted to, they could just march right in and get me with little to no interference from my roomies. The Dad and Lulu do not good security guards make. Seeing as how *mi padre* can sleep through his own snoring, I am assuming he would not be awakened by any activities up to and including a Third World War or at the very least an invasion of clown-creatures determined to kill. I assure you, unless one of those evil beings actually changes the TV channel from ESPN once inside the house, he'd be safe from The Dad. And Lulu would sell me down the river for a Beggin' Strip. Know that.

If I had my druthers, I'd take my chances with the gang members who reside, I've been told, on the other side of the interstate. I hadn't really thought of it as a perk until now but living on a *cul de sac* on a hospital campus makes my house very difficult to locate. I mean, if the intrepid drivers for Pizza Hut can't find my house, I think I'm safe. I have to believe the Killer Clowns (proper noun) don't have a GPS. Or if they do, I hope it wasn't a gift they got at a GSA conference. Apparently, we have rules about those sorts of things.

God Bless America, y'all.

Saturday, May 5, 2012

Cinco de Own It?

I've come to find it's fairly difficult to take over the world without either start-up capital or a doomsday device. Seeing as how I have neither in any capacity I am at a crossroads, dear readers. And I'm not referencing fellow Southern icon, Ms. Spears', movie debut. While it was not so horrible as to give rise to thoughts of gouging one's eyes out it was also not so great as to admit having seen it without the relative anonymity of great distance twixt you and me. Sometimes Netflix runs out of options, y'all.

This morning I got dressed in one of my favorite outfits: teal cardigan, teal, navy and silver striped skinny tie, navy chinos and grey suede wingtips. I thought I looked ever so cute, but when I presented myself after breakfast, The Dad paused for moment before he continued clippity-clopping toward the door in his house shoes, saying nothing, which is quite the feat for someone who is known to share all his thoughts, appropriate or otherwise.

We were on yet another yarn run to the part of town where I'd prefer never to sojourn. My Inner Snob is appalled, I admit, traveling to Wal-Mart. My Inner Old Lady reminds me of the great value. This is what takes place in my head. Is it any wonder I can't concentrate on what others are saying most of the time? I'm not self-involved, I'm merely distracted. I accept your apology.

Now, you know that I am not above sinking to a level of mundane from time to time, but today has taken its toll on me both psychologically and gastronomically. After fighting the 67% of the citizenry of Guatemala who inhabit the geography around this particular shopping center, The Dad suggested a stop at Taco Bell for an early lunch. I assume this was his way of celebrating Cinco de Mayo.

Considering it was 10:00 am, I thought it should have been considered a poorly chosen brunch, but since he had consumed his breakfast at 5:00 am prior to taking the first of his many naps, I figured he was probably hungry. Having learned to chaperone him lest he feloniously consume grapes from the produce department, I can attest he had not eaten anything in the store other than the amount of oxygen needed for him to punctuate his every step, between the sad little greeter and the extravaganza of color and foliage of the Crafts section, with a fart.

As I prepared to say no, my Inner College Student reminded me that I needed to try a Dorito Loco Taco Supreme. A taco with the shell made of Nacho Cheese Doritos; a dish that will be served in heaven along with iced tea and fried pickles. Of course, the College Student won.

The Dad chose a #11 (two bean burritos, two tacos, drink). He can't remember his ATM PIN or that he should change underwear more than once a week, but he can recite the Taco Bell menu, a place he has frequented exactly zero times in the last eight months. I just adore selective memory loss.

I haven't blogged much in the past few weeks as I have been traveling the highways and byways of this fair land completing many projects for our esteemed federal government all with your tax dollars. And I thank you. I had the luxury of dining out on my most recent visit to DC which helped bookend a delightful week with my group of management trainees.

One of the duties I retained from my previous position is National Program Manager for my division's management trainees. There are, at present, 27 scattered across the VA system; VA being Veterans Affairs, not the State of Virginia. They were presenting their research projects and did a marvelous job, as they had been subjected to a patented Dustin-critique on several occasions throughout their year of data collection and analysis. I spent the first day of the conference, where they would present to the national leadership, micro-judging everything from their jokes and wardrobe choices to their speaking skills and eye contact. It's almost like preparing someone for Miss America. Hyper-scrutiny is par for the course these days. Once they make it past my micro-judgment, they are ready for anything, do you hear me?

When they finished their presentations, they surprised me with a tribute for all my hard work and support with a thank you and listing of what they called Dustin-isms, like my brutal honesty which they described as "[he] isn't afraid to call an ugly baby, an ugly baby." They said they liked some frequent phrases like, "Just saying", "I'm Awesome!" and "Nobody's Perfect, but Jesus". They also presented me with engraved cuff links and a business card holder that was engraved with my name and their favorite Dustin-ism, "Own It and Move On". This has become my career mantra because owning it and moving on is something you must do when you don't understand why something must be done but it's mandated, and you can't change it. Welcome to public service, y'all.

Full disclosure: I didn't realize I used that particular phrase so much until last year when the participants at my Procurement Training Conference in San Antonio created a dance move using the hand gestures I apparently use while repeating the phrase. The motions are somewhat like pulling fruit off a limb above your head and then brushing it to the side.

I can tell you the presentation from the trainees left me overwhelmed and, in a rare occurrence, speechless. I admit I teared up just a bit and had to just hug some people and have a seat. I felt like Sally Field in the graveyard in *Steel Magnolias*, without the convenience of Shirley MacLaine to slap in order to laugh through the tears.

I said all that to say this: I may have found a way to dominate the world after all. I am making the world, if not better, at least a better dressed place, one management trainee class at a time. I am helping make the federal government more efficient, friendlier and more attractive as well. You are most assuredly welcome. Trust me, it was more selfish than altruistic; I have to work with these people. Cute, smart and fun trumps apathetic, double-knit swaddled and angry any day.

And nothing gives me a greater feeling than taking my "life as an art project" approach and, if not actually grooming any followers, at least making unique more acceptable through a stealth campaign with more awe than actual shock. Although most passersby, The Dad included, don't quite know how to react to my fuchsia chinos. I just tell myself their look is one of envy and carry on with my head held high, Diet Snapple Peach Iced Tea attached to my lips, eyebrow arched just so.

In other words, I have owned it and moved on.

Sunday, May 13, 2012

If a Redneck LOL's, does it make a noise?

I've just finished reading *Drop Dead Healthy,* the latest memoir of sorts by one of my favorite authors, AJ Jacobs. I am a lover of all things non-fiction and Mr. Jacobs has documented all manner of activities in his life, like reading the entire Encyclopedia Britannica in a year or literally living the Old Testament for a year. *DDH* is about his quest for bodily perfection. In it he talks about androstenone, which causes people to not be able to smell things like sweat, urine and pig spit. That this could apply to The Dad should come as no surprise as the man does enjoy his Vienna sausages or as he calls them, "vie-eenie weenies". They seem to be no more than potted meat in the shape of a tube. Not appealing in any manner or circumstance up to and including a plane crash in the Andes Mountains. I'd rather eat a soccer player. Well, not really, but you get my point.

The revelation there is the possibility of an ounce of truth in all The Dad's protestations of "I cain't smell what you say you smell" caught me by surprise. He might truly be biologically incapable of actually identifying the funk that is him. As it is a complex aroma (part sweat, part flatulence residue and part old man smell) it has caused me much grief and has been the main source of friction betwixt us since he moved in.

This is not the only reason I bring up the book. Another issue that sprang to mind whilst I was reading is this: Mr. Jacobs is a witty writer, an enjoyable writer, a writer of great talent. He is not however, an author who causes me to "LMAO", otherwise known as laughing my a-crooked letter-crooked letter off. (If you don't get that joke, I'm to assume you never spelled Mississippi as a child). No offense to Timothy Ferriss, who praised him on the book jacket. First of all, what's with all the vulgarity being thrown about with abandon? I weep for our future people. Weep.

Don't get me wrong, AJ, as I would like to call him should we ever meet, is vastly entertaining. When I read his books, and this is the fourth one I've read, I am enthralled, educated and happy. I do not, however, LOL. Not once. And that means laugh out loud, not lots of love as my best friend Christopher's mother originally thought. Full disclosure: we discovered she thought LOL meant lots of love when she made some random comment about the ethnicity of Christopher's fiancé and threw in a few "hell fire and brimstones" and ended the statement with LOL. Now I've known some judgmental Evangelicals in my time, but that was a little too far into Fred Phelps territory for my comfort and I asked Christopher just what was up with his Pentecostal mama. As he did not know, he asked her what exactly she meant by her use of the phrase. I think it might be a generational thing because I asked The Dad what LOL would mean to him and he said lots of love, too.

I'm not trying to say I have never LOL'd. However, I have only LOL'd when reading a very few select people's work. John Kennedy Toole, Tina Fey and Jenny Lawson are a tiny minority of writers who make me LOL. I have also not LMAO'd and I don't know anyone outside of possibly fraternity brothers in the throes of post-finals celebrations who have actually ROFLMAO. That, as you may know is rolling on the floor, LMAOing. Nothing in the history of mankind except possibly Eddie Izzard (in his *Dress to Kill* concert), Robin Williams doing stand-up in the late 80s or Katt Williams and/or Kevin Hart is *that* funny. Dane Cook is not that funny. Amy Schumer is not that funny. LOL funny? Sure. ROFLMAO funny? No.

But what are we to say when we find ourselves in the throes of a reaction that needs to be documented? In order to educate as well as entertain (in the mold of Mr. Jacobs himself) I have decided to create a new language to cover the bases of the reactions I have had while reading, Facebooking, etc. Use it as you see fit.

GAB – (pronounced like you'd think) giggle a bit.

SAL – (ditto) smile a lot.

OMIA/OMID (ditto) open mouth in anger or disgust.

AEBIS/AEBII – (ditto) arch eyebrows in surprise or interest.

SHIW/SHIS – (ditto) shake head in wonder or sadness. Usually follows OMIA/D.

TLMHWHN – (pronounced Tulim Hewin) tight-lipped mm-hmming with head nod.

GAWL – (pronounced like you think) gesture accusingly while laughing. Usually at a person who you have discovered is "so (that person) it's not funny", which ironically is funny.

LCASFATR – (pronounced Lucas Fatter) look condescendingly at someone from across the room. Of course, I'm referring to the theoretical room that is Facebook.

LSHILAFSTLWRIAAAIDTPITF (no pronunciation offered) laugh so hard I look around for someone to laugh with, realize I am alone and immediately decide to post it to Facebook. Of course, I could have inadvertently spelled the name of some obscure city in Wales. If I have, I apologize.

GMFHBNLMFP (ditto) got my feelings hurt because no one liked my funny post from the LSHILAFSTLWRIAAAIDTPITF.

So, there you have it. I hope I have established a new common language to assist you in getting your point across in cyberspace. Now, I realize some of the pronunciations can get in the way, but if we were being honest, how often do we really say LOL in person? I'm hoping not at all, because if you are then it's just sad and I will, at the very least, AEBIS and more than likely SHIS. Just saying.

To return the focus of this missive to The Dad, I will say his possibly biological inability to smell certain things has also, apparently, affected his judgment in many ways especially in relation to acceptable behavior in the home. Now I know I am persnickety about many things, but I truly don't feel it is asking too much to expect him to close the door when using the restroom. He doesn't, regardless of the activity being executed. I believe the street vernacular is #1 and/or #2.

I also don't feel it is, to use his words "actin' like Queen Elizabeth is comin'", to require a properly closed trouser (buttoned and zipped) for any and all meals, snacks and TV viewing. What he does when I am not home would, I feel quite sure, both alarm and unnerve me and I'd just rather be in the dark. His level of comfort is much too close for me, if you are picking up what I'm throwing down.

Additionally, I have made small requests in relation to meal time conversation. I have asked clinical details of bodily functions, fluids and various other words which begin with an F be saved for his actual physician. I do not want to know what came out of where while I am trying to enjoy my "concoctions" as he likes to call anything with which he has no familiarity which can be something as mundane as hummus and pita.

When I described the ingredients, he just stared at me. Chickpeas "sounded weird" and tahini sounded like "somewhere rich people go for vacation". In my zeal to establish a frame of reference using things he understands, I ended up calling it a Mediterranean version of refried beans, which lessened my enjoyment, can I just say.

Sunday, May 20, 2012

Fat Rednecks and Gangstas: Style Cousins?

It has happened. I have crowned myself America's Next Diet Guru without the need for an exhausting reality program hosted by someone of questionable British heritage. The evidence, you ask? I present, for discussion, The Dad and his 40-pound weight loss (since September 2011). I have dragged him kicking and screaming toward physical health. Well, his version of kicking and screaming which is more pouting and angry looks as he is often tired and intermittently ambulatory.

I discovered the exact degree of weight loss (39 pounds 11 ounces) when he entered the dining room this morning and asked, "How is it that I've lost 40 pounds and I'm wearing the same dad-blasted pair of pants?" He did not like my answer of, "Those pants have been, and remain, too small. Belt buckles should sit at your waist, not the middle of your thigh."

Men of his generation, the offspring of those called "The Greatest" by Tom Brokaw, are an interesting group. I'm not sure if this is a Southern thing or not, but all I know is most of the men I knew growing up in the South begin in high school a lifelong relationship with the same waist size of pant, regardless of issues of proper fit. Baby Boomer is the name for their generation and although it probably wasn't a term created to correspond with the alarming rate of waist expansion, the moniker is more than apt, wouldn't you agree. I was going to say ample, but there's no need to be rude.

It strikes me as humorous my father's pants have slowly slid ever toward his knees like a child who has been instructed to clean the yard; a slow, meandering walk, gradually easing toward the intended destination, which I can only assume, is around the ankles, as these people spend an inordinate amount of time in bathroom. I have never known him to be a fashion pioneer, but he and his meaty brethren have been (grammatically more accurate) bursting a sag since, at the very least, October 1970 AD, translated 'After Dustin'. I know there are those who will say it's actually *Anno Domini* or something else Latin, but my interpretation makes more sense, *n'est-ce pas*?

Due to the reduction in the protuberance subjecting the upper portion of his lower torso to extreme shade, his pants are now somewhere in the, medically inaccurate, upper-middle-thigh area. This is just low enough to cause concern but high enough to lessen the likelihood of a glimpse of 'welder crack', as he has never plumbed to any degree. The citizenry of the South San Francisco Bay Area is appreciative, whether they know it or not. I am accustomed to working behind the scenes, trying to make the world a more pleasant place one person at a time. Your silence reeks of gratitude dear readers. You are most welcome.

If you know anything about me you know once The Dad proclaimed his weight loss, I immediately began to deconstruct each section of his person to see if anything else had changed. Other than wearing the new shirts I bought him to replace the ones somehow misplaced in an incident in the laundry room, he has maintained his look. As the incident was un-witnessed by anyone except myself and Lulu it shall remain a mystery.

Throughout my life I have noticed his stomach had increased at a rate equal to the disappearance of his buttocks. I did not notice any change in his lack of posterior. Full disclosure, I try to avoid eye contact with that particular part of anyone's anatomy prior to my morning coffee. I prefer my wake-up to include only caffeinated beverages.

Now, I am no physician, but having worked in the healthcare field more than a decade and as I am hyper-observant to the point of criticality, I can say most men of this generation are equally disproportionate. As in all real estate transactions, location is king, and it seems their buttocks, tired of the view, have migrated *en masse*, to a better spot. I suppose the betterness of the spot is an opinion to be validated by someone else interested in the anatomy and physiology of "old men parts". I would have said this would include their female counterparts, but I have been assured on more than one occasion by the alumnae of my alma mater, Mississippi University for Women, this is simply not true. As I am a student of criticism, not anthropology, I will leave this academic discourse to others. I do know I have seen much more old man crack, plumber or otherwise, than I have ever wanted or imagined; mostly within the safety of my own home.

On a positive note, the weight loss has afforded an improvement in his diabetes, or The Sugar (pronounced 'Tha Shugah') as it is known in the boonies. His blood sugar is relatively under control. I say relatively as his scores are better than his siblings, for whom gravy is still a beverage. He has said on a number of occasions, usually in the throes of some dramatic invitation to one of his patented pity parties, RSVP not required, "You know tha sugah is gonna take my feet."

I typically do not engage when this is presented as a topic of conversation because I, and he, have grown tired of my constant refrain of "carbohydrates are as harmful to your body as sugar." His practiced inability to retain this information causes me much frustration. Each time we discuss the fact that crackers, bread, potatoes, rice, etc. are all carbohydrates he feigns confusion as if he expects to go to the bargain market and find a box emblazoned with the word 'CARBS'. His avoidance of this particularly labeled box should allow him *carte blanche* when it comes to eating a meal containing pasta, potatoes and bread, with crackers as a vegetable.

By simply creating pre-portioned meals to give him what he wants in moderation and forbidding the purchase of items such as soda, ice cream and chips, he has unwillingly lost the afore-mentioned "near 'bout 40" pounds. Helping him choose cottage cheese and fruit over Peanut Butter Snickers is also a way to remind myself to consume a healthier diet, as I must eat by example. He has not cottoned to sharing my love of salmon and Mediterranean food, but he has agreed to mashed cauliflower as a substitute, sometimes, for mashed potatoes and he will infrequently allow "hippie hamburger" in his meatloaf or breakfast omelets. The rest of society refers to it as ground turkey.

I predict he will be able to reasonably fit into his current clothes once he loses about 25 more pounds. Only at that point might he be at the appropriate weight for a 44x27 carpenter jean; his pant of choice. Yes, you read that correctly. With my measurements of 36x29, I am the Heidi Klum to his Melissa McCarthy.

As Dr. Phil is unequivocally larger than I and has several weight loss products on the market, I feel it would be acceptable for me to launch a second career. I could call my guidebook the *Shrinking Redneck Population* to trick unsuspecting Yankees into buying what they are hoping is a sociology treatise.

Sunday, June 10, 2012

Isn't this a Tom T. Hall song?

At 4:45 the other morning I awoke to such a clatter, I sprang from my bed to see what was the matter. The noise seemed to involve wood, ceramic and metal. I was soon to discover it also included denim and whatever material constitutes a tractor supply hat. The Dad had fallen; like a Redwood in the forest, except with more cursing. This couldn't have come at a worse time as when I awoke I realized I had been sleeping on my right arm; it was numb, and I couldn't move it.

I am a typically unadventurous sleeper. Until my significant weight loss, I used a CPAP machine to help me breathe and had to learn to sleep (1) on my back and (2) without moving. Making my bed in the morning is not an exhaustive task. My sister has said it's slightly creepy how I don't move; like a dead person. However, for the past month or so I have been tossing and turning like Bobby Lewis. Some of you will get that joke; others will need to ask their parents.

Anyway, I rush into The Dad's bedroom and see him on the floor, having somehow taken the entire contents of his bookshelf and the top of his dresser except for the TV, thank goodness. When I attempted to help him, he insisted he could get himself up and lurched away from my one good arm and proceeded to get up on one knee and summarily collapse onto the floor, emitting more curse words than a truck stop waitress who has "been done wrong" by some no-good trucker with a double name.

Trying to help him with my good arm, while flapping my other arm around to get the circulation flowing and him wiggling all over the floor, threw Lulu into a state of confusion and happiness as she bounded from her doggie bed wanting to play. Have you ever tried to help lift an overweight man who is trying to fight you using your one good arm and fending off the dog? No, Dustin, just you. And while it may be funny now, it was most assuredly not funny then. Well, except maybe to Lulu.

I felt bad about him falling and I know older people can break things when they do fall. He complains about aches and pains non-stop, so I knew I could look forward to an uptick in the woe-is-me-ing later that night and especially the next day and even the day after that. As someone who knows (somewhat) the pain of working out, I can tell you the next day is not as bad as the day after.

Although his falling and my working out are not the same, they both involve sweating and someone on the floor cursing and usually followed by someone regaling all and sundry with the specifics of the incident and detailing the aches and pains long after interest has waned and even the memory of the pain has subsided. Full disclosure: I did kick boxing for about 5 months (from October 2009-February 2010). I still talk about the pain. Yes, Virginia, I see the irony.

Of course, he is still talking about the fall and the aches and pains and it's been like a week and a half. His toe hurts, his ankle hurts, both knees hurt, his ribs/thigh/shoulder/lungs/kidney/uterus hurt. This is in addition to his typical refrain of "my back, a-double-s and neck hurt". When I ask if he has taken a pain pill, for which he has a prescription, he always says, "Nah. It's not *that* bad yet." Really? To hear him you would think his pain was mind-numbing. He has likened it to child birth. He has actually said, "On a scale of 1 to 10, this is a 25", but in his estimation, it is not enough to take a pill. Get over yourself old man.

What do you think is going to happen? Just because more than your fair share of relatives (on the Thompson side) have become pill addicts doesn't mean you will. I am hardcore anti-drug but even I've started acting like the sketchy best friend in a coming of age movie saying things like, "Come on man, it's no big deal. It's just one pill."

I have even resorted to just getting one out and putting it in his hand and giving him a bottle of water. No questions, no judgments. Just like one of those meetings you see on TV where you tell your name and your addiction. They don't have one for thrift store shopping; I checked. They should have one for gossiping but those kinds of meetings usually take place in church and although we'd discuss how we feel guilty talking about people, we'd end up talking about people while describing why we felt we had to and it would be sort of a breaking even situation and nobody wants that. Not even for really good chess pie. Ok, maybe for really, really good chess pie.

And although he is prone to exaggeration, I really do think he is "stove up" a little as he has turned down the last two invitations to breakfast at Jason's, his favorite place, as well as the latest trip to Wal-Mart leaving me to navigate the waters of Little Guatemala, *mano*-a-nada. *Como se dice*, 'Alone'?

I felt like the hero in an action film who has been abandoned at the gates of the castle/den of thieves/cave, on a mission from some hard to please despot who requires things I wouldn't normally buy like yarn, XXL underwear, Stetson cologne and denture adhesive. I can only imagine what people were thinking when they looked into my cart. *I used to say buggy but that can be shamed out of you by New Englanders who call them carriages.*

What? You mean you don't look in other people's carts, scoping out their items and using what you see to parse out their back story? No, Dustin, just you. I guess it is true what my mother always said, "Just because you're talking about people doesn't mean they are talking about you."

Well said, nomadic Southern Baptist. Well said indeed.

Wednesday, June 13, 2012

I knew I liked the Golden Girls, but...

As I suspected, my father, never one to suffer in silence has been milking his fall like a dairy farmer, y'all. His rants are usually forlorn and punctuated only by heavy sighs and head nods. Well, let me tell you, today he was in rare form. He got irritated at Lord only knows what, probably when I refused to buy his diabetic self a cupcake, and he began to loudly protest the pain and suffering he was experiencing and while I didn't quite understand everything he was saying I can attest to the fact that I have never heard a-double-s used so many times in a 5-minute period. I liken it to the number of times Al Pacino says the f-word in *Scarface*. For those who haven't watched that family-friendly flick, let me just say it was a LOT.

Now I don't know if my father became so adept at cursing once he began working off-shore or if he entered marriage with my mother pre-packaged with a filthy mouth, but throughout my life he has taken his cursing to a Master level. If there was a certification in potty mouth, I can assure you he could serve on the curriculum team. Of course, I have cursed in my day but usually only in the most trying of circumstances like when an inanimate object won't do what I want it to do, like stupid socks, an uncooperative umbrella or that irritating napkin that REFUSES to remain covering the dish in the microwave while it rotates ever so slowly. I also dislike people who can't drive, which includes most everyone on the road except me and the relative few of you who can navigate our nation's highways and bi-ways. What is a bi-way, I wonder?

And, honestly, one cannot live in a curse-filled household and it not affect your speech, although my mother remained above the fray. I did pretty well with no cursing until I was in college and, just like eating potato chips, once you start it's hard to stop. Now, I don't curse at work and I definitely don't at church and I don't typically in public, but boy howdy I sure do when I'm alone and I get irritated. And I try to keep it under control but like my best friend Christopher says, "Screaming 'strawberry' doesn't have the same satisfying effect."

Am I proud of this? Absolutely not. Am I working on fixing this? Absolutely. Have I been successful? Depends on your frame of reference for success. I have tried substituting different words and phrases for some of the fouler sayings in my verbal arsenal but that often leads to confusion for those around me. Hearing someone say, in a loud annoyed voice, "Brenda Fricker!" is cause for concern. The full statement, depending on the level of irritation at the person, place or thing, "Brenda Fricker won an Oscar for *My Left Foot*!" makes no sense to anyone other than Oscar trivia buffs and, including me, that consists of about three people. And even they would wonder why I am so passionate about an actress that no one remembers, if they ever knew her to begin with. I have learned to wear my ID photo badge on my nightly walks around the hospital grounds lest anyone suspect I have managed to escape from the locked ward.

I was discussing my new thrift store finds today with my management team. We had an off-site retreat and, wanting to set the right tone for an informal gathering that would generate ideas, I chose to wear and multi-colored-striped button down and white chinos with matching navy suede belt and wingtips. I have been told that my three-piece suits with coordinated tie and pocket square were intimidating to some and I wanted to take a much more casual approach for this particular session. During the course of the day, I was speaking to them about the unique situations you encounter when you supervise people.

There are three staff members who have recently been promoted to management positions and their co-workers have been treating them differently. I said, "You have to develop a thick skin (in leadership roles) because people will invariably talk about you. I have a very thick skin; I couldn't dress this way and expect to not have people question everything from my political leanings to the state of my soul."

One reason I love living in Menlo Park is that no one bats an eye when I wear my outfits as the majority of the denizens of this fair burg are wealthy older people and the women love my ensembles; odds are the shirts and pants belonged to their dear departed husbands. I have been hugged on several occasions by exquisitely-coiffed, teeny tiny ladies who tell me how "adorable" I look. If you'll pardon the poor grammar, I loves me some older ladies, y'all.

It just occurred to me, I may need to start looking to this older group for dating and possible marriage. As someone who is uncomfortable talking about, much less contemplating, "relations" with anyone, I feel the odds are pretty good of finding someone who shares my love of seersucker and doesn't want to degrade themselves (or me) in the boudoir, if you're picking up what I'm throwing down. I have it on good authority many women would love a husband who would voluntarily take them shopping, understands the need for multiple pairs of black shoes and doesn't want to "mess with" them.

Also, no awkward first dates. Really, no dates at all. Getting them coffee before the church service one Sunday could count as second base. I'll be like Truman Capote, when he escorted all those society ladies in New York. Eww, wait. Okay, *not* Truman Capote. I know, I'll be like Bernie from the movie *Bernie* except I wouldn't shoot Shirley MacLaine; I'd just give her extra wine and put her to sleep.

This might actually work. Look at the things I have in common with this particular crowd. I go to bed at 10, get up at 6, like to eat dinner around 5:30, hate to wait in line for anything, think most young people are disrespectful, am very conservative in my dress and have always been partial to Lincoln Town Cars. Plus, I make a mean pone of cornbread, always have a can of cream of mushroom soup in the pantry, hate most TV shows because they are filthy, enjoyed *The Best Exotic Marigold Hotel* and am usually cold.

Well, this wasn't the outcome I was expecting. I mean, I don't mind being an old soul; I just assumed I would be an old man.

Friday, June 22, 2012

Time after Time

For the first time in quite a few years I am with The Dad on Father's Day. I have always called him and sent him a gift but it's the first time since probably college where he and I are staring at each other on the exact date. Staring at each other in a good way…I suppose. It's more a testament to our confusion over shared genes than an actual competition although he would win by utilizing the time-honored weapon known as "pull my finger". Knowing full well a refusal to approach much less yank the digit in question will in no way impede the intended result. And sitting on my almost non-existent butt with my oddly short legs swaying in the breeze, I know beyond the shadow of a doubt I am a younger version of The Dad except I have cuter clothes, computer skills and an aversion to eating protein out of a can.

This day coupled with the fact tomorrow would have been my parents' 47th wedding anniversary has put in mind things for which I am grateful in relation to my family and my life. I used to think and say I wish I had grown up in different circumstances, financial, geographical and otherwise. I know now I am glad things happened as they did for a reason. I would not be the person I am if my life had been any different. For a long time, I wished I had grown up in an urban area as opposed to various boonies throughout the South, but as an adult I truly appreciate the rural nature of my upbringing. It has given me a foundation of civility and simplicity which seems down-right quaint in comparison to today's slightly skanky society. Drugs and pornography were not even on our radar; alcohol was easily with reach, seeing as how Walthall County, although a dry county, was within inches of Louisiana, a state always on the cutting edge of sketchy behavior. And although my peers imbibed from time to time it wasn't as if we planned our social life around it. You're welcome for this revisionist history ladies and (one) gentleman.

As is typical for small town mama's boys, most of my friends were girls. I've always found them to be more interesting, fun and clean. Their activities, while sometimes odd and uninteresting to me, were at least indoors, where I was determined to be. It wasn't as if I were opposed to the outdoors. Full disclosure: I was opposed to the outdoors. I attended my fair share of pasture parties and soirees at the river, but it was more for a sense of camaraderie than any zeal for nature. And by camaraderie, I mean popularity, peripheral or otherwise. While I was usually well-liked I have never been cool, by anyone's definition. I tried to make up for my natural uniqueness by being funny. And for this talent I look to my father. While my mother had many wonderful traits, and was humorous, The Dad was the comedian in that marriage, in the broadest definition of that word. He found himself peerlessly hilarious; we often found no humor in what he was saying, usually because we were horrified or embarrassed for the repetition. At what age can you hear the phrase, "fine as frog hair" in response to someone's inquiry into his well-being and actually laugh and/or not feel instant shame? Apparently age 12, as this phrase has caused internal groans and external reddening of the face since somewhere around 1982.

One of The Dad's unusual traits I have recently discovered is his need to put a time to every action. For example, a week or so ago he was complaining he forgot to charge his cell phone and he was about to go to sleep. I inquired as to why he would need his phone during slumber as he doesn't often use it while awake and he said, "I need it to tell the time during the night." As it was also my bedtime (I feel old, y'all), I refrained from continuing the conversation lest he not get the 11 hours of beauty sleep he most assuredly needs.

The next morning, I discovered the reason for his complaint. He proceeded to tell me each and every time he woke up throughout the night and what time he arose to start the morning. Apparently, "I got up 4 times to pee" is not scintillating enough conversation. He feels I would do well with more detail. "I got up at 1:43, 2:18, 3:36 and 4:27 to pee" is more detail than I need to start my day off adequately. Sadly, dear readers, caffeine is not what wakes me up.

Along with the punctuality of his emissions, I am also privy to the exact time (3:44) his a-double-s started hurting and he had to move himself to his bed. This is followed by the exact moment (5:11) his side began to bother him requiring a return to his trusty recliner. Without his phone, his stories would be down-right boring. Smell that? That's sarcasm.

Even though we had celebrated with a Father's Day dinner the night before, as I had a full day with church, brunch and heading to San Jose to greet the attendees for my training conference this week, he somehow finagled a BBQ as well. At 2:34 we fired up the grill (yes, I have a grill) and at 2:37 he wanted to know exactly what was taking "them dad-burn pork chops so long? I could cook them faster with a stick and a match." At 2:38 I said, "Look here old man, sit down and wait; you're the farthest thing from starving I've met in a long time." Actually, I said it in my head. What I said out loud was, "They'll be done in a minute. Go get your Kool-Aid and check your blood sugar." That was at 2:42. See how much more interesting this story is when I include the times?

Author's Note: I now check my phone each time I get up at night. Touché, Old Man.

Monday, July 2, 2012

Are you called a butler if you don't get paid?

My sister, niece and niece's boyfriend were here for vacation last week. The Dad couldn't fit it into his busy schedule to accompany us on our trip south, so we had to make it to LA and back bereft of the stimulating conversation he would surely have provided. He wasn't far from our minds however, when on our trip back, we noticed the most wonderful sight in the world; a walmart.com delivery truck. The wording on the side said they delivered groceries to your home. Have more beautiful words ever been spoken? If I could just go online and click all the things The Dad needs from The Wal-Mart I would never have to have my passport stamped in Little Guatemala again.

I don't mind being around those for whom Spanish is their only language, it's more the crowded street market feel of the whole experience which does not meet my expectations for a fun-filled Saturday morning. If I were a betting man I would give you ridiculous odds there are in fact live goats and chickens tethered in the regions of the store into which I fear to tread, notably the "Home and Garden" and "Sporting Goods" sections. Several years ago,

I found, to my dismay the H&G section was more garden than home, so I have not returned.

As the parent of exactly zero real children (lest we not forget the imaginary Kinley) I keep forgetting a vacation with a teenaged girl is not so much a family outing as it is a trip with her highness and the wait staff who cater to her every whim. Now I personally have no memory of my parents ever asking me what I wanted to do, however this new generation doesn't wait for an opinion to be requested. They offer theirs up with greater frequency than a Kardashian plans a new marriage.

Typically, growing up, we didn't so much take a vacation than spend the summer at my grandparent's farm, or after my grandfather's death, at my aunt and uncle's ranch. All I remember is spending every summer surrounded by the flora and fauna typically found in either the Louisiana Delta or East Texas, which included cows and poison ivy based on the disasters that befell me each sojourn. I guess I should also include horses as I have spent more than eight seconds on one.

Suffice it to say I haven't willingly gotten back on the horse since. Note I said willingly. Again, not sure if it's this new generation or not but I don't remember ever, not even once, being asked, "Would you like to (insert horrifying proposition here)?" Things as random as "camp out on an abandoned flatbed trailer and sleep directly on poison ivy because you hadn't begun studying The Cub Scout guide for indigenous plant life" or "ride in the Grand Entry of a rodeo even though you have squat experience and if horses can sense fear, yours is aware of the terror-filled youth in ill-fitting denim sitting in a quasi-sidesaddle position as one foot got stuck in the wrong stirrup and the chubbiness of the legs and agility of the youth did not allow for proper or speedy correction".

Granted they didn't go into much detail, I'm assuming, because no one in Texas would have imagined someone could do those things outside of a 1930s screwball comedy starring Myrna Loy or Rosalind Russell. At least they had the excuse of being snooty society types from "the Manor" whereas I was not a society type unless you count 4-H as a society. You'll notice I declined to discuss the manor from whence I came. You'll notice the declination is still in effect. I thank you for your cooperation.

I trailed behind Payton and her long-suffering boyfriend Chad, paying for everything and offering trivia as we went (one of the costs of Uncle Dusty's financial support is the required interest (feigned or otherwise) in whatever manner of infotainment tidbit I decide to share. Sometimes Uncle Dusty himself is surprised by the (admittedly) fascinating anecdotes).

We made our way northward from Anaheim to LA to Santa Monica and finally back to Menlo Park, our home base, where we returned to this reality: whenever left to his own devices, The Dad will attempt to batter and fry the contents of my home. There was a thick layer of country wafting through the air. For the uninitiated, country is my word for grease, smoke and flour; the least health conscious Yankee Candle scent ever.

Such is the vacation for this year. I am familiar with the idea of a stay-cation where you're just off work but stay near or at home. But I'm not sure what to call what my family did. Was it a poor-cation? Country-cation? Whatever you called it we would travel to a relative's home and like houseguests in *Downton Abbey* days, we'd stay at least a fortnight, if not a fortnight squared. Sleeping eight kids to a pallet on the living room floor, trying to stay quiet lest you be beaten into submission; stifling giggles, persistent only because we weren't supposed to giggle; never rooted in anything actually funny.

Payton has never known the joys of floor sleeping, her vacations always involve an upgraded suite at a Marriott as my guv'ment job affords travel point accumulation at a rate far above my income level. Left to my own dollars spent, I would be platinum only at Motel 6 or at the very least Super 8, who probably base their levels of appreciation for patrons on something like lunch meats. I'd like to think I'd be black forest ham, hand sliced in the deli. Truth be told I'm so cheap when it comes to spending on myself I'd probably be clearance priced hogshead cheese.

We trailed behind Her Highness who, like other members of the royal family, does not carry cash. Although she has more purses, handbags and wristlets than a shoplifting starlet, she never seems to carry anything on her person that would cause her to have access to necessities such as sunglasses, lip balm or snacks because her mother is there for such things with her giant bag. We're like a Butler system sponsored by Coach. We've butled (?) throughout many ports of call, New Orleans, Colorado, LA, San Francisco, Hawaii, and New England. She has stated the desire to go to Minneapolis and the Mall of America, but I feel my credit cards wouldn't survive this particular destination, intrepid though they may seem.

Trying to be the host with the most and attempting to cater to all whims, both ridiculous and carb-heavy, I juggled all house guests (including the permanent ones) like the over-caffeinated clown we saw at Pier 39 on the Bay. Remember how I hate clowns? Well I really, really hated this one and not just because he thought his seersucker pants were "ridiculous". It was almost enough to keep me from enjoying the bag of mini donuts which were in my possession for approximately three seconds before it was snatched away by Her Highness, who had become hungered as apparently posing for a caricature is hard work, y'all. She shared my pilfered treats with Chad who was ravenous as apparently mooning over a 6' tall 16-year-old is also hard work. Kids these days don't know a thing about real work, said my inner old lady.

Of course, there are those in the Boomer generation who reside in my home who feel they should be rewarded for waking up and mass-producing afghans at a rate which is the envy of the Japanese auto industry. So, I guess it's not a Millenial thing; it's a thing for people who are used to being waited on hand and foot. And that's where this lovely Wal-Mart idea will come into play. I can give The Dad his heart's desire; at least those desires which reside within The Mart which, truth be told, covers everything on his list except Harley Davidson motorcycles. And I never have to leave the comfort of my home. Now I just have to convince them yarn is food.

Tuesday, July 10, 2012

Is burnt chicken really patriotic?

I apologize for the lateness of my 4th of July-themed blog. I was trying to wait until my eyebrows grew back but it was taking a long time, so I figured I might as well spill the beans. I had decided it might be fun to have a few friends over for a cookout on the 4th and celebrate as our forefathers did, or so I've been educated by beer commercials. I find it hard to believe George, Benjy and the lot partied down after their victory over the British by hosting a kegger and burning red meat and poultry. However, The Dad took hold of the idea of a BBQ like a raccoon to a penny so off to The Wal-Mart we went for a new grill purchase; the previous grill was a hibachi that didn't survive the fact I forgot I had it and left it practically hidden from view beside the central A/C unit and it rusted in the Silicon Valley rainy season or what people in other parts of the country call winter.

As to his choice as a grill merchant, did you really think he'd go somewhere else? If Crate and Barrel offered a grill, I'd have purchased one in either kiwi or melon but alas 'twas not the case.

We went on a Tuesday afternoon. I should have been paying more attention to what he was tossing into our buggy, but I was too busy fending off his attempts to purchase his favorite sugar-coated treats. Have you ever tried to wrestle a package of bear claws from an overly aggressive elderly redneck in Little Guatemala while wearing pastel chinos and trying to maintain some sense of decorum so your

141

disdain for the locals doesn't seem out of character? No Dustin, just you.

The next morning, after we laid out the various cuts and types of meats to be grilled, I reminded him we had invited exactly four people besides ourselves to this little shindig. There were enough hamburger patties to feed every laborer who built the Panama Canal with enough leftovers to end world hunger if we can convince third-world citizens Spam is food.

I left him to fire up the grill while I went to pick up our fantastic desserts, cupcakes from my favorite new bakery, SusieCakes in Menlo Park. The blueberry pancake cupcakes are so good they ought to be illegal.

When I returned, he was dousing the charcoal with lighter fluid.

When I asked him why, he said, 'So it'll burn, boy. Lord, have you fergot ever'thing I taught you?"

I replied, "Of course not, I can still curse in five languages. The proud Thompson legacy lives."

When I reminded him that the charcoal was manufactured to light with a match he wanted to know how I knew such things. My pointing to the words "Match" and "Light" on the bag was deemed hateful and I was asked to retire to the kitchen with the other women folk, meaning, I guess, Lulu and the ghost?

Before I could turn to get inside I felt whoosh of heat that singed my eyebrows from behind do you hear me? It was heat on a Dante's Inferno scale; like backpacking on the sun, y'all. After he put out the fire which had consumed his most treasured Tractor Supply hat, I asked him what happened. He replied, ever so innocently, "I guess I put too much lighter fluid on the charcoal."

"You put more lighter fluid on it?"

"Well, I wanted it to light."

"But the bag said Match Light. I literally pointed it out to you 10 seconds ago."

"Hmpf. What does they know about charcoal?"

"As the manufacturers of said charcoal, I would say Kingsford knows just a bit more than you."

"Just go get the meat."

Later my guests enjoyed any number of crispity, crunchity treats, which is good if you're eating a Butterfinger, but not so much when it's supposed to be chicken and burgers. The fire was so out of control, he actually charred the corn wrapped in foil sitting on the bun warming shelf. Go big or go home, I suppose. Luckily the cupcakes were perfect. *Thanks Cheyenne! Can I have my free cupcake now?*

The weekend came and as I have previously reported, my new normal Saturday routine involves me chauffeuring The Dad to "town". Mr. Daisy he is not. This particular Saturday, we had to go get his truck weighed as he cannot find his registration papers with the weight listed and this is a requirement for a license plate in California as they consider all pickup trucks, regardless of their use, to be commercial vehicles. Yes, the bureaucracy in the land of the heathen is enough to make a good Baptist talk about somebody, do you hear me?

Lately I have been refusing to run some of his errands, hoping to force him out of his recliner and into the community at large, to no avail. Now that I've sold my recently paid-off car to my sister and I have yet to decide what mode of transport I will choose, I must depend upon the truck as my chariot. Of course, The Dad has seized upon this situation with the glee of a cheating diabetic who finds a gallon of chocolate ice cream with no one to stop them from eating every bite. Not that it happened. It's purely conjecture at this point, although the fact the trash can was emptied into the bin outside while I was at work is suspicious. On a positive note, yay him for leaving the house, if only to venture to the curb.

The reason I am giving you the back story is we had a very interesting discussion on the way to get weighed. It involved the level of "macho" of various cooking oils, if you can believe it. When we grilled out for July 4th, I invited people from work. Per my father, the attendees were three geeks (me included) two macho men (him included) and one lady.

One of my managers is an intimidatingly large person. He looks like a Hell's Angel, but is one of the kindest people I have ever met. Imagine Gandhi on a Harley but less hateful. Seriously. When I asked The Dad why he felt I was a geek (not that I was arguing, I was simply curious) he said everything about me was geeky right down to the "grosh'ries in your pantry." When I asked *"por ejemplo"*, he said, "What?" When I repeated "for example" he cited my purchase of grapeseed oil as geeky.

So, to school you the Redneck Scale of Macho for cooking oils, just in case you were wondering and even if you weren't. I have decided if I must know it, so do you.

Sunflower oil – "Sissy."

Grapeseed oil – "Geeky."

Safflower oil – "What the h-e-double-l is a safflower? You mean sunflower? I already said it was sissy."

Peanut oil – "Squirrelly. 'Cept for fried chicken. You remember that place in Clarksville (TX)?"

Olive oil – "Hmmm. Sounds fancy, so probably Sissy."

Vegetable oil – "A'ight I guess."

Motor oil from an old lawn mower – "Macho." Just kidding. What he actually said was, "If you're not gonna take this serious, then why're we talkin' 'bout it?"

When I asked what kind of oil he found appropriately masculine, he said, "Grease. With bacon."

"Aren't grease and vegetable oil roughly the same thing?"

"How is oil and grease the same thing? You don't have them check the grease in your car every 3,000 miles, do you?" Noticing my confusion, he muttered, "Knowing you, you prob'ly do. Where'd you come from again?"

"Your loins, old man. Don't remind me."

The frequency of odd conversations in my house is on par with the level of cholesterol in my father's blood, which is comparable to a really good credit score. Like 0% financing good, y'all. Pray if you feel it's appropriate.

Sunday, July 15, 2012

World Peace has a new mascot

As you know I have been buzzing around town in the redneck truck for about a month. It hasn't been too terrible, but I am simply not a truck person. There are specific things about The Dad's that aren't standard on most Ford Rangers and they require a level of skill and patience I just don't possess. For example, the tailgate lever (?) handle (?) thingy is missing so you're forced to reach in the bed of the truck and pull one metal rod one way, while twisting and pulling another metal rod in order to open the tailgate. If I were that mechanically inclined, I would be an engineer instead of a bureaucrat, I assure you. Well, maybe not, but at least I would be able to give more information to the computer help desk at the hospital other than my computer is black and I am in room 110B, Building 5. I always tell myself the sigh of pity that meets my description is "noise on the line", which I understand is a legitimate computer term.

You would think someone who had been tailgating on more than one occasion would be more familiar with the inner workings of the gates on which we tailed, but I tailgated at Ole Miss and those gates are not of the Ford Ranger variety to be sure.

I had to let down this particular tailgate to remove his scooter, so I could see out of the rearview mirror. When his machine is in the back, it looks like I'm being tailed by a floating lawnmower– like the skateboards they promised would be around in 2012 in the movie *Back to the Future*. There is also the issue of the side window. His edition, which is ironically called a king cab, is not royal by anyone's definition as there are roll-down windows. I didn't even know they made those anymore.

It's not like his truck is a 1921 model; it's a 2002. Who on earth, besides The Dad, would buy a vehicle with roll-down windows? Okay, there are those people, but I am simply not one of them. I never realized how many times a day I need to roll down my window. I assumed it would be slim to none since I do not frequent drive thru establishments nor do I litter, flip someone 'the bird', smoke or any other behavior that would require someone to lower their window. However, attempting to use the drive thru car wash, valet parking at work or freeing the random insect that somehow decided to ride shotgun.

As I have the soul of a trust fund baby but the spending habits of Scrooge McDuck, I was torn on what sort of vehicle to purchase. I wanted it to be something stylish and attractive but not so expensive as to induce nausea each month when the payment was due. I know that Dave Ramsay says you should buy a car with cash, but I could not stomach driving that truck any longer.

I had completed quite a bit of online research comparing gas mileage, body style, level of awesomeness, etc. I wanted a Mercedes for the sole reason of saying I had one. It's the only reason to buy a car like that. If people were honest, they would admit the main reason you buy luxury goods is to show others you can.

I have a Louis Vuitton wallet. It cost a ridiculous amount of money and it's not even leather; its waxed cotton. I bought it because it made me feel fancy. Am I *that guy*? Apparently. The only reason I paid full retail is that LV has no outlet. I love nice things, but I do not like paying full retail. My Coach attaché was purchase on clearance at the Coach Outlet, people. All my Brooks Brothers clothing was either procured at the outlet mall or a thrift store.

The only other items for which I must pay full price are shoes and Spanx. The shoes are specific and expensive because I have old man feet with a potent mix of neuropathy and arthritis. Sexy, I know. I need Spanx undershirts to keep my post-weight-loss-pre-plastic-surgery midsection in some semblance of a midsection, y'all. Plus, those people are doing the Lord's work. Can I get an amen? Oh, really? Ninety eight percent of the people reading this right now either have purchased, are currently wearing or truly desire Spanx. If I was the only one, the inventor wouldn't be something like the 3rd wealthiest woman in America.

The clothes and accessories are minor purchases in comparison to buying something like a car. That is serious money, dear readers. Not to get all street on you, but that's a lot of Benjamins just to feel fancy and be obnoxious. I can be *that guy* for much less money, do you hear me? I was *that guy* in my Chrysler Concorde. Full disclosure, I was *that guy* in my '77 Plymouth Volare. I've always been a little uppity per my family.

I bought a 2013 Hyundai Sonata. It looks somewhat like an S-class Mercedes if you squint and only use one eye. It is fat and full of cool things and I got a great deal and I am happy. So happy in fact when I returned home, and The Dad asked me to fry some chicken, I said yes!

I have never fried chicken in my entire life. I have eaten more than my fair share, but I wasn't really paying attention to how it was prepared. Apparently, he had been wanting some chicken for quite a while and was waiting for me to be in just the right frame of mind to agree. It seems that last Sunday, Norah Jones, the singer, was interviewed in *Parade* magazine. She talked about how her family used to cook fried chicken when they were growing up. I guess Ravi Shankar, her father, either married a woman from the South or his real name was Reggie and he cooked it himself, because the recipe that was remarkably like my mother's, according to The Dad.

So, I bought buttermilk, flour, and oil on purpose and without too much shame. I always have a little; its residual shame from when we lived in the motel in Texas when I was in high school. Man, I'm being all "Oprah Moment" with y'all today. Anyway, I fried it up with some onion rings and turnip greens and cornbread and sauerkraut with smoked sausage. Apparently, I have become even more of an old Southern lady. Am I right?

The best part about the fried chicken incident was it gave me some interesting insights into my family. I now know why my mother ate very little at supper; she was full, from snacking while cooking. I personally "taste tested" about 4 or 5 onion rings and ate more "goodies" than I should. Goodies are the crumbly pieces of crust that fall of the chicken. The Dad coined the term when I was very young; I had forgotten I even knew that word.

I was also forced to apologize to him for being mad that he always makes a mess when he fries something. I was all OCD in the kitchen today and still managed to get grease on a number of surfaces including my suede saddle oxford. I know, who on earth fries their food while wearing suede? Lastly, it puts The Dad in a most festive mood; on par with someone who has won $20 bucks on a lottery scratch-off.

From within the haze of chicken grease (apparently, I got the scald just right), he has volunteered to watch both *Queen and Country*, a BBC documentary about my favorite royal QEII, and *Drop Dead Diva*, an over-the-top sitcom on Lifetime TV.

Maybe they should serve fried chicken at the UN and solve all these pesky world issues in one fell swoop. Maybe they should serve it to everybody in America and end all this partisan bickering.

I do believe that deserves an 'Amen' from somebody. One of you Baptists needs to put down your chicken leg and get to it!

Sunday, July 29, 2012

Epidurals and saving grace

It has been a few weeks since I've posted anything. And for that I am truly apologetic. Not apologetic enough to have posted anything, mind you, but apologetic nonetheless. I have been working very hard serving Veterans and could use it as an excuse, but I believe we are close enough for me to admit, I've just been tired, y'all; as tired as a quickie mart manager at the end of a double shift who suddenly remembers they have to go to the 24-hour Wal-Mart to buy Huggies for their grandbaby whose trifling mama can't be bothered to stop partying and take care of her child.

Work has been tiring. Some people have likened managing people to herding cats. I describe it as more akin to herding birthday balloons; the ones that have been haphazardly and unwillingly inflated The Dad and Uncle Herschel. They float lazily along, skittering hither and yon from the ever-present breeze stemming from the slow exhale of apathy. Of course, you understand, this is absolutely not descriptive of my staff. No, sir. Those in my office are the very picture of efficiency and zeal.

The tiredness has been compounded by the hourly briefings from The Dad about his post-surgery condition. As I may have shared, he recently underwent minor outpatient surgery. He had a cyst on his...well, let's just say lower back, which "sprung a leak" from the description he gave, and he had to return to the hospital for a follow-up procedure where he informed everyone in the operating room that their parents were in fact never married. I really can't blame him for his outburst although I denied any knowledge of his connection to me when asked.

It seems they were forced to give him four, count them, four epidurals before it worked. Of course, he couldn't walk for about six hours after the procedure. Too bad they couldn't have given him an epidural in his mouth. I can assure you if it was (1) medically possible and (2) remotely legal, they would have. Taking your doctor a hand-crocheted afghan doesn't really remove the sting of a large red-head questioning the moral fiber of one's mother while you are waiting to remove a growth from the nether regions of said red-head who comes complete with anger issues, questionable hygiene and the inability to be knocked out without using rhinoceros tranquilizers from the zoo, y'all. Those poor clinicians.

At least they're all getting matching scarves to go with their afghans because it's a typical gift pairing per The Dad. He tried to blame his behavior on the epidural, but he might as well have blamed it on the bossa nova for all the good it did him when I found out about the incident. Never in the history of man has an eyebrow arched in such a judgmental fashion. I may have sprained something.

He has been living with me, as you know, for about 10 months and we are still trying to get used to each other's peculiarities. He is supposed to be trying to lose weight and understand I am not his maid or even a home health aide, although from the activities that take up most of my free time, it seems I am something akin to a nanny who cooks. Like Mary Poppins without the magic umbrella or the inclination to sing while cleaning.

I am trying to get used to having someone in my house for all 24 of the blessed hours allotted in each day. He is never *not here*. He does not leave the yard on his own. I guess I should be happy he goes to the bathroom unattended. If ever he requires assistance in that realm, we are either calling in an agency or getting some adult diapers. I love The Dad and will honor him like the Bible says, but unless you can show me a verse that specifically states "Thou shalt assist your parents in their daily ablutions" you can count me out.

This morning, as every Sunday morning, we have coffee and share the newspaper prior to me going to church. He only attends when the pain of sitting on a pew in the Presbyterian Church is outweighed by the need for pancakes and sausage. The pain is a mixture of physical and liturgical; him being a semi-devout Southern Baptist. His devotion is directly related to the amount of casseroles and frequency of dinners on the ground. I'm kidding, of course. He attended church on a semi-regular basis throughout my childhood. He was one of those Christmas/Easter/my Mother needed to prove he actually existed kind of church-goers. And the occasional wedding.

I myself was a faithful church attendee from birth through my junior year in college. Then I fled from the constraints of religion as I was an art major and trying to find myself; an excuse more convenient than true. I stayed away from church throughout graduate school and it's no coincidence the dumbest and most life-altering mistakes I made were during this time. I won't bore, or titillate, you with the details. Suffice it to say my testimony is a bit spicier than I would have liked.

I used to wish I had a more exciting life story. Now my autobiography reads like an Afterschool Special with parental warnings and includes certain experiences that would necessitate a revival of Oprah's talk show and a heated discussion/prayer intervention by Mike Huckabee and Sarah Palin. In retrospect, I would much rather have had the mundane "saved in 4th grade, taught Vacation Bible School, trying not to feel/appear holier than thou" backstory. Be careful what you wish for, indeed.

The great thing about being a Christian later in life is I can truly see the redemption God granted me. I have a career I love; that gives me the success I enjoy despite the ridiculous paths I sometimes chose. God can take even the crookedest path and find you a new route if you let Him. Rand McNally has nothing on Jesus when it comes to navigation. Looks like I'm trying to have church before church this morning. Can I get an Amen?

I'm not sure how I started talking about The Dad's surgery and ended up talking about salvation but that's just how it goes sometimes. You know a conversation with me is all about the digressions more than the topics.

One reason I haven't finished the sequel to *A Gone Pecan* is I am also working on my memoirs (is it called memoirs if you're not famous and possibly not interesting?). All the statutes of limitations have expired, I think, and I only share to help whomever it can help and at this point I don't know how or even who that would be. I *believe* all these things must have happened in my life for a reason other than to teach me a lesson. Sometimes the lesson was learned quickly and sometimes it's taken a while, but a lesson has always been learned.

I don't know about you, but I'm just glad God doesn't have a last nerve. If He did I would have been on it, do you hear me? Now I know that deserves an Amen. You Baptists sitting on the back row need to give one up.

Thursday, August 2, 2012

What came first, the chicken or my opinion?

Before I left home this morning I wrote The Dad a note telling him where I was going as he was asleep and I signed it. He thinks it's funny I sign it because there is no one else in the house. I think it's funny he gets mad when food is eaten, and it wasn't me who ate it and he swears it wasn't him. As if Lulu is dexterous enough to forage for, say, a leftover quesadilla someone ate but apparently didn't even like, when confronted and ultimately admitted to eating and then felt no guilt about it even though it was on the other person's assigned food shelf and the act violated all manner of agreements. But I'm not one to hold grudges.

I always try to keep him informed of my whereabouts, so he won't get confused about whether I've forgotten him or am purposefully avoiding spending time with him. He sometimes laments he feels as if he lives alone. I would love to feel that feeling again, even if for just one day. Although, truthfully, I do like having him here with me. I didn't really expect to and at first second-guessed myself, but we have a good time most of the time. Of course, I am an absolute dream to live with. I am relaxed and easy-going. I am not persnickety about my space or belongings and I am amenable to the point of being a pushover. If we're going down that road, I can also fly, walk through walls and read minds.

Anyone who has met me knows the afore-mentioned personality traits are not true, but since I am the only one involved in my family that is writing a blog/book, my opinion should count as his too, right? Someone must capture the real me before my biographers start interviewing people in my life and begin piecing together the truth. Truth has no place in social media, as you well know.

Never has this seemed truer than when I perused the comments on my YouTube video recently. In 2008 I was in a leadership training program called Leadership VA. In this program, we had to write and deliver a 5 –minute speech on any topic. I chose "Leadership and Life Lessons I Learned Playing Football against My Will in Junior High". You can search "Funniest Leadership Speech Ever" to see it. I was a full 220 pounds heavier and swathed in a lime green polo shirt. You can see me from outer space; prepare yourself.

But that's not the point. The point is someone who watched it (3.5 million views as of October 2017) has asserted I am a failed stand-up comic with the stage name of Tub O' Lard and I recently got into the "Leadership Racket". I don't know whether to be offended or proud or at least invested enough to remember my password and add my own comment refuting his.

While there is a 91% "like" rate, this one guy thought I was unfunny enough to make up something or there is someone who looks and sounds like me who is an unfunny comic. Now, I may have a physical *doppelganger*, but a vocal twin would be a new experience. I have a distinctly odd voice, as anyone who's ever heard me talk can attest. My voice has been described as "Mr. Garrett from *South Park* and Scarlett O'Hara have a son", yet, somehow, they pay me to make speeches. Thank goodness, I'm funny, right?

And that was the part that hurt a little. I would like to think if I were a stand-up comic I would at least be 'Chuckle Hut' funny, for pity's sake. Since I don't curse (in print) and don't talk about nasty stuff, I probably wouldn't make it these days, but I like to think I am, at the very least, funny during a toast at a wedding. I guess I now know what celebrities feel, on a very, very basic level. Of course, many of them invite scrutiny.

Anyone who has left home bereft of panties or wearing police tape as a brassiere are begging for comment. However, normal celebrities like Helen Mirren and Larry Hagman shouldn't be open to scrutiny just because they are marginally famous. And I'm not even marginally famous. I'm not famous at all. If I were I'd have more money, right?

At the very least, if he was going to malign my character, he should have bought my book. The link is in the video description.

Getting back to my point, when did it become okay to absolutely make things up about people and post them online? Where is the integrity of the public, he asked, ruefully? I think it's just ridiculous, no make that, depressing what passes for manners and even discourse these days.

Over the past few weeks, I have seen much more information and opinions about people's sexual politics than is warranted outside of marriage. No one should feel surprised that the CEO of Chik-Fil-A supports what he calls the Biblical model for marriage; it's his right. He doesn't open on Sundays and that is his right. This is America, isn't it? He is entitled to his opinion and if he wants to deny me Chik'n minis on Sunday mornings, he can, although it's just rude. It doesn't matter if you agree or disagree. It is simply his opinion and he can have it if he wants.

I have had a lot of people ask me my opinion on gay marriage and I am wisely staying out of that whole argument because it shouldn't be an argument. It should be a discussion instead of a name-calling, for-or-against shouting match. Why do I have to agree with everything you say or be your enemy? Am I not allowed to have my own opinion? I don't even always agree with everything I say; why on earth do you expect me to agree with everything you say.

While I am not a Biblical scholar, I did compete in Bible Drill and have been going to church since long before I came out of my Mother's womb during the second of her three virgin births, as we have previously discussed. I know what the Bible says. I also know what many Biblical scholars and theologians have said about what was considered law and what was considered Jewish custom at that time in history. And if these people, who have spent their entire careers studying the Bible, can't agree on the interpretation of a word, then how the heck do you expect any of the yahoos who are butchering the English language in a sound bite on a cable news show at this very moment, to make sense of what Jesus did or did not say.

Who cares who somebody parties with/dates/marries/ lusts after, etc.? I surely don't care who Bo Jimmy Jack, She'quan or Kieran have decided to join together lest many men put asunder, if we're going to bring up traditional marriage/divorce statistics, Mr. Gingrich. If they don't consummate their love in front of me or within earshot, I let them be. I don't want you to be interested in what I do in my house because I can assure you I have far too many other things to worry about than what you are doing in yours. Lord knows, managing The Dad is a full-time job. And managing your life should be.

Maybe if you spent more time worrying about your own stuff you wouldn't have an unhappy spouse and/or horrifyingly rude and disrespectful children who ran into me with their shopping cart because you left them to their own devices at the Safeway while you drank your mochaccino at the Starbucks stand chatting with your equally offensively dressed friend of indeterminate gender.

What we should be paying attention to is the state of our nation and the crooks who seem to be intent on running our country into the ground. We can't be bothered to pay attention or fight back against the politicians who are spending us into becoming the largest colonial outpost of mainland China and reducing our educational system to not even a memory of what it was, but, boy howdy, we will take up arms to support a chicken franchise that "took a stand" for "American values".

And you know what this accomplished in the end? All you did was make people who already planned to eat there take three times as long to get their food, made them late getting back to work and cost taxpayers (of whom many, but certainly not all, of you are) a ton of money in lost productivity. And nobody bothered to bring me a sandwich. Selfish.

I don't normally get off on a political tangent, but I have had enough of this mess clogging up Facebook. I want to see important things like whose kids won what sporting event, how many weird foods my friends have eaten and the eleventy-hundred hourly postings from my friend Stacy O'Quinn Kidd.

And by the way, just so you'll understand, if Jesus were living among us today, He wouldn't be the gleaming-toothed, overly styled televangelist preaching a life of monetary success for a few minutes of prayer each week. He would also not be a white guy; there is no enclave of white Europeans in Palestine, despite the paintings that you and I grew up seeing at the Baptist Church.

He would be the Middle Eastern man who makes you nervous when you're in line at Starbucks, especially the Starbucks at the airport. And he'd be hanging around with all those that some segment of society deems "less than", like gays (who I mostly like; drag queens are a bit much at times) or politicians (who I sometimes like; pundits are a bit much at times) or people riding Segways and think they're cool (who I never like and want to push over all the time). Why? Because He loves, say it with me, *every*body.

And for all the people who have just been offended by this portrait of Jesus and who just inhaled very sharply and are now trying to calm themselves before they unleash the fury of what they feel is righteous anger, calm down, for pity's sake. You shouldn't even care what my opinion might be.

But I would like to point out if, during the course of your life and based on your actions and the outward expressions of your heart, you must constantly remind people that you are in fact a Christian, odds are you aren't acting like one. Said one sinner to another.

The Dad ate his favorite meal (ribeye steak with taters,
onions and gravy) every Saturday and, of course, had
to prepare the dish on my custom designed dining
table, because that's what you do, apparently

I have Nordstrom, he has Pep Boys. This is not long after he got
to my house and needed brakes on his truck. After he saw this
picture, he allowed me to put those pants out of their misery

Lulu loves to go for a ride to the store, just like
I did when I was young. I miss her

Meal prep is how I monitored his diet and kept him on schedule.
He got to choose his entree. This is meatloaf, broccoli and
cheese and mashed potatoes. It's all about portion control, y'all

The Dad dressed up, at church and much
thinner after six months with me

The living room of my house in Menlo Park with original
art by me and a sofa from which The Dad was restricted.
When I can't find art I want, I make it myself.

I was clearance shopping and apparently decided I looked awesome so I took a picture. You can't tell but the pants are fire engine red

My favorite picture of my mother. This was taken in 1985 in New Orleans, the year before we moved to Mississippi. I was 14, she was 40 and so beautiful

With my niece Payton, being fancy for her 18th birthday

With The Dad and my brother, who was in town visiting
while on his way to training in the Air Force.

The Dad was rarely in family photos as he was always working.
This perfectly captures my sister's feelings about me when
we were in high school. Of course, she adores me now.

His truck as he left, heading back to Louisiana. I have my
mother's gift for packing and The Dad's gift for tarp usage.

Sunday, August 5, 2012

Forced Lesson in Anatomy

This past week friends from the East Coast were in town and I spent the day with them in The City, otherwise known as San Francisco. Jane and Mark had decided we would spend part of the day exploring the touristy things like the trolley and Lombard St. They also wanted to rent bikes and ride across the Golden Gate Bridge (GGB) to Sausalito and then take the ferry back. For reasons I still haven't quite figured out, I agreed and met them on Wednesday morning. We walked the mile or so from their hotel to the beginning of the trolley lines.

Since my weight loss, walking this far is not a big deal. It used to be a chore to walk anywhere. Forgetting something in my car once I was inside my loft at the height of my weight (422) and sickness (sarcoidosis) was cause for stress, anger, tears and then the realization I could live without said item until the following day, unless it was food. Then I would send my trained parakeet, Excelsior, to fetch the foodstuffs. Full disclosure, it wasn't a parakeet and his name is Christopher, my long-suffering best friend.

I am down to 200 pounds and not afraid of a little exercise and I felt I was fully capable of accepting whatever challenge lay before me. And all was good until we hit Mile 2 on the bikes. Ignoring the fact everyone looks ridiculous in a bike helmet, I realized far too late to rectify the situation that the seat of my bike was made of, apparently, a new material; an iron/cactus hybrid. My butt cheeks were in agony, y'all.

We have previously discussed my lack of hind quarters inherited from The Dad and I can assure you the sad remnants of my "butt that never was" were on fire. If my butt could talk, there would have been choice words, dear readers; choice words indeed.

According to Jane, George Dubya's former physical therapist, I am bereft of developed quads. It seems although outwardly I look like I am in reasonable shape, I am more akin to an Olympic Spectator than, say, an Olympic Athlete. Apparently, there are different muscles you use when peddling than you do when walking. Who knew? Apparently, many people who didn't major in a liberal art in college. All this time I thought a quad was the grassy section in the middle of college campuses in movies that need a central point, so the completely implausible couple can "meet cute". If that couple had gone to the college where I received my undergraduate degree (Mississippi University for Women, or The W), the meeting would have taken place in the cafeteria and the adorable words he/she would have attempted to utter would have been drowned out by the voices of 300 people, mostly women, singing. We sang a lot at The W.

Now quad-less and suddenly fully aware, I wondered could people tell I had immature quads? Is it a bad thing? Do I want mature quads? I decided, yes, I did. Should I be ashamed I don't have them? Would my legs have hurt anyway? And what does it have to do with my butt hurting? Are your quads linked to your butt like that whole leg-bone-thigh-bone song? Can one acquire quads? According to Jane, yes you can, but it requires things like squats, lunges and mountain climbers and I remember all too well those horrible things from my kickboxing classes and I have sworn (literally) on more than one occasion I shall never again partake in any of this vile, gym-related activity.

However, I am a trooper, as Jane continuously said, and I pressed onward and upward. Seriously upward, like scaling the side of a mountain. Have you seen the GGB? It's tall, y'all, and I'm not talking like "water tower tall"; I'm talking like "state fair roller coaster tall." Don't judge me. Have you tried to ride a bike fabricated in some evil Eastern European factory to torment capitalist pigs in America to the top of a ferris wheel without a break for water or a panini? What? I was hungry from all the quad development.

Full disclosure: I pretty much walked a bike to the top of the hill to get on the bridge. I had tried everything to stay on the seat. I pedaled furiously then stood on the pedals and coasted. I even tried to ride sidesaddle. It was as successful as you would imagine. So, I created my own rhythm, if you will. I would bike until I could no longer take the pain, which was around 5 minutes and then I would leap/stumble from the bike and push it along. Now anyone else would have been irritated to stop and wait for me to catch up, but Jane and Mark are (1) very patient and (2) very much in love. If they weren't so darned adorable it would be sickening.

Once we got over the middle of the GGB, I was assured, nay *promised*, it was "all downhill" to Sausalito. LIES! Okay, there is some truth to the downhill-ness of the other side of the bridge, but they didn't mention the continual use of the brake due to the crazed pedestrians who were either high or stupid or both. Everyone seemed to have the reaction time of a pothead. For those not in the know, that means slow, like Aunt-Maudie-blowing-out-her-95th-birthday-candles, like waiting-for-Christmas-morning-when-you're-8-years-old slow. And although medicinal marijuana is legal in CA, I find it hard to believe there has been an outbreak of glaucoma among the 20-somethings in the Bay Area. Once we left the confines of the bridge, I was again assured of the downhill journey and the fun that was in store.

Again, LIES! Lies and vicious rumors! There was a slight downward change in grade but not enough to have recalculated the vectors or tensile strength or other random things I vaguely remember as a Journalism major taking Physics in college. Once I walked my bike through the remainder of the path before reaching the road into Sausalito, I realized the bike path they encouraged us to take was not a path at all. It wasn't even a narrow, designated lane beside the road. There wasn't even a shoulder for the road. We simply rode in the road as if we were cars. As the people behind me came to realize, I am the vehicular equivalent of a '77 Plymouth Volare with faulty brakes and a driver who learned to use a standard on the column a full 15 minutes before getting in front of them.

Then suddenly there was a downhill. A frightfully steep downhill. And I'm not talking "roller coaster" steep, I'm talking steep "like the mountain they race down at the end of *Better Off Dead*", that John Cusack movie from the 80s. Using gravity for its purpose, I flew past both Jane and Mark, due to my lack of familiarity with proper braking techniques and my zeal to de-bike. I leapt from the velocipede and walked it reasonably quickly considering I had just escorted it 10 or so miles, through the quaint, overpriced town; my final destination, the reservation desk for the ferry to take me back to the mainland so I could release the beast to its owners and flee as quickly as one can having walked a bicycle the 627 miles it takes to cross the longest bridge in the known universe.

Having been rebuffed in my quest for something other than "first come, first served" seating, I left my bike on the rack, unlocked; hoping against hope someone would steal it and I would be free, brothers and sisters! Free! The $100 deposit would have been worth it. I almost felt compelled to throw the bike in the water and feign ignorance of its whereabouts.

Truth be told, I hadn't ridden on a bike since the age of around 11 and I remembered quite vividly the reasons and they were two-fold; each representing a butt cheek. I have never felt pain like this, people. It was as if an angry nightclub bouncer had punched me in the butt crack, if you'll allow a vulgar metaphor.

After some great Mexican food (guacamole can soothe even the most ravaged beasts), Jane, Mark and I walked those wretched bikes onto the ferry and once we landed back on the Pier, we carried them up a flight of stairs (no, I don't know why either) and found ourselves at Pier 1, the actual pier, not the trendy home goods store. We were supposed to have arrived at Pier 41 which is where we rented these torture devices. Here's a tip for the people running Guantanamo Bay; forget waterboarding, simply rent a bike and make the prisoners ride across the GGB. They'll sing like canaries. Canaries that've been punched in the butt crack.

"It's only a 7-minute ride to Pier 41", chirped the thinking-she-was-being-helpful-but-realizing-it-wasn't-true-when-she-saw-my-facial-expression young lady who greeted us at the information booth. Ever the trooper, I attempted to "saddle up" and try once more. It was not to be. The buttocks made one last valiant effort to throw me from the bike and I was compelled to do what made the most sense to me, I hired a pedi-cab to pedal me, holding my bike, to the bike rental stand.

I was so tired and hurting I begged off dinner and returned home where I made the mistake of telling The Dad what happened. As I write this, he is still laughing. And if my physical pain won't get me a hastily organized prayer circle, my shame should at least get me onto the prayer list somewhere near Aunt Maudie. She's 95; it's an assumption.

Monday, August 13, 2012

Do teeth in your pocket count as yours?

A recent encounter with The Dad was disarming to say the least. I was cooking his requested "country" food and took him a small bowl for taste-testing purposes. He usually tells me I need to add salt and pepper and, even though I never add the salt as he has high blood pressure, I always tell him I do, and he deems it "just right" upon the second taste test. The dish tonight was shrimp stir fry. What? China is a country.

Anyway, when I took him his little bowl, he had to get his teeth out of his shirt pocket to take a bite. I was so taken aback I simply stood there, trying to process the information. Besides the fact he had them out of his mouth, they were sharing the overly stretched confines of his shirt pocket with his glasses, phone and a crochet needle.

As someone who has spent a small fortune on dental care in recent years, I am hyperaware of both my and other's teeth. You could have purchased a car with what I have paid for dental surgery. Not a new car, mind you, but at least a mid-90s Buick LeSabre; definitely more than you need to spend to have an award-winning smile, as if there are awards for that sort of thing. Even if there were, I wouldn't be winning any as the small space between my front teeth is not sexy like Lauren Hutton; it's simply a space. A small imperfection in an otherwise normal face, if normal is what you call someone whose eyes are so small there is an assumption of Asian heritage.

I've always heard you can tell someone's financial health based on their hair, teeth or shoes. Having had my hair snipped in both hoity-toity salons and chains like Super Clips, I can tell you there is scant difference between the two (for men, at least) other than you won't get a hot towel facial at a Super Clips unless your stylist dumps her latte on your head because she is texting/drinking while she cuts. There are texting dangers outside of driving, people. Where's the advocacy?

And I definitely have excellent shoes. It's amazing what you can fit your former canned ham of a foot into when it shrinks right along with your waistline. Yay me.

As someone who did not receive regular dental checkups as a child, due to the lack of dental insurance, I can attest to the fact poor dental care is a factor of poverty difficult to overcome; hence my over-priced but still not award-winning smile, but it's ok. I am single-handedly funding my dentist's daughter's year abroad and I know she would be grateful if she was aware. And I'm glad to help someone go to Europe, although if I had my druthers it would be me or at least someone who would share photos.

But, back to the teeth in the shirt conundrum. What does one say to one's parent who has just (1) retrieved their teeth and (2) from the confines of any location other than their mouth? How does one tiptoe past it? Does one address it? Does one ignore it? Does one blog about it? Apparently, yes to the last question.

I don't say this to malign The Dad; he is who he is. But it's one of the starkest differences between us. When I was discussing my upcoming dental surgery, and told him the cost, he was as taken aback as I was when he asked his home health aide if she'd ever heard a gnat fart. When I added how much I had already spent, he informed me I "coulda had all them teeth pulled and got (you) some false teeth and then used all that leftover money to buy me a Harley".

And I thought about it; not the Harley part but the pulling teeth and saving money part and I realized truly in my heart of hearts I wanted to have the teeth with which I was born, still in my head and not in my pocket.

I don't carry change in my pants pocket as it breaks the line of my trouser. Why on earth would I want to put teeth there? I don't put my phone in my shirt pocket as it skews the drape of the shirt and makes me look messy. Why on earth would I place teeth there? I don't want my teeth anywhere heretofore considered unseemly unless it's biting into a Susie Cakes cupcake or a corndog at the Franklinton (Louisiana) Fair.

Now I don't know the reasons behind his false teeth, but I do know his health has been an issue for quite some time. In all honesty, based on his diet and his lack of exercise since he hurt his back off-shore in 1989, I am surprised he is still with us. The man has had eight, count them, eight heart attacks and a stroke (he says) and I still have to fight him on whether or not he gets to fry the one steak he is allowed per month as I am doing everything I can to keep from becoming an orphan at 41. And I must constantly watch his crazy diabetic butt to keep him from ingesting ice cream and donuts, all the while lamenting "the sugar" is going to "take (his) feet".

And even after I bullied and tricked him into a 40-pound weight loss since he moved in, he remains 65 pounds overweight and it's been an issue for some time. Based on photographic evidence I have recently uncovered, he transitioned from pudgy to officially fat sometime in 1974, y'all.

As a former fat boy, I can tell you that the more weight you have on your body, the more pain you will feel. Doctors have said for every pound you are overweight, it's like four pounds of pressure on your joints. Imagine walking around with your best friend strapped to your back, unless of course your best friend is crazy skinny like mine was in high school. Then imagine walking around with your best friend and her Mama strapped to your back.

As someone who has lost 200+ pounds in the last four years (yes, I am bragging), I can attest to the feeling of being able to leap like a mountain goat from peak to peak once you shed the equivalent of a normal-sized person from your person. However, that feeling quickly passes at the first failed attempt to jump to anything other than the premature conclusion that you are actually in decent shape.

I was also sad to find the only thing that changed with my weight loss was a thinner me. I had the same issues, same problems, same everything, both good and bad, other than a more stylish wardrobe. And while that is awesome, it wasn't the only thing I thought would automatically change. To find skinny people are just people who are skinny was an unexpected let down. And here I talked about y'all all those years. I apologize.

I have tried everything I can think of to motivate The Dad because further significant weight loss will not take place as his only exercise is walking between his recliner, the bathroom and the kitchen table. Driving at "full rabbit" on his scooter doesn't do anything for anyone except keep those in his way unexpectedly exercising lest they be rundown by an aggressive Santa look-alike in a Tractor Supply hat, a stash of contraband Almond Joys hidden in his basket underneath assorted crime novels and packs of Freedent, the gum of choice of denture wearers nationwide.

The only part of his body in any sort of reasonable shape is his mouth, as it gets a constant workout due to his sudden singing of random songs like "Rainbow Stew" and "Why Me, Lord?" and whistling with a talent on par with a songbird, y'all. It's a truly amazing sound, like he's kidnapped a bird and hidden it, like everything else, in his shirt pocket.

I thought about comparing him to the Hager Twins or any other minor members of the *Hee Haw* gang, but I'm still reeling from the residual shame of admitting I knew the identity of Faron Young in Senior English in high school. The only other people with similar knowledge are in a nursing home and think a blog is something "your Daddy useta get. It'll pass."

Sunday, August 26, 2012

If Queen Elizabeth goes to Mexico I can get her a watermelon

As I write this, it is 8:43 am and The Dad is asleep. This is an unusual event and, after checking to ensure he is breathing, I celebrated quietly. I haven't had a morning to myself since he moved in almost a year ago.

It is an amazing thing. It is so quiet in my house. No slurping of coffee, no muted strains of 1960s country music, no random snorts from Lulu; just peace. It is so quiet, in fact, I can almost hear the Hispanic couple in the parking lot of the *Super Mercado Y Taqueria* across the street from my neighborhood arguing over something which sounds vaguely sinister in their foreign tongue but is more than likely a spat about the mini watermelons that are 2 for $1.

I looked up what they said and *sandia* does mean watermelon; I thought, at first, they were saying Santeria which is some sort of voodoo black magic thing. The odd part was the sentence they used online *por ejemplo* (which is Spanish for "stop saying stuff in Spanish") was "The watermelon is corky". *"Esta sandia esta corchosa".* What does that even mean? Corky? I have never used corky in a sentence about a fruit or other foodstuff. The few times I have about 1980s TV characters from *Murphy Brown* and *Life Goes On,* respectively.

All that aside, it is unusual for him to be asleep this long. I know he awoke at his usual 4:45 am as I started to hum "Up on the Housetop" in my sleep due to his clip-clopping into the kitchen. And I know that he made and consumed his oatmeal as the remains were left on the table, countertop and sink. It's interesting how he remains overweight as a good percentage of his meals and snacks end up on various surfaces of my home, including the toilet.

I once asked him why on earth he would eat food in the bathroom and he asked me, without a shred of shame, "Ain't you ever needed to (use the restroom) while you were eatin'?" My reply was to assure him I had not. When I followed up with the statement, "If you have to use the restroom, I think you might not actually be hungry", he looked at me, confused, and said, "But my Popsicle would've melted if I waited." There are no words, people.

Caffeine is a stimulant for the average person. It says so on most packaging. However, I have come to find what works for most, does not work for him. He derives no alleviation from pain with the use of morphine. I, on the other hand, can't remember my name when on prescription meds. I once was issued Vicodin for tendonitis and after I left the doctor's office, I went home to take one Vicodin tablet and go to bed but before I went to sleep, I called my office and told my assistant that I did not want to be disturbed. Apparently at some point in the afternoon I called her and yelled at her for calling me. I remember none of this.

The Dad has taken three Oxycodone at once with no effect. None. On the other hand, a pint of chocolate ice cream can cure most any ill, he swears. He once prescribed a ham sandwich to cure my sore throat; it worked.

People drink coffee to give them an energy boost; to wake them up. The Dad can fall asleep while drinking a 2 liter of Jolt cola. I, on the other non-macho hand, can simply say the word caffeine after 6 pm and be up half the night. It is a sad thing.

I was never a coffee drinker. It's not that I don't like it; I just never really had a craving for it. At least that used to be the case. Now, The Dad makes coffee each morning and I drink a cup with him. What I drink is an actual cup of coffee in a regulation sized coffee cup, which if I were to measure probably holds an exact measurement of a cup. My father states that he drinks two cups per day. What he means to say is that he drinks two tureens of coffee per day. I use a cute little cup and saucer that I got at an estate sale. It is red with multi-colored polka dots; just enough whimsy to start my day on a good note. The Dad uses the beer stein my brother brought him from Germany.

As I like to structure my day in my head before I leave for work, I am not much of a talker in the morning. It has nothing to do with my mood; I am a morning person and thoroughly enjoy embracing a new day. Sleep to me is overrated but necessary. If I am tired, I find if I can get comfortable and just sit quietly for an hour or so, I am capable of recharging and seizing another part of my day.

My father's days are pretty much the same and I know this because he gives me a play-by-play each and every morning at coffee and each and every evening at dinner or when I come home, if I've had dinner with someone else. He even gives me the run-down if I've had dinner and played Pub Quiz (and won and, yes, I'm bragging) and don't get home until after 10 pm. He will wake up and regale me with the minutiae of his evening. How many times he peed, what he did or did not eat (mostly lies based on the food wrappers poorly concealed or containers hastily washed) and what TV shows he did or did not enjoy in between bouts of sleeping, followed by furious crocheting. In the mornings I am entertained by the hourly trips to the toilet and the position and length of times sleeping in those positions. On his left side on the hospital bed for 45 minutes, on his right side on the bed in the guest room for two hours and on his back with his left leg cocked up over the side arm in his recliner for the remainder of the time 'twixt ten and 4:45.

I am like one of those parents whose child left the nest and then returned, unable to find employment thanks to those yahoos in DC. Full disclosure: I hold a mixture of suspicion and disdain for all political parties unless they are approved by John Stewart.

The only difference between these parents and me is I have a bouncing baby boy of 71. Such a fun age, full of wonder and excitement. Potty-trained only in the sense that he knows there is a special room for such activities, but has poor aim. Like a cat, he does not like baths and like a child who has just received the JC Penney Christmas Catalog, he wants every shiny thing he sees. Fortunately, this child o' mine can be left for extended periods of time alone, although he would never throw a party in my absence. He doesn't like people enough to do it, except for his home health aide.

I guess there is a pressure to chat to someone whilst they doctor your nether regions every other day. The Hows and Whats of their conversations are beyond me as he is hard of hearing and she is El Salvadorian, not "Messican" as he reported after their initial meeting. I can only imagine the conversation that took place for that piece of information to stick.

I do know they have at least discussed me on more than one occasion as she seemed oddly familiar when she chastised me for giving him a slice of cake for his birthday the very first time we met. It's an odd feeling to have to defend yourself to someone who you've never met but is privy to your activities, clandestine or not. They have also discussed London of all things as he asked if she could borrow (Lord Mayor of London) Boris Johnson's witty book on the history of that city. As I have what my father has described as a "metric crap ton" of books, I offered to let her keep it. I have a rule that I must give away a book each time I buy a new one, so this presented an opportunity to raid the local Goodwill for a new tome; this one about the royal sisters, QEII and Margaret. I love QEII (Queen Elizabeth II, for those not on my wavelength). I know it is viewed as a betrayal of my generation to not prefer Diana, but I simply do not. A lifetime of service before self and 60 years of fantastic hat/coat ensembles deserve our admiration.

As I try to remember, although she is the Queen, she is somewhat of a regular person to a point and Prince William's Granny, I wonder do her ladies-in-waiting get bombarded with the minutiae of her nights and days at breakfast or bedtime. I would love to read QEII's diaries. I wonder would she read mine? I recently re-read *Andy Warhol's Diaries*, pilfered in 1993 from a friend's ex-boyfriend's house, and I use that information to this very day although it's mostly to recognize the names of those people in those photos of parties that appear in the front pages of *Vanity Fair*.

I suppose I should be happy with The Dad's information. All knowledge is good for something, right? And it means he is still around to generate said information and that's a good thing. If only they had a pub quiz category like "Sleep Patterns and Bad Habits of a Displaced Country Boomer". Maybe I'll suggest it next week. What? It's not any more esoteric a topic than "Bridges of Eastern Europe" or "Attendance Statistics for Sporting Events", of which I somehow knew the answer for the first Super Bowl. Incidentally it was not called the Super Bowl, but the NFL-AFL Championship Game.

The answer is 61,000. And, no, I don't know how I know that.

Sunday, September 2, 2012

Have Dad, Can't Travel

In the last month or so I have been thinking a lot about moving. Not me moving but those who I've come into contact recently who are on the move, so to speak. I spent a wonderful day with a high school friend, Stacy O'Quin Kidd – she of the eleventy-hundred daily Facebook posts – as she was en route from Phoenix, AZ to her new home in Tacoma, WA. As someone who has moved multiple times throughout my life, I understand the excitement and trepidation of a new move.

My nomadic Southern Baptist parents moved us for a variety of reasons throughout my formative years. From birth through high school graduation, we lived in 18 houses in 10 cities in five states. It's a lot, I know. I don't remember feeling as if we were running from something. From what I could tell, with my frame of reference for reasons to move, we were chasing a good paying job for The Dad. As my parents were of the generation who did not include children in adult conversations, we were not privy to any information prior to the general announcement of, "get in the car, we are moving to Mississippi."

Since I have been in charge of my own life, from 1988 through today, I have lived in 25 apartments/houses in 17 cities in 12 states (including college and graduate school). Again, a lot, I know. I am also not running from anything. I used to use the excuse I was chasing "a grade" to use government employee lingo. It's not unlike chasing a promotion and I have moved each time for a position with increasing responsibility or more meaningful work.

Tobey Mac, a Christian artist, has a song called *Me without You* and the chorus strikes a little too close to home for me. The words are something like "(without you) I'd be packing my bags when I need to stay…" And prior to this current living situation, I really didn't give much thought to moving. Of course, I prayed about all the moves and opportunities and I didn't make the decisions with a cavalier attitude; there were definite career-enhancing reasons. Moving from New England back to DC was for the opportunity to do good things in the education realm, which remains a passion of mine.

The move to CA from DC last year was the opportunity to get back to the field and make a tangible difference on a local scale, instead of theoretically on a national scale. Some of my more skeptical friends have asked me if I'm antsy since I've surpassed the year mark out here in the land of the heathen, but my answer is, somewhat surprising even to me, a big 'No'. And it's not just because I really love CA.

Before, I was always able to make a moving decision quickly as I had only to gather the opinions of myself and Jesus. And I was typically already on the same page as me and Jesus seems to respond quickly, sometimes. However, as I have an aging teenager sharing my home, I can't be so quick to entertain ideas about moving. I can't even entertain ideas about entertaining in my home as The Dad is, well not exactly anti-social, but the mere thought of persons invading his space without an express invitation, medically necessary task or delivered foodstuff, puts him in a panic.

When I casually mentioned I might want to invite my Singles Bible Study group over for a game night, the sharp intake of breath and look on his face made me immediately reach for his inhaler. When he questioned why I was handing him his "li'l breathin' thing" I said, "I thought you were having an episode. What's with the face?"

When I answered in the negative to his panicky query of, "Am I gonna have to talk to all them people?" he visibly relaxed and went back to playing his electronic solitaire game, the most anti-social game there is. I truly feel in my heart of hearts if he didn't have to hang out with me due to it being my house, he wouldn't miss me too much.

Well, that's not necessarily true. He constantly complains he feels as if he lives alone, I'm supposedly gone so much. Other than dinner with friends on Tuesdays and running errands for him, I am at home much more than I care to be due to the noise emanating from his general direction. Although, in the last week or so, I have had reasonable peace and quiet at home.

His back has been bothering him and the muscle relaxers he takes (only when offered, never on his own) make him sleepy. I simply do not understand having to remind someone to take a pill expressly prescribed for pain when one is in pain.

I came home yesterday at 3:00. He was sitting at the dining room table eating *my* chips and drinking his weekly Coke Zero. When I announced myself upon entering the house, as I always do, I assumed he realized I was, in fact, in the house. As I rounded the corner between the kitchen and dining room and said, "Hey!" he jumped like he had been kicked and said, "Lord, boy, you scared the mess outta me!" Then he grabbed his back and groaned like it was killing him. When I asked, "When was the last time you took a muscle relaxer?" he said, "Yes'tidy".

How on earth can someone not remember to take a pill which would theoretically alleviate the pain they profess is more than they can handle? Is it me? I situate the bottle of pain pills on his placemat, next to his Solitaire game so when he has a spasm and wonders, "is there something around here to stop this pain? Perhaps a pill?" they will be directly in his eye line. Yet, he still does not remember to take them. And he's not lying, I've counted them. He only takes the ones I place into his hand, wordlessly encouraging him to take it. And it works. Maybe I should do the same with clean underwear?

He has been stating for the past couple of days he feels too "poorly" to eat. However, upon just a round of very rudimentary snooping and questioning, he admits to having eaten the same amount of food as a normal day, just not at the scheduled meal times of 5 am, 11 am and 5 pm.

I brought him into the conversation because I now have to take into consideration what I will do with The Dad were I to move in the future. I am truly happy with my current job and my current location and I have no plans to leave, but as I am a mere lad of 41 and 7/8ths (birthday in one month, buy yourself something fabulous from a thrift store in my honor) I figure I will move again at some point in the next 20 years, which is right about the time I anticipate retiring and starting my second career as President of Southwest Mississippi Community College, Director of a medical center in Palm Springs or a full-time writer if this book sells well. *Authors' Note: Don't let your friend(s) borrow your copy; buy them one instead. Thank you.*

In the days leading up both the landfall of Hurricane Isaac and the anniversary of Hurricane Katrina, the Weather Channel allegedly designated my home state as the "Land Mass between New Orleans and Mobile". Whether they did or not I don't know.

What I do know is Mississippians didn't curl up in a ball and cry. Oh no, that is not the way we do things. We took to the web because we have internet in the South, and computer literacy, too, contrary to what some people seem to believe. There are, at this very minute, a good many of my fellow Southerners, wringing every dollar they can selling the t-shirts they printed with all manner of logos and plays on the phrase "Land Mass" and using any remaining pent-up energy to drink, overeat and/or relentlessly post updates on Facebook after watching their SEC teams dominate the various sporting events this weekend.

For that I am truly indebted. Now I don't have to suffer through ESPN with The Dad. I can just wait to see their posts about what ref made a terrible call or what tight end made some momentous catch and my water cooler chat is primed and ready for the next work day, although with the holidays I will have to wait until Tuesday.

The programs I watched this weekend, the season premiere of *Dr. Who* and the Miss Venezuela pageant, aren't typical subjects for water cooler topics as I do not work at a Silicon Valley tech start-up or a beauty shop in Venezuela. And while *Dr. Who* talk is seemingly popular with my Facebook crowd, The Dad thinks it's because I have nerdier friends.

I understand the need for the media to find "real" people for interviews on TV. And, yes, there are those Southerners who are at present sitting between two double-named men at a bar in a building that used to be a single-wide trailer. And there is probably a woman named after an alcoholic beverage or soap opera character on her way there once she puts the final coat of shellac on her teased hair and smokes one more Marlboro Light.

However, to designate them as the spokespersons for all Southerners is mean-spirited and un-Christian. You can rest assured we are as horrified at the prospect of these people talking for us, even if they are related much more closely than we will admit without somebody pulling out that big old Bible with the family tree in the front that sits on top of the piano in Aunt Maudie's front room.

And it begs the question, why on earth would anyone want to ask the opinion of someone who hasn't been sober or employed since Carter was in the White House other than to poke fun? Those involved in TV production love, love, love to take the person with the least number of teeth and the most questionable DNA and parade them around for the rest of the country as a typical Southerner. And it just chaps my hide, do you hear me? Especially if you've ever seen an episode of the recently, and thankfully, cancelled *Jersey Shore*. All you have to do is change the designation of double-named men to those whose names end in 'io' or 'ie' and who have more hair gel-based products on their person than felonious Johnson & Johnson lab tech and you have the same level of ignorance on parade.

And you can think what you want about us. We know who we are; we of the literate South; of gentility and respect and rules about the wearing of white. Of charming accents and biting wit. Of "yes, ma'ams" and "no, sirs" and other manners that seem to escape the rest of our fellow Americans. If CNN and TWC and other media outlets had to navigate a section of the country where toothless hillbillies were truly as ubiquitous as they'd have everyone believe, then they wouldn't have had access to satellite feeds, comfortable bed and breakfasts and good food.

However, most Southerners (apparently not me) don't let that sort of thing bother us. They simply smile and shake their heads and maybe even roll their eyes just when someone named Catfish, Cornbread or other food makes a statement too inane for comment. And it's because we know they don't know any better because they weren't raised right. And you can't blame Tater Red or Biscuit for wanting to be the center of attention. They've been trying to figure out how to get on TV since the half the family was on *America's Funniest Home Videos* for the tape of the incident with the backhoe, four dozen Roman candles and a Shetland Pony. The other half was on *Cops* for the same thing.

As someone who has lived all over America, I can assure you there are stupid people everywhere and my New Jersey example was but one. Unfortunately, these other states don't get as much press as our characters do because, I guess, we're just so darn colorful.

One day when they option my book for a TV movie and I get a big fat check and I cash that check and it clears the bank and I spend that money, I assure you I will go all Julia Sugarbaker on them. But let's not get ahead of ourselves. And I truly thank you for buying this book, unless you stole your copy. If you did, I'm flattered. Somewhat horrified, but still flattered.

Sunday, September 9, 2012

Southern Hospitality?

I recently read an article on CNN.com that listed the most diverse cities in America. The top five are all within an hour's drive of my current home, which, as you know, is about 25 miles south of San Francisco. The clear majority of the citizens in this area are Asian and Hispanic. And I have learned all manner of things about other cultures I never knew. Like how there are differences between northern and southern Chinese and not just in relation to height. How, even if you have no way of distinguishing from which South or Central American country someone hails, woe be unto you if you mistakenly insinuate they are from the wrong one. To all you politically correct people out there, I have been assured in more than one dialect that there is no place called Hispania, so the catch-all 'Hispanic' is not any more popular than The Dad's designation of "brown people".

This discussion of differences and accents reminded me of my previous post and some of the more colorful language that my, and to my horror, Honey Boo-Boo's, family use more often than we should. I refuse to watch their show, but grudgingly admit I have heard or used sentences printed in those publications found by the gum, batteries and candy bars at your local grocery stores.

They recently were quoted as saying 'beautimous', which is familiar to, and in use by, my immediate and extended family. I hope against hope they do not use the term I am loath to admit I used at work recently.

Several of my managers and I were discussing something, and I meant to use the term 'tiny' but instead, in a rare moment of letting my guard down, probably due to my mild Diet Snapple Peach Iced Tea addiction, I let fly a term my family uses when referring to someone short of stature. We say 'tee-niney', instead of tiny. There is no way to recover from using that phrase, dear friends. You can't simply un-say it. You just have to "stop that train" so to speak, and redirect the conversation. And while I was able to steer the discourse in another direction, I feel quite sure there were tongues just a waggin' when I stepped out of the room.

Recently, my new management trainee Susan stopped by to talk and asked me about my colorful language. It seems due to my dress, accent and sometimes folksy vernacular, she finds me intriguing, "like something out of Tennessee Williams". As she is from the Midwest, she isn't used to Southerners outside of their natural habitat or, really, inside it. She moved here from Michigan to start her new job, not expecting to be getting such a big dose of Mississippi right here in Silicon Valley.

I have visited Michigan only once, but I am a big fan due to Michigan being one of the most competitive Miss America states. They have had five winners including the lady who was the catalyst for the social platforms which are now required for all contestants. Kaye Lani Rae Rafko was an Oncology Nurse when she hula-danced her way to victory in 1988 and spent her year as Miss America touring the country speaking about AIDS and hospice care. I got to meet her in 2011 in Las Vegas. I know another Michiganian (I looked it up) named Jason Morgan, from when I lived in DC. He will one day be President. You heard it here first. I know precisely where each of these Michiganders (also acceptable) live(d) on "the mitten". If you don't know what that means, you have never met someone from Michigan as they will hold their hand up as if they are stopping you in the name of love and show you where they reside. If you look at a map (go ahead, I'll wait) you can see that the regular part of Michigan looks like a mitten; a giant Mrs. Field's cookie cake of a mitten (What? I'm hungry), but a mitten nonetheless.

The other part of Michigan called, I believe, the Upper Peninsula is part of their state although no one seems to know how or why. It may have been stolen from Canada or Wisconsin. I am imagining a frontier politician desperate for re-election, sizing up a "vacant lot" across the water and paddling over to stake claim for Michigan and using the votes of the indigenous peoples of Canada (who were kind and quiet and fond of socialized medicine) to remain in either the Senate or House; whichever one wastes taxpayer dollars.

It's no wonder Flint, MI (which is on the peninsula according to Michael Moore and it's up to your political leanings whether or not you believe him) died a slow, tragic death as some towns do when the main employer (car factory) closes its doors. There was nowhere to go for fun except Wisconsin and how many times can one wear a hat made of cheese before the reality of shame seeps into your unconscious? That's actually a bad example as I have seen these Cheeseheads (and who would voluntarily call themselves such?) each and every year in the stands at football games in the snow, bare-chested whether they should be or not. It doesn't seem to happen as regularly in the South. Of course, I'm talking about towns dying, not people who are inappropriately semi-nude in public. The resilience of Southern towns is admirable.

These hamlets, many of which are too small to warrant inclusion on most maps, can weather any storm, literal or figurative. They will survive when there is nothing left except a store, a church and three houses. There may only be five people and two cows, but they retain their identity and always with a "City Limits" sign. Even if that sign states your simultaneous entrance and exit.

Transylvania, LA is where my Mother's people are from. Yes, I know I just ended that sentence with a preposition. That one, too. Based on my last visit there in the late 1990s, there was a gas station, what used to be a cotton gin, a tiny elementary school and some houses. But they still have a post office and a bait shop, and I dare you to suggest they are too tiny to be considered a town. Go ahead, I'll wait.

Cities up north lose one store and the rest of the town is immediately shuttered, all citizens fleeing as if from a natural disaster. In the South, you close the one sawmill in town, someone will immediately open a business making t-shirts proclaiming: "Tater Junction – Useta be the home of the Sand Road Sawmill" and selling them to Yankees who are lost on vacation trying to find the Mississippi River.

Of course, those Yankees and the citizens of Tater Junction and surrounding communities will be in need of all and sundry, well, sundries. So, they will add purveyors of drinks, food and other *accoutrement* (like pecan logs and pralines) and the next thing you know the Sand Road Sawmill is a flourishing mini mall full of items that would have previously been donated to the White Elephant Sale at the Tater Junction Baptist Church, but are now advertised as antiquities of Southern heritage. You may be asking yourself, why someone would stay in a place like that? My answer is there is only so far most Southerners will move before they plant their feet and say, "That's it. We're home."

As someone who was informed by his parents "because we said so" (when he asked why we were relocating to Mississippi), I can attest to the fact Southerners are not leaving *God's Country* and that particular designation stops not too far north of Memphis and not much further west than Dallas. Most of Tennessee we will take; Kentucky, we're not so sure about. And the only thing West Virginia is good for is keeping Mississippi from being last place in education. I know, I know, that's just downright Un-Christian; not untrue, but definitely un-Christian.

As my Mother always said, "When you start acting like that, you know it's time to just hush and go to bed."

And with that, I bid you good night. Well, good night in the sense that I'm stopping this post; I've had more than a tee-niney bit of Snapple and shall be up way past the time decent people have called it a day.

Sunday, September 16, 2012

It's Not Gossip if You're Eating

I received my e-mail notification from AT&T that my monthly bill was ready to be reviewed. As I have multiple phones on my account (The Dad, me, Payton) I always double check to make sure no one is going over their minutes or whatever. It's really somewhat of a joke as everybody and their mother in my family is on AT&T and therefore we do not get charged for calls betwixt ourselves. This has granted us an account balance akin to the money held in the Cayman Island by unscrupulous politicians.

I do, however, have a limit on data usage each month and my niece Payton and her never-ending search for "awesome stuff" leaves us precariously close to overage charges. Much to my surprise, however, this month it seems the majority user of minutes that caused us to dip into our rollover account was The Dad. I am as surprised as you.

My father's usual contributions to conversation are a complex series of grunts, burps, protestations of ill treatment and demands for fried things and this is only because I am seated directly in his visual path and am the purveyor of said things.

When someone visits our home, he beats a hasty retreat unless there is food. Then, and only then, will he begrudgingly entertain people with jokes at my expense while scarfing as much food as possible to allow social hibernation for the remainder of the entertaining activity.

When someone calls him on the phone and it's not his home health aide telling him she will be late again or a Pizza Hut delivery person needing more specific directions to our home, he is less than thrilled. He looks at the phone with the same look of revulsion I have for any article of clothing that has snap-closures (i.e., western shirts, coveralls, etc.).

However, it seems he will talk to his sister Gladys on a weekly basis for up to 40 minutes. I have never witnessed one of these marathon conversations, so I can only deduce there are a lot of 'mhmms' and 'a-yeahs' and more likely than not, several periods of the phone being placed on the table while he attends to his business of eating, abluting and crocheting, in that order. Not being overly fond of phone conversations myself, I can understand his aversion. However, his lack of engagement in simply discussing of his lack of engagement is almost humorous.

There are many interesting and useful things you can glean from a simple phone call. For instance, my sister just enlightened me to a heretofore unknown three-pronged approach for housing money in one's unmentionables; brassieres to be exact. Mind you, my sister is not the person for whom this is a means of insuring her money is safe. I prefer FDIC-backed security; however, my maternal grandmother, the sainted Mama Dot, has recently embraced this method of safekeeping for her net worth. Off shore bank accounts are just not done by good Christians from the South.

It seems my sister was visiting Mama Dot when she was made privy to her new idea (the first prong) on how to keep her money safe from "those people". Who those particular people were, was never really revealed as my sister solemnly agreed she *knew* who those people were when Mama Dot's revelation was transferred *sotto voce* (which is Italian for whisper). After slipping the *dinero* (Spanish) into her brassiere (French?), which is, as you may have guessed, the second prong, Mama Dot rose to journey to wherever it is a grandmother will travel when they leave the room and are gone for seemingly months on end.

After she left on her sojourn, my sister noticed the money lying on the floor. Apparently the third and final prong in this approach is to actually be wearing the brassiere, which was invented a long time ago by a guy who then had the idea stolen from him by a patent thief, if I am to believe the song from the musical Bette Midler stars in, inside the movie *Beaches*; a movie that makes me weep unashamedly and without reservation, not unlike one does when one hears the song *The Christmas Shoes* for the first time. Seriously, I had to pull over to the side of the road as I could not see through the tears, y'all.

I am happy The Dad will listen to the stories his sister tells as they give great insight into the human condition. Case in point, recently there has been a bit of drama in their tiny not-even-a-town. As one who has lived in the boonies for the first 24 or so of my 41 7/8 years, I can assure you there is typically drama afoot in these particular necks-of-the-wood, but this latest incident is worthy of a repeat, which he gladly did over morning coffee.

It seems his older sister Gladys has a neighbor who had two of her children visiting; one of them for the day, the other for roughly 32 (of 48) years, so far. Anyway, there was some melodrama about cigarettes or beer and someone had a seizure or a wrestling match or a really impassioned game of Twister (there were people on the floor, fully clothed – I've learned not to ask for details) and in the midst of the thrashing about, one of the tiny dogs, named Tootsie Muffins or Mitsie BooBoo, was frightened and fled through the doggie door.

And while she is not feeble by anyone's definition, her friend is close enough to 80 to read over its shoulder, so it was with great exertion she raced after Tootsie BooBoo to ensure she would not be kidnapped by a hawk. That she moved so quickly out the front door caused great alarm in those involved in the entanglement on the living room floor. Not enough for them to follow her and assist, but enough to give them pause for a moment or two before resuming their activities.

Apparently, her fear was valid as one of her previous dogs, which I believe was a poodle as it was named Poodle, was abducted by a hawk or a hawk-like creature. Additionally, you don't want your almost-octogenarian mother coming to fisticuffs with anything winged, unless it's fried on a platter or in a bucket if you're too lazy to cook.

I am happy to report the lady and the dog are fine but the various family members, who had been otherwise occupied at the beginning of the story, met their karmic fates once they decided to help. I won't get into details, but I can report there were multiple falls into a single mud puddle, an accidental mooning, the loss of someone's underwear (off their person or off the clothesline was not specified) and a back-porch shower by water hose (due to the previously mentioned mud puddle).

As someone who has experience with mud (voluntary or otherwise) a back-porch shower is embarrassing enough when you're 8 years-old. I can only imagine it happening at 48.

So, the next time someone calls, and you don't want to talk, go ahead and answer your phone anyway. Odds are the other person doesn't want you to interrupt them as they instigated the call and obviously have something to say. As you can see, some stories simply can't be relayed properly in a text message.

Sunday, September 23, 2012

What if Goldilocks was a Red-headed Dude?

We celebrated The Dad's one-year anniversary in California with the purchase of a new recliner. *He also celebrated with a bag of iced animal crackers he stole from my shelf in the pantry and he thinks I don't know, but I do.* This new recliner is leather because it is less prone to retaining smells and subsequently my monthly Febreze supply can be at least halved. This will free up significant cash reserves to be used for all manner of fun things like SusieCakes salted caramel apple cupcakes and thrift store sweaters, as the fall season is upon us. Well, not so much 'us' here in the sorta-western-central-just-south-of-Napa-Valley part of CA, but for the rest of you people who have to suffer through extreme weather outside of the 55-80-degree year-round range. Apparently, money can buy happiness.

I'm not saying anyone out here in Silicon Valley used their significant brain power to harness the weather and make it as wonderful as it is. I'm simply mentioning the two Steves, Jobs and Wozniak, had to have spent their youth doing something besides playing three-dimensional chess, paintball and inventing computers, if I am to believe the hobbies and interests portrayed by the nerdy geniuses on the *Big Bang Theory*. If Sheldon built a CT Scan in the wilds of Texas, one of the Steves could have built a weather-controlling device at the behest of a golf-loving father.

The unnervingly nice weather is one of the things which delights and confounds my father, who has spent all but three of his 71 years in locations where the presence of any moisture is heavy in the air in the form of humidity. The one three-month stretch he spent in California, during the summer before my senior year in high school, was as a welder in Boron, which is reportedly as fun as you would imagine a town named after an element in that section of the periodic table would be. My niece Payton once described humidity as "I feel like I can grab a handful of air, Uncle Dusty". A wise nine-year-old, indeed.

As The Dad has a shoulder injury from long ago, I was able to talk him in to getting a remote-controlled chair which will recline the back and lift the feet with the push of a button. As persnicketiness is apparently hereditary, he was adamant that he had he audition the chair prior to purchase. This required a sojourn to the La-Z-Boy showroom in Santa Clara, about 15 away. He is a lifelong customer of this merchant as they are sole producer of what is known as a 'Big Boy' recliner. To the uninitiated that pretty much means a loveseat with elevated leg supports. This recliner, while just a smidge smaller than his previous chair, is still wide enough to necessitate full size sheets were one to outfit it properly for sleep, which is the activity most enjoyed in this particular piece of furniture.

You can only imagine the circumstances that arose when he, not unlike a dog, felt the need to 'mark' his territory by subsequently farting in each chair. He ambled his way around the showroom and sat in every chair including those I knew he would never buy, like ones with floral chintz or wooden legs. This was while he was still using his wound vac from the "lower back" surgery. The vac is housed in a shoulder harness that looks like a tiny messenger bag. He was very self-conscious about the bag when anyone of any level of brain power could see there were tubes running from his "man purse" to his body and deduce it as a medical device.

However, to ensure all and sundry knew he was macho, he, very loudly, stated he was "not carrying a man purse". He was but a simple macho paratrooper forced to wear a "contraption" because of my "a-double-s surgery". My face turned the color of my orange chinos and I immediately took up with an Asian family standing nearby, convinced them I was an in-store designer and helped them find the perfect sectional sofa.

He was looking forward to getting his chair that day, but it had to be special ordered because he wanted one with an extra-long leg rest for reasons known only to him. His inseam is 27" but his patented way of sitting (a series of leg hikes, contortions and scooting) and his need for

100% of his feet and shoes to be supported by the chair make it almost impossible to find the perfect chair. And the perfection of the chair is important because he spends all day and all night in this *de facto* bed.

Lately, however, due to his increased pain from his back he has been spending an inordinate amount of time in an actual bed. He has a hospital bed from the VA, but he says the mattress is "too hard". I put an egg crate mattress topper, but he is adamant it is still too hard, like an overweight Goldilocks but with red hair, and, yes, it is still red at age 71. He is forced, he says, to sleep in the guest bedroom, which is the most attractively decorated room in my home.

When I first moved into this house, I chose this bedroom for its central location and it became an art deco haven filled with my favorite furniture like a cream linen headboard and mirrored dresser, nightstand and lamp. The boldness of the purple accent wall is tempered by the pewter comforter and occasional chair with pops of pink and lime green found in the wall art, throw pillows and vases. It is an amazing room from which I was summarily roused on his first night, by the brouhaha due to his, and apparently, Lulu's, sleep apnea.

I now reside in the former guest bedroom which while it is well decorated with a leather wrapped sleigh bed and a color scheme of coral, aqua and off-white, is not a room to make one feel fancy which was one of the main purposes of the art deco world I attempted to create. If one cannot make up for childlessness with fabulous décor, what is the point of celibacy? I would have ridiculously fabulous children were I to ever find a woman brave, forgiving and fantastical enough (like, say, a former Miss America) to undertake a life filled with more pizzazz than is warranted outside of a theatre. I am the physical manifestation of jazz hands, dear readers, and I am aware I am a bit much, at times.

My father protests there is too much "fancy" in this house, but I think it interesting he chose the best bedroom with little fanfare. I came home from work one day and there he lay, like a dead sea lion oddly placed in the housewares section of one of the better department stores. Don't look at me like that; Tractor Supply hats and suspenders do not scream art deco. What it does scream is, "Help Me!"; a moot point to be sure. He looked so out of place I almost thought there had been an attempted burgle from a narcoleptic criminal.

He has insisted the mattress, a pillow top from Serta, is "too squishy" but it seems it is more than "just right" as he has slept in the bed for the last two weeks, on a blanket on top of the comforter lest his 'old man smell' ruin the ice-pink 800 thread-count sheets from the people who brought you the pyramids. What? I'm not being mean, it's not like the man sleeps in pajamas; he sleeps in the same clothes he wears all day. The only difference between his 'awake and going to Wal-Mart' outfit and his 'dozing/sleeping' outfit is the latter doesn't include the hat, glasses or teeth, but does include the phone.

It has fallen to me to break in the recliner, if you will. I spent most of Saturday afternoon watching a *Big Bang Theory* marathon while he slept away the effects of his medicines and it was a revelation. You would imagine something so large would seemingly envelop you and you would be right. I was so comfortable curled up in that chair, I chose to skip my snack as it was all the way in the other room and my body said, "Seriously dude, do not get up". Apparently, my body's inner voice has assimilated to California-speak much more quickly than the rest of me.

With the level of comfort I was experiencing, I made the decision to watch the latest *Dr. Who* episode without the added delight of Snapple or Garden Salsa Sun Chips, my latest favorite thing, when The Dad chose the stroke of 6:00, the start time of said BBC sci-fi selection, to arise and request assistance with medicine, food, etc.

No worries, I told myself, it will re-run at 9:00. You can already guess he arose again at the stroke of 9:00, demonstrating timing is everything. And the timing in the future shall be that of a move to the nursing home nearest Shreveport, LA and his sister, if he makes me miss another episode of one of only four shows I watch in any given week.

Sunday, October 7, 2012

The Psychology of Chili and Cheese

The hallmark of humor is honesty and I although I have over-shared in certain areas I haven't been truly honest about some of the realities of living with The Dad. I try to find the humor in our everyday differences but of late there has been less and less to amuse or share.

I admit, I was naïve about his moving in, expecting to be gaining a roommate, but since he has been here he has devolved into a difficult and depressed person or he was always depressed, and I never noticed. It's confusing and draining. We have never shared a bond in the traditional sense of father-son relationships as seen on TV. Ours is more of a familiarity with each other's reputation than anything else. I know him well enough to accurately predict most reactions or behavior but in a vaguely anthropological way. I'm Jane Goodall and he's "Redneck in the Mist".

There is, however, one behavior which I simply have not been able to become accustomed; the crying. I do not remember my father crying at any time in my life before my mother died, including when his father died my freshman year in college. I saw him cry for the first time at my mother's memorial service, but the impact was lessened by the fact everyone was crying.

Now my father cries randomly and often. He sometimes cries when he is unaware. He'll be sitting at the dining room table and get this far-off look in his eyes and the tears start and when I ask him why he's crying, he says, "I'm not crying. What are you talkin' about?" Then he wipes his eyes, stares at the wetness and looks at me accusingly, as if I'm responsible for this unmanly moisture.

He cries over any number of things but mostly it's my mother. He's mad at her for "leaving", as if she chose to die. He's mad at God for taking her away. He feels God is punishing him by taking her and leaving him here. What he thinks he's being punished for, he will not say. I have asked.

He cries when he talks about her. He cries when he can't dream about her. It's all rather unsettling to me as I have been indoctrinated by him that crying is a weakness to be pitied. And while I do not pity my father, I am at a loss how to respond to his tears.

If I acknowledge them, he gets embarrassed and then angry. If I ignore them, he feels like I am cold-hearted and gets his feelings hurt, which causes him to be angry. So, I become the anthropologist; I question the root cause and keep a clinical distance from the response. Of course, this makes me feel somewhat callous and detached and truthfully its taking a toll on me.

When my mother was very ill and (we had been told by her doctor) was about to die, I spent the night in her hospital room, simply holding her hand. Having no frame of reference for how to act when losing one's mother, I didn't really know what else to do. We didn't say much; she was too sick, and I was fighting a sense of helplessness. I ventured a question, "Why you?" She responded, "Why not me?" And that was what made her life so remarkable; she was always so wise, so loving and so important to everyone around her.

My father, apparently, learned nothing during his life spent with a prayer warrior and eternal optimist, as he continually laments, "Why me?" He questions why she left and why she loved him. The first answer is easy; the second answer is unknown as she is not here to say.

Unable to ask her myself, this is nothing but conjecture, but I think she was attracted to someone who embodied the opposite of her good girl, church-going self and she was drawn to the "excitement" and by the time she realized the complexity and level of emotional baggage he had, she was too much in love and too far along in the marriage to simply abandon it. Baptists just don't do that. To her dying day, she loved him; literally holding on until she heard he had come through his surgery with no problems, before taking her last breath. He had been in a car accident in front of the hospital while he was visiting her and required shoulder surgery.

I know he is angry and he has every right to be, but he also needs to realize no matter how much he wants it, she is not coming back. She is gone from this earth. She lives in my heart and my memory and I visit her often; sometimes with laughter, sometimes with an exquisite ache, but I don't let it stop me from living; this is not what she would have wanted. She did not abide self-pity. As someone who was adept at planning pity parties as a teen, I know whereof I speak.

My first year of graduate school afforded me the opportunity to take several psychology and counseling classes as my major was Higher Education Administration and I have worked in federal healthcare for 14 years. My frame of reference for recognizing depression in its various forms is fairly strong. The Dad is depressed and not in that "I'm sad because they cancelled the *Rockford Files*" way.

As his frame of reference for proper mental health is himself, you can see why he would be unaware. As he talks only to me and then only to share the litany of woe involving his random aches, his unquenched desire for chocolate ice cream and continuous fart jokes, he doesn't realize what he is feeling is not normal. He thinks he's fine and I suppose he is feeling most of the same things he has always felt, about himself and the world. He has been somewhat irritated for as long as I can remember and my memories, however vague, begin somewhere in late 1973.

As I am the "weird one" among his offspring, he doesn't think I am qualified to dissect the intricacies of his psyche or offer suggestions for how he should feel. He didn't actually say that. What he said was, "Stop tryin' to get in my head. You ain't a shrink." And it is true.

But as his primary caregiver I felt he needed to talk with a professional and his doctor agreed. They assigned someone to help with his chronic pain management. When he asked me if this (new) doctor was a psychiatrist, I said, "No, she is *not* a psychiatrist." Then I stopped talking. She is a psychologist; there is a difference. Judge not, y'all.

You see, his constant back pain makes him feel bad, which worsens his depression, which makes him more susceptible to pain. It's a vicious cycle and is not going to improve through my wishing and hoping. It's also not going to improve through the ingestion of Krispy Kreme donuts, as he continually suggests, but that is an experiment I support once every three or four months. You know, just in case.

In the last couple of days, there has been an improvement. He has requested to accompany me on tomorrow's Columbus Day-inspired jaunt to the outlet mall in Gilroy, home of any true Southerner's favorite duo, Sonic and outlet shopping. Nothing says happiness like clearance-priced Robert Talbott neckties followed by a cherry root beer.

Whether he will be able to maintain his improved outlook once he has witnessed the carnage of an outlet mall clearance event remains to be seen. Regardless of how tomorrow goes though, I know there is nothing so bad a foot-long chili cheese coney and tater tots can't temporarily fix.

Wednesday, October 31, 2012

Pac Man wearing Mickey Mouse ears

How appropriate my father has become an officially licensed heathen (i.e. resident of California) on National Pagan Holiday or whatever evangelicals call Halloween while still buying Snickers in bulk...for the children. His free gift with purchase was a fair amount of attitude from a woman in a multi-colored wig which was apparently not a costume (again, I apologize Shelisia) and stickers that make his Grapes of Wrath truck legitimate but only in the sense it is no longer illegal to drive it. It is still illegal to think you're cute in it, as I am continually reminded each time I must commandeer it to transport him for the purposes of healthcare or yarn procurement.

This has been an arduous process the likes of which I have never seen. When he moved to this great state in September 2011, his tags had expired the previous month. When I asked him about it, he said he'd get around to it sooner or later.

As the sole driver of said vehicle, I was nervous every time I drove it, afraid I would get a ticket for expired tags. And CHiPs are serious about tickets out here, believe you me. If you don't know what CHiPs means, you are far too young to understand my humor and should laugh at random intervals so grown folks think you 'get it'. The nervousness was apt when I was stopped back in January for an illegal U-turn while attempting to wrangle a prime parking spot outside Armadillo Willie's BBQ.

If it hadn't been for the scooter in the back of the truck I would have noticed the car directly behind me was a full-on police car with lights and everything.

When I got out of The Dad's truck wearing kelly green chinos and said, "I'm so sorry, I didn't see the 'No U-Turn' sign; it's my Dad's truck and I'm not used to driving it", the cop took pity on me and only gave me the U-turn ticket. I informed my father we were getting tags post haste or even faster.

To make this story as short as possible, I have been attempting to get him California plates and a license since February. We made it through the written test communicating across the room with more hand signals than an indecisive first base coach. California requires you to take a written test if you are from another state, regardless of how long you've had your license.

And the rules out here are different. There are questions about smoking in your car (illegal), phone use in your car (illegal except when dialing 911) and other random things about light rails, child seats and something about twin babies in a back seat both I and The Dad missed and still don't understand.

Once he had the license, we could get the tags. That's when I realized we were in for a treat with the lovely people at the DMV. My father had, in his assortment of important papers, a Colorado license plate, a Louisiana registration and a title transferred from Mississippi to Alabama. When I asked how that was possible, he accused me of being too picky. When I informed him it was the state of California and not I who wanted these three items to be from the same state, he told me I was just trying to figure out a way to make him look dumb.

So, cut to me, spending four different days of vacation time over several months attempting to get unwilling state employees to tell me what was acceptable as they changed their minds more than a political candidate. Then I had to contact the respective states, finance companies and insurance companies to get the necessary paperwork while *mi padre* sat and watched loudly complaining it was taking too long. Don't make me type out the thoughts running through my head because they are not fit for mouth or print.

I don't know if the impending legality of his truck was the primary motivator for change or he was simply inspired by the political climate, but he decided very recently he can drive himself to the doctor. He was forced to drive himself while I was away for nine days in the last two weeks. However, upon my return he decided he was fully capable of taking himself to and from his appointments for the foreseeable future.

This past Monday, I was headed to work around seven a.m. while The Dad had an appointment at 9:30. That he left the house before me should come as no surprise. I was so excited about it the prospect of a day not interrupted using family care leave to cart him home I took a photo of his truck when I was behind him at a red light. He drives so slow, I almost had to pass him.

It's a strange photo because his scooter with side mirrors looks somewhat like a ghost from Pac Man wearing Mickey Mouse ears, but it was a beautiful sight indeed. If a picture is worth a thousand words, I would've posted it to the blog and not actually written anything. Alas, it is not worth so many words, but it was worth about the same number of calories I ate, as I celebrated with a turkey and cheese croissant from Palo Alto Baking Company which is serendipitously on my drive to work, if I take 5 extra turns and go about a mile and a half out of my way.

And driving himself has continued including yesterday and today and tomorrow. I know that is a lot of appointments but we (the doctors and I) are trying to fix everything from bad feet, gnarly toenails and obesity to poor circulation, lung disease, diabetes and depression. There should be a reality show about 'refurbishing' The Dad to some semblance of good health. We could call it 'This Old Redneck'. I'd be the unwilling family member, forced to share the screen and subsequently steal the spotlight and finally get my own TV show as everyone tells me I should have. And when I say everyone, I mean my sister.

Monday, November 5, 2012

If we pawned America, how much would we get?

I was out to dinner with a friend Friday night. As per usual, I texted The Dad and reminded him of my plans as he gets irritated if he doesn't know where I am. As per usual, he ignored my text. Had he bothered to open his flip phone, he would have known it was not the morning when he awoke at six. Since I wasn't there to inform him of his error, he thought Friday evening was Saturday morning and proceeded to make coffee and eat his oatmeal. He also took his morning meds, one of which is a diuretic.

When I got home about 9:00 pm he was confused as to where I had been and why I was carrying a box of leftovers. However, he was not confused about his desire to eat the contents of my doggie bag and he happily munched on half a turkey burger with black bean and corn salsa, while I asked to what I owed the pleasure of piping hot coffee an hour before bedtime.

He said, "It's almost nine in the morning, boy, what chu talkin' bout bedtime?" When I pointed out it wouldn't be pitch black outside at nine in the morning, even if there was a storm a-brewin', he looked at me as if I had stolen the last bite of the burger. It never occurred to him why I would have a turkey burger for breakfast. "Food's food," was his reply, accompanied by the burp one would expect from one as uncouth as he.

Once he realized it was, in fact, not Saturday morning, he spent the next hour berating himself and wondering aloud how someone could be so stupid. I told him it could happen to anyone, although usually it's only when one is doped up on cold medicine or hung over from too much partying. Since he is fairly well doped at night as I save all his "may cause dizziness" medications (and there are several) for right before bedtime, it would have been understandable. Due to his current physical condition, partying like a rock star would include things like heading to The Wal-Mart without his scooter or walking outside to check the mail more than once a day.

I thought it was funny he had made an error, but I very quickly swallowed my giggle when he threw a look my way I haven't seen since my Southern Baptist mother found out I voted pro-choice back in college.

When I reminded him that the time was going to change again on Saturday night, he asked me, "You like messin' with me?" When I assured him that it was not a ruse to confuse him, he told me, "If you don't mind, I'll ask somebody who didn't eat hippie hamburger what time it is tomorrow."

He awoke Sunday morning at a bright and early 4:00 a.m. Even though I had changed all the clocks in the house, he was using his watch which he had refused to allow me to change. His clippity-clopping on his way to the kitchen to make the coffee was bad enough but he decided to fry a steak for breakfast and the ensuing noise was enough to wake the dead, myself included.

We have discussed before how I cannot keep up with his swirling vortex of filth. To keep some semblance of cleanliness in my home without losing my sanity, I hired a service to come in every other weekend to clean. And while they are the nicest people, I feel odd sitting there while they clean so I decided we would venture to the outlet mall as they were having a clearance sale at my favorite shop (Robert Talbott) and The Dad was lured by the promise of lunch at Hometown Buffet.

We were forced to take his truck as he refuses to get into my car, which he says is too fancy. It's a Hyundai Sonata. And while I think it looks much more expensive than it is, it is still a Hyundai Sonata. When I asked him to define fancy, he said, "It's too nice to fart in." I would like to think I am too nice to fart near, but when I posed the question, I was met with a resounding "No". Well I'm assuming it was a no; there wasn't actually a word offered; he simply lifted his left leg and farted. When I asked why he did that, he replied, "Because I'm left-handed."

We pile into the *Grapes of Wrath* truck and head toward Gilroy, Garlic Capital of the World. When I got in I noticed there was a grape tomato on the floorboard of the driver's side. As The Dad had driven himself to his doctor's appointments on Wednesday, he had stopped by the farmer's market on campus. Apparently, he had purchased tommy-toes, as he pronounces them, and left one behind. I laughed and put it in the drink holder of the console, intending to throw it in the trash once we reached our destination.

When we arrived, and got out of the truck, I noticed him chewing something. When I asked what it was he said, "My tommy-toe. Why?" Being used to things like that at this point, I just said "alright" and continued my quest for discounted designer ties.

Inside the store, I searched for fabulous things while he wandered around, loudly excoriating any company who would charge so much for "somethin' that's not even clothes", laying down on their couch, using their Employees Only restroom and making an un-PC reference to people of Hispanic origin having used my trouser seat as a domicile when explaining to the salespeople why I chose to not purchase the chinos I had tried on. I think the deep discounts they offered were to hasten our exit especially when I told them I thought the loud older gentleman might be homeless and I couldn't figure out why he was following me.

We had an interesting lunch at the buffet, which he informed me was less-than-enjoyable due to the large number of people, including thousands of children. Okay, maybe not thousands, but when you get a dining room with a maximum capacity of 150 and a full 100 of those are children hopped up on orange ice cream and cotton candy, it can seem like you are trapped on Bourbon Street at midnight on New Year's. Not that I would know anything about that.

I concurred with his discomfort and understood when he was only able to polish off three plates (including one of just ham which he declared, "I've had better") before he was forced to flee to the confines of his truck. Well, flee in the sense he walked as fast as he could on feet that work correctly only about every third step.

When we were driving home he asked who I was voting for on Tuesday. As I voted by mail two weeks ago, I told him I wasn't sure, just to avoid any discussion, but wondered who he would vote for, were he registered to vote in California, which he is not. When he told me that he would pick either Charles Bronson (who is dead) or Rick from *Pawn Stars*, I felt somewhat happy he isn't going to cast his vote.

A lot of pro-Romney people say we need a businessman in charge and if making a living running a pawn shop isn't a sign of a business-minded person, I don't know what is. So, if you don't like Obama but aren't really jazzed about Romney either, you could just choose "Pawn Stars for President!"

Would it really be any worse?

Monday, November 26, 2012

The Perks of Knowing a Good Ol' Boy

Throughout the time I have shared with you the ins and outs of living with The Dad, I haven't done a whole lot of reminiscing about the more interesting perks of having a good ol' boy for a Dad.

I recently spent a week in Hawaii with my family for an early Christmas. My "family" currently includes my niece's boyfriend who is saddled with the unfortunate nickname Rica.

This very nice young man's parents named him Chad. My sister started calling him Chad-rica, for reasons known only to her. And as she is prone to do, she shortened it to simply Rica and refers to him by that moniker in all our conversations. I have started calling him Rica in my head; for example, when I was making my Christmas list I actually wrote "shirt for Rica". The Dad even calls him Rica and thought he was Hispanic, which made for an odd conversation when they arrived at my house this June and in walked a blonde boy.

The Dad ever so eloquently stated, "I ain't never seen a blonde-headed messican. Are you sure that's Rica?" When I attempted to make light of the situation (due to the reddening face of Rica himself) by stating Castilian Spaniards can be blonde, The Dad flagged down that train with his usual bluster, "There ain't no such thing as a blonde-headed messican."

I returned from my trip on Wednesday night, Thanksgiving Eve, if you will, and reminded The Dad he had promised to eat dinner at co-workers Greg and Louise's home the following day. Well, you would've thought I had asked him to wear a tutu or volunteer at a nursing home considering the look he gave me. To clarify, he doesn't like "old people".

You see The Dad is not a social person, which comes as a bit of a shock to some of you. Granted he can turn on the charm when he wants to and if you can get past the shockingly un-PC statements he is prone to make, he will make you laugh, albeit sometimes nervously and always looking around to see who heard you laugh as it was probably slightly vulgar. He can "act right" in front of company when he wants to. Unfortunately for me, I am not considered company.

To ensure he remained in a reasonably interactive mood, I plied him with breakfast at our favorite diner, Jason's, and let him get in a nap before we left for Greg and Louise's.

One of the only reasons my father agreed to attend is Greg is one of his favorite people partially because he looks like a biker and owns a Harley. I think he likes Greg more than he likes me. Scratch that; I KNOW he likes Greg more than me as, and I quote, "Greg is macho". Shockingly, I am not considered macho; a term used exclusively by my father and the Village People.

When we got to Greg's, I distracted him with football on the big screen and Ruffles with onion dip until dinner was served. Thank goodness, they had a Honeybaked Ham, The Dad's favorite holiday protein. After we ate, he sat back down with Greg and watched football and told lies about Vietnam (the country with the fighting back then) and Germany (the women back then) and other standard *après* dinner conversation topics.

After a couple of hours, which was very much surprising, he said we needed to go as his a-double-s was starting to hurt. On the way to the door someone asked why The Dad calls Adam (my management trainee) George. I tried to explain the nicknames my family doles out and the odd names my father loves to give to the various animals who have had the joy of being members of our household. Dogs named Missy, Goober, Digger, Licker, Snoopy, Satan, Sophie, Pepper, Hot Dog and Lulu. I just adore my Lulu although I wish her name was not the same as a now-deceased, overweight, reformed stripper who became a Christian and sang on *Hee-Haw*. Since The Dad has claimed I have "stole" his dog (which is accurate), I have tried to get her to answer to Paisley, but she will have none of it. You can take the dog out of the patch...

The conversation then turned to the odd assortment of other animals we have owned such as horses, cows, sheep, guinea pigs and parrots. One parrot in particular was named Seymour. Christmas 1981, we drove the 13 hours from Oklahoma to my grandparent's farm in Alsatia, Louisiana, population 27 (not counting goats or horses). My mother was driving. I, my sister, brother, 694 Christmas gifts and our poodle (Pepper) were in the backseat with The Dad riding shotgun with Seymour on his shoulder. Yes, you read correctly. As he was slumped in the front seat sleeping, some random heathens mistakenly thought my mother was the only adult in the car.

Somehow finding enough confidence to terrorize a family while driving a Ford Pinto, these ruffians proceeded to pass us and then pull over in front of us and slow down to 20 miles an hour. As I inherited my lead foot from my mother and because back then Oklahoma highways had no posted speed limit, my Mother easily passed them, making great time on our sojourn toward the farming community of her youth. After several episodes of the passing and subsequent slowing down with these hooligans, The Dad woke up and asked her what was going on.

When she explained the situation, it poked the proverbial bear, and he asked me if I had brought my early Christmas present, a knife. My sister wondered aloud what good a pocket knife would do, having apparently forgotten my father somehow mis-interpreted my Christmas wish list to include "Bowie knife with 8" blade and snakeskin handle" when what I had actually asked for was "Electronic Battleship". *Being an Almost Odis requires a poker face when receiving gifts, not unlike the time I asked for a monogrammed*

218

*button-down and argyle sweater and received a .22 rifle with
a scope.*

I grabbed the knife and we had a mid-air swap as he
threw the parrot into the back seat and proceeded to hang
his upper torso out of the window and wave the knife asking
the "M-Fers" to politely join him in a discussion of the merits
of leaving us alone. For some unknown reason, assumingly
alcohol, the threat of a large bearded fellow waving a Bowie
knife was not enough to distract these wayward souls from
their intended mission of, I am guessing, harassing people
because they repeated the pass and slow down routine
several more times.

Having more than enough of the situation, The Dad
asked my mother ever so politely if she was finished with
her (glass bottle of) Tab. When she indicated she was, in
fact, no longer in need of the diet refreshment, he asked her
to pull alongside the Pinto.

When he could see the whites of the driver's eyes, like
General Washington taught us, he proceeded to introduce
the half-full bottle (to quote an old basketball cheer) "smooth
upside the head" of the driver, causing an abrupt departure
of the Pinto from the pavement. With that, he turned to my
mother and said, "Solved that problem, Mama. Let's get on
to Alsatia."

Actions do speak louder than words, y'all.

Wednesday, December 5, 2012

Rhymes with Google

This past week I had the opportunity to visit Stanford University's campus for a lecture series. As they are located about two miles from my office, it is a convenient way to learn new things without signing up for an actual class, which I will only do if Condoleeza Rice is the instructor. This speaker was going to discuss Emotional Intelligence and I am all about self-betterment through knowledge.

I headed there straight from work and surmised, based on the number of people who knew the location of the School of Education, the next great generation of teachers is matriculating elsewhere.

Before I took my seat, I had to take a rest, so I found a room specifically designed for such activities. When I finished my business, and was washing my hands, I noticed the gentleman at the next sink was cleansing his hands with the dedication of a surgeon about to operate. Having worked in healthcare for the last 15 years, I practice proper hand hygiene and after I dried my hands with a towel, I kept it for use as protection when I opened the door to exit. This gentleman, instead, grabbed the door handle with his bare hands and held it open for me. Then he smiled this maniacal smile and I thought, "Good Lord, I hope he's not the speaker" and chuckled to myself.

Not surprisingly, I entered the auditorium and there sits Mr. Nasty Hands in a lotus position in a chair with his shoes and socks removed grinning wildly, waiting to fill our minds with glitter hugs dipped in rainbows, I imagine.

But, as I am not one to judge, I decided to see what he had to say. After all he is an executive with an internationally known and respected company. I won't say which one, but it rhymes with Google.

He starts to talk and mentions he is a Buddhist, which was unexpected as he spent the first 10 minutes or so talking about how awesome he is and based on my limited information about Buddhism didn't think arrogance was one of the basic tenets. Although based on the activities of the Dalai Lama, celebrity stalking might be. However, he made a statement that got my attention. He shared he was listening to a Buddhist nun and in the instant she said a particular phrase, he became a Buddhist. This must be some phrase, I thought. It was 'the answers are all inside you'. Yes, you read that correctly. Glitter hugs indeed.

What he said next confirmed the opinion that I needed to exit. He said, "In that moment, I understood EVERYthing." And he wasn't kidding. Well, it was more than I could take, so I quietly left the auditorium and headed to Starbucks to get my Venti Black Iced Tea with 3 Splenda and no water and ponder this preening donkey's statement. He knew everything, huh? Well, you don't know proper hand hygiene. You don't know the proper footwear for public speaking. You don't know how goofy you sound and that's just off the top of my head.

But it got me thinking. Would I even want to know everything? Cate Blanchett, at the end of *Indiana Jones and the Kingdom of the Crystal Skull*, learned everything from that big ol' alien whatever and all it got her was an exploded head. No thanks.

I know lots of things, most of which don't matter to anyone, but which help me win trivia. However, I do know lots of things I wish I didn't, so I decided to compile a list.

I wish I didn't know:

1. What Coca-Cola tastes like with cigarette ashes in it. Thanks to The Dad in 1978.

2. How to haul hay or hoe cotton.

3. How a pickled pig lip tastes. Stacey Morgan and I shared this experience.

4. There is a 24-hour gay bar in Birmingham, AL.

5. Acid-washed jeans sometimes disintegrate while you're wearing them.

6. How to involuntarily cliff dive on a trip to Canada. Full disclosure: involuntarily means they pushed me. I am still ticked, and it was in 1993.

7. What it feels like to avoid walking past storm drains at night because the movie *Stephen King's It* messed me up, y'all.

8. What it feels like to be forced to watch overweight middle-aged hippies make out to progressive art rock songs that last 25 minutes each while waiting for Yes to play their one hit song…and then they don't.

9. Liver gets bigger when you chew it.

10. The feeling you get when your calf is the only competitor in its category at the county fair and it still comes in third place.

11. What it feels like to go tubing down the Bogue Chitto River for eight hours with no sunscreen and end up with burns so bad you miss all but one of your high school senior parties.

12. What it feels like to watch the third *Twilight* movie.

13. What it feels like to play football against your will in junior high (see YouTube video "Funniest Leadership Speech Ever").

14. The dimmer switch on a '77 Volare is on the floor by your left foot.

15. What it feels like to have to hitchhike, after you hit a deer on New Year's Eve, and catch a ride with a man in a Ford Pinto station wagon with the passenger door roped shut through a hole in the roof who ends up being the uncle of your cousin's boyfriend.

I think that's enough of that, don't you?

Dusty Thompson

Saturday, December 22, 2012

Two Girls, a Dance and a Ham

Recently I assisted a friend (Alisa) who is a teacher by helping her chaperone a middle school Winter Formal at a private school in San Jose. I haven't spent much time around kids in this age bracket (5th -8th grades) since I was a junior high boys' Sunday School teacher before I fled Mississippi for Alaska in 2002. However, I looked forward to this experience as I am always curious about whether kids these days are much different than those in my day, due to the many changes in society and technology.

I am thankful I am not a teenager in this decade. There is far too much access to nasty, trashy stuff of which I was unaware in the veritable Mayberry where I grew up. You can accidentally come upon something nekkid in any number of places these days, including TV shows. Not in junior high, but toward the end of high school, we knew where the nekkid was (behind the counter at the truck stop) but we were unable to access it.

I arrived early as has been my routine since the infamous band picture debacle of 1986. I was late to the group photo and they had already arranged the trumpets on the first row, as trumpets are the coolest people in band besides the drummers. I, a trumpet player, had to go on the back row with the flutes and other instruments no one can hear during the performance. All apologies to Stacy, Paul and other talented flautists I've known, but a flute in a marching band is almost pointless unless there is some random Revolutionary War theme and there usually isn't.

As I was early, I could watch most of the kids arrive in their dress clothes, if that is really the term to use. It was an odd assortment of jeans with un-tucked dress shirts and clip-on ties for the boys and party dresses with Chuck Taylor sneakers for the girls. Is that a thing now? At least some of the sneakers were sequined. Since the clothes had changed I wondered if the social hierarchies were in place in California in 2012 as have been in place for decades in other locales like Mississippi or cable TV. I paid specific attention to those who seemed to be armed with posses, or whatever the plural of posse might be.

There was one pony-tailed young lady who seemed to have declared herself head decorator as she held very strong opinions about balloon placement. Balloon Girl, as I named her, seemed to be the Queen Bee until the arrival of another girl, who I named Sparkly Skirt. She was wearing what I can only assume were her mother's clothes and shoes. Otherwise, she's not being raised right, y'all.

Balloon Girl and Sparkly Skirt eyed each other from across the room, like it was a reality show. Apparently, it was 'ON'. Color me intrigued. Sparkly Skirt started dancing once Johnny Moustache (he of the overly-styled, barely visible (count them) seven upper lip hair follicles) broke out his laptop.

After one too many renditions of the weirdly popular Korean dance song *Gangnam Style* (which everyone including some of the more aggressive teacher-spouses seem to know the apparent required choreography), Johnny Moustache was replaced by Aggressive Girl in High Tops with her trusty iPod. I am not ashamed to admit, she and I shared many dance favorites. Okay, I'm a little ashamed. But the music was only the background for the drama unfolding.

When the room became entranced upon Sparkly Skirt's entrance, Balloon Girl started dancing while playing slow motion volleyball with the balloons. Never has power shifted so quickly outside of a South American country as all the children followed suit.

As far as I was concerned, it was going along pretty well, and I was introduced to the teachers, not realizing my appearance as the 'friend' of the single teacher was the juiciest thing that had happened there in quite some time. Feeling as if all eyes were on me, I texted my sister, also a teacher, and she confirmed I was not being paranoid and at that very moment each and every one of the whispered conversations were in fact about me; specifically, the level of my relationship with the single teacher which would have enticed me to accompany her to such an event.

The announcement of the voting for the Winter Formal Court caused a ruckus that refocused everyone's attention. Never in my life have I felt relief to no longer be the center of attention. And speaking of me, I found my tiny doppelganger. Wearing the same gap-approved uniform as his classmates, he seemed to be the only boy with any semblance of rhythm. He would dance with abandon as if no one was watching; however, he was definitely aware of everyone's placement as he halted his moves if no one was looking and traveled nearest whichever Queen Bee the crowd was surrounding and start dancing again, to ensure the largest audience. Oh, sit down, Dusty, Jr., I laughed to myself.

While we waited for the votes to be counted, we were distracted by a new drama unfolding just outside the entrance when Johnny Moustache was apprehended trying to sneak off with his girlfriend who, only after I caught sight of her, was summarily nicknamed Invisi-Justice as she had somehow escaped my notice while wearing a hot pink and black floral dress from the tween clothier I loathe. How do I know? Well, let's just say they've been selling that very dress for quite some time since I bought it for my niece Payton in 2006. Mr. Moustache, when he was denied whatever nefarious activity he had planned, was furious and refused to re-enter the gym, believing to the very depths of his almost-teenage soul we did not have his best interests at heart.

This sounds just like The Dad, who does not believe I have his best interests at heart. He feels I purposefully keep some of his wishes unfulfilled. Over the past few weeks he has asked me to find what he calls his favorite "lunch meat".

I have tried to explain to him they don't have this type of meat product anywhere outside of a six-foot radius of Bethany, Louisiana (population 1,100 if you count individual cans of beer at the Quickie Mart), but he will not take no for an answer, even when said with considerable disdain. I have looked for what he described but I feel as if he is accidentally combining the traits of several of his favorite foods, vile though they may be. The description was something akin to a thinly sliced potted meat/Spam hybrid. As my friend Dawn from Memphis would say, "Ooh-to-the-wee".

I had attempted to provide him actual deli ham, thinking I was splurging on something he would prefer to this luncheon loaf. I was wrong. He told me he would, "eat it, I reckon, but I don't like it that much." Assuming he would just give up and find another item over which to hyper-focus, I was surprised to see that he apparently ventured out of the yard, for the first time in about five months. Never underestimate a redneck on a mission.

I returned from my recent trip to DC to find he had braved imminent death to cross the street to the *Super Mercado y Tacqueria* to ensure no stone had been left unturned in the search for this favored protein. I found his butcher-papered bounty was labeled *Jamon*. When I asked what he was eating, he haughtily replied, "I found my lunch meat at the messican groshry store. And you said they didn't have it."

I smiled and said, "You realize *jamon* is Spanish for ham, right?"

I believe the correct spelling of his reaction is, "Hmpf!" followed by the dismissive smacking of lips and judgmental clicking of false teeth.

Tuesday, December 25, 2012

Your name is what?

It's Christmas morning and I have put the big one down for a nap and I am clearing the pantry of everything fattening or sugar-filled by creating desserts to share with co-workers tomorrow. It's for our own good. The Dad is diabetic, and I am determined to remain "not fat", so yay for the hospital staff; they'll think I am selfless. 'Tis the season, y'all.

My absolute favorite holiday candy is haystacks. I use my mother's recipe which calls for potato sticks instead of chow mein noodles. They are buttery goodness and taste ridiculously yummy. Of course, the ingredients necessitated a trip to Little Guatemala as no other store had even heard of potato sticks.

I like the fact Wal-Mart does not change their inventory dependent upon geography with the notable exception of TJ Blackburn syrup and Snapple. It has been my experience, you can't find Blackburn Syrup, the only decent pancake syrup on the market, outside of the South and you cannot find Snapple inside of the South.

When I was spooning the haystacks onto the tin foil (because I'm Southern, he said in response to the query of the reason he said tin instead of aluminum), I thought about who named these and other candies and how important it is, apparently, that a cook not only be creative in the invention of, but also the naming of, said desserts.

Haystacks look exactly like little haystacks. It's a perfect name. I'm not sure if they were so named by the creator (little c – I've not speaking of Jesus at this particular junction) or if there was a clever family member who said, "Ooh, those look like little haystacks" and the name stuck.

I have to think those sorts of things cannot be left up to chance; names are important. If it was left up to the cooks, we'd have an entire section of the cookbook called "tiny nom-noms or hunks of gooey goodness".

While I don't necessarily think the first First Lady actually invented her namesake treat, I like the regal nature of a Martha Washington. And divinity fudge calls to mind religious intercession as the sugar content is enough to cause Type II diabetes from simply walking slowly past the decorative candy dish on the dessert table at your

Grandmother's house. In fact, one of my back teeth just turned black from typing that sentence.

And speaking of names, *mi padre* asked, just this morning, if I thought Terryll was a typical Southern name. Terryll is pronounced like Errol. As in Errol Flynn, for those over 50. For those under 40, go on IMDB and educate yourselves. My response was, "Number one, I don't think there is such a thing as a typical southern name and, number two, if there is, it is most assuredly not Terryll."

On a side note, I learned my name (Dustin Terryll) is interesting to be sure. Per a study I read, Dustin is ranked 4th on the list of most common names for white boys in California and Terryll is ranked 6th on the list of most common names for black boys in California.

Which begs the question, what is a typical southern name? My best friend from high school (Paige) sometimes sends me our hometown newspaper so I can see the interesting names of the populace of the bustling metropolis of Tylertown, MS. Tykevius, Jakevius, Idaya, Todrick, Antisha, Catavious, Zaman, Traquarius, Latavius, Dartavian, Amari, Arkale and Kendrioun; and those are all boys on the football team. It sounds like roll call in the Roman Senate.

You don't even have to leave my family for some of those people with resoundingly Southern labels. We have the men: Hubert, Searcy, Sherman, Thurman, Thornton, the aforementioned Terryll, Odis, Lynch and the James-doubles (James Allen, James Oscar, James Melvin). There are also quite a few with names which are initials which don't stand for anything like RC, AV and JD. On the women's side we have Waynette, Perrilyn, Arilla and Ercel and the doubly good Myrna Rae, Jimmie Sue, Lucy Jane, Rhoda

Lee and Billie Evelyn. And that's not counting friends and acquaintances Catfish, Cooter, Johnny Boy and Tater. I also know both a male and a female JoJo, but we are not related; a fate which saddens me a little bit, although more color in my family tree I do not need, *n'est ce pas?*

If you've read my first mystery (*A Gone Pecan*) you are familiar with interestingly named people such as Marcetta, Deltrenda, Crespo and Billie Shannon. Now you know more about my background, it's easier to see these names are not much of a stretch.

Would a name have to be doubled like Bobby Merle or Willie Nell to be considered Southern? At least Southerners aren't as bad as some celebrities with children named Pilot, Apple, Moses, Moon, Inspektor and Kal-el. Of course, it depends on your point of view whether those are preferable to Hilma Fay, Spur or Shadynasty (pronounced Sha-dynasty). At least little Apple will have a big bank account.

I feel sure most children in the next generation will be named Bella or Jacob, but don't some of the newest names sounds like they are from specific TV channels like Soap Network (Fallon, Channing) or Nat Geo (Savannah, Dakota). There are an alarming number of female Kendalls and Kinleys these days and more than a handful of Dylans and Brandons. I blame 90210 for those last two. There are also those amongst us that have delved into the categories of special characters and random capitalizations like De'Quan, She'Angelique, RaShad and LaMiracle. If your child requires assistance to spell their name upon entering fifth grade, you might have gone too far out of your way to be unique.

So, you tell me, what is the typical Southern name? I would continue our discussion, but I am, in the words of my dear sainted mother, "…too ashamed to look at you because I have done nothing but lay around and eat the live long day" and I am tired, y'all.

With that I'll bid you a Merry Christmas. I'd offer to send you some haystacks but somebody, I won't say who, ate them all.

Monday, January 7, 2013

Would you give fake sugar to the Dowager Countess?

Having just survived the holidays and trying to decide if MLK Day is enough of a reason to break out the haystacks once more, I realized that sugar is all around us and is an integral part of what makes a Southerner Southern as opposed to merely from the South. Our tea is sweet, our belles are sweet (at least as far as you know) and our desserts are diabetes-inducingly sweet. We even coat our criticisms with a sugary, 'Bless their hearts' when we meant what we said but needed the recipient to still feel as if the Junior League wasn't suddenly out of reach.

The reason I bring this up is I have been fake sugaring all sorts of things of late and today, I am loath to admit, I sugared my chili. Now, before you get all judgmental, bear with me. I merely added 3 individual Splenda packets to a pot of chili that contained 2.5 pounds of hamburger. It's not like I was trying to make a red meat soufflé; I was simply trying to recreate this amazing chili I had as an appetizer at dinner last night. It was some of the best I've had (Willow

Pizza in San Jose, check it out) and had a slight sweetness that was just divine.

So, I bought the ingredients for chili and was trying to figure out how to make it sweet. I add grape jelly to my baked beans and they are loved by all and sundry. But I thought that wouldn't be quite the flavor profile I was seeking.

It is a known fact that Clara Herrington of Tylertown, MS makes the best tuna salad in all the land. And I'm not kidding. As someone who used to weigh 422 pounds, I know food. As someone who lost 220 of those pounds, you should trust my tastes. Why, you ask? Well, I'll tell you. I have great taste in clothes; as I write this I am wearing fuchsia chinos and a navy cardigan with navy suede wingtips and a matching belt, and my most recent fortune cookie fortune stated, "You are admired for your impeccable tastes". So, there you go.

Now, I have never been known for violent tendencies other than scathing remarks about tacky people or bad drivers, but I can assure you if you were to stand betwixt me and Ms. Clara's tuna salad, fisticuffs would ensue. I am not proud of that reality; I am simply being honest.

A couple of years ago, I was visiting Mississippi on a tiny book tour (buy my book *A Gone Pecan* online) and had an offer to stay at the Herrington Family's house on the Bogue Chitto River. As I was taught to do, I politely declined at first (we are very British) but when they upped the ante to include, not only Ms. Clara's tuna salad, but Ms. Clara herself, I would have been a fool not to accept. I love me some Herringtons, do you hear me?

Now, I realize having just admitted to spending the night alone with Ms. Clara is tantamount to a scandal is the not-otherwise-occupied minds of Tylertownians, unless you think about it for, I don't know, say, 4 or 5 seconds and you realize the players in the story are Ms. Clara and me. I think Andy Griffith's Aunt Bea was more scandalous than the sainted Ms. Clara. Well, sainted if Baptists had saints, whose designations I assume would be somehow tied to popularity of casserole recipes or number of prayer circles started.

I said all that to say this, her secret ingredient is sugar. I apologize if that was meant to be a secret, but Sharon told me at the river one time so it's her fault, Miss Clara.

I know sugar is bad for you. We all know it will one day take The Dad's feet. Fear not, however, as I have been using fake sugar for quite some time. Sweet 'n' Low (the pink one) is the first I tried and used to be the only one. It reminds me of old ladies' perfume and/or the soft drink Tab. I switched to Equal (the blue one) when Cher started advertising it in the 90s, I think. The Dad and I had been using it for our morning coffee until recently. A friend, who is a nurse, told me some story about Equal having the same effect on your organs as formaldehyde or somesuch. I don't know if this is an urban myth, but I switched to Splenda (the yellow one) as I was told by this same friend at least Splenda was real sugar that had been altered to be bereft of, well, sugar. I assume it was some chemical engineering process, but I like to think it was magic like in Harry Potter.

And speaking of Harry Potter, The Dad and I have been enjoying *Downton Abbey*, which he calls *Down Town Abbey*, then wonders aloud (each week) why they're in the country, not the city. He can't remember who is who so there's a lot of questioning throughout the show, which requires the use of close captioning. Not so much for him, but for me.

I am adept at understanding English accents, idioms and slang, being an unabashed Anglophile. He, on the other hand, being a citizen of Ala-Miss-La-Tex, doesn't even understand me half of the time, much less someone British. Watching with him is not unlike sitting beside a child with ADD and no Ritalin. Who's that? Why's she wearing that? Boy, that one sure is ugly. She'd make a haint take a thorn thicket! Why'd they pick an ugly girl? Why do you need a house that big? Would you like a house that big? I wouldn't. I like log cabins. I want a Harley. Why don't you let me eat candy bars? Did you bring me a Coke Zero from town? You know I lost 2 more pounds. Why're you lookin' at me like that?

We were watching TV this past weekend as I do only when he complains I don't spend time with him as his activities consist of sleeping, eating and crocheting while watching TV. I had found a Harry Potter movie and we were both enjoying it when he suddenly said, "Hey! There's that old lady from *Downtown Abbey*!"

I responded, yes it was, in fact, the Dowager Countess and although she is a two-time Oscar winner (1969 Best Actress for the *Prime of Miss Jean Brodie* and 1978 Best Supporting Actress for *California Suite* in which she played an Oscar nominee on her way to the ceremony) she is best known to the Millenials, which apparently includes 71-year-old rednecks, as Professor McGonagall.

This set him off on another tangent: Boy she looks terrible, don't she? What year was that movie made? Can you look it up on your little computer? I wonder how old she

235

is? How old is Ziva from *NCIS*? I know Abbie is older than she looks. You know she's from Loozeeana? You find out the year yet? What's takin' you so long? How old is Abbie? Who's that old man? Can I grow my beard and tie a ribbon in it? Why d'ya always make that face? Is it time to eat yet? I'm hungry. I sure would like a chocolate shake, this big. Where you goin' butthole?

I just realized it is almost 6 pm and time for *Downton Abbey* out here on the West Coast. I will bid you adieu and head to the TV viewing room. I must prepare myself to read my new favorite TV show because The Dad is wide awake and while over-medicating a crazy old man isn't actually illegal, it borders on rude and being British, I'd rather someone think I were poor than rude.

Happy New Year, y'all!

Wednesday, January 23, 2013

Funk in the 80s means something different

As we have previously discussed, The Dad is a very generous person. He would give you his last nickel. And by you, I mean just that. You, me, anybody. Familial connection is not a pre-requisite for this generosity. Of course, unlimited generosity has its downside. Recently, he told me that the button had come off a pair of his jeans. Or whatever you call that metal fastener thing. It doesn't have an interesting name like aglet (the tip of a shoelace).

He told me, by way of instructions for disposal, to donate them to "them poor people at the Goodwill." My response, "Haven't they suffered enough?" was met with offense, which I still don't understand. Did he really think anyone would want to own a pair of jeans that have been assaulted with malice aforethought and essentially rendered inoperable?

Now, I could tell you I was simply thinking Rustler jeans are not a quality garment when they are new, I swear you get a pair free with a Big & Tall underwear purchase at Wal-Mart, but what I was truly thinking was if those pants could talk they would either weep, throw up or beg to be sent to wherever socks hide when they escape from your dryer and disappear. Someone told me they go to be with Jesus and as I don't really know that it's not true, we'll just let it lay there like other statements that make us unsure whether to laugh or pray for the speaker or in this case, the writer.

I know I have discussed the fragrance of my father more than is necessary, or so I've been told by my boss, but I just don't understand why there has been little success in that particular department. I have curbed his natural tendency to judge others aloud and have forced him kicking and screaming into a 60-pound weight loss without any exercise, but I simply cannot make headway in the olfactory department. And although his new recliner is leather, which does not retain smells like his previous velour one did, I find that I am forced to walk throughout my house every other day, with a Febreze bottle continuously spraying over my shoulder like a dragon fruit scented mosquito truck, ever-vigilant in the fight for a house that "smells pretty".

But, it's the price you pay, I suppose, for housing the elderly, as I have discovered while discussing The Dad with others, like ½ of the set of twins who were my best friends

7-10th grades in Texas (Hi, Juliann!). We were madly in 'like' (also known as 'going together') for somewhere in the neighborhood of 3-4 weeks in 8th grade but as young love does it went out of style right around the time Panama Jack t-shirts came to prominence. For those who don't know or remember, Panama Jack was an overpriced t-shirt that was never owned by yours truly, he said with only a trace of bitterness. Juliann and I met for dinner on my recent trip to Dallas and in the midst of our laughter, gossip and story-telling, we somehow found ourselves in the territory of older men's hygiene habits in the absence of their wives. Old men are simply old men and they have an odd fragrance if you will. I always assumed my father's particular odor was a combination of bologna, feet and onions with a dash of ornery and a smidgen of righteous indignation at my insistence that he "smells...odd".

I assumed that his hygiene practices were learned on the turn row, modified in the wilds of Vietnam and subdued throughout my childhood by the sheer force of my mother's will. That explains why she always seemed wore out at the end of the day. That must be it, right? It couldn't have been her children. I don't speak for my siblings, but I can assure you, based on my recollections, I was quite simply a joy throughout my youth and remain so to this day. What? The Dad says it's not bragging if it's a fact.

I did, however, assume that people who are a bit fancier would have habits that are more in line with what you would imagine. And as Juliann's father is in a much higher tax bracket, I naively felt he wouldn't be gross, to use 80s parlance. She informed me, over two different kinds of queso, that old men are old men.

Apparently, it is not directly linked to income, education level or any other arbitrary categories and that is a sad statement indeed. I thought the great equalizer was Wal-Mart' apparently, for old men, it's butt and feet. I wonder what age you start to smell? Is it just old men or is it all men? I asked my sister and her response was "All men, besides you, are gross." Well said, sister of mine. Well said indeed.

Also in January, I began a 75-day detail as Acting Associate Director of my healthcare system. When I won the national Prosthetic Service of the Year award, I thought about my next career step. This detail would be an amazing opportunity for me and one that would help me decide if this is what I wanted to do; be an executive. This included the time our facility underwent our triennial Joint Commission Accreditation Survey. I knew this would be a more stressful time as I would still need to keep an eye on my service; I have issues with letting completely go of something, afraid others cannot do as good a job as I can. I'm not proud of this trait. I told The Dad that I would need him to be more helpful around the house and be prepared to see less of me and the fact that I would be tired and not wanting to watch as much TV or talk as often.

I had talked to The Dad about my need to be able to relax when I came home because the job as Acting Associate Director was too important to mess up. My inherited anger is pronounced when I am tired and/or stressed. I know I need to be well-rested to be able to handle whatever life throws my way. Prayer is a powerful weapon, but sometimes my anger seemed too strong for even that. His immediate reaction was to take offense at my suggestion that he wasn't helpful. When I tried to massage the message, it didn't help. I apologized, and he eventually agreed, in theory, but he was adamant I had not inherited the temper from him as he assured me he was not an angry person.

The next morning, he told me he was proud of me, but in the same breath warned me about forgetting where I came from. I wasn't sure what he meant by that and when I asked him, he said, "Just don't be getting' ideas that you're better'n other people." I just stared at him. He had been living with me for 15 months and saw me daily not forgetting where I came from. We had already had several conversations about my self-esteem and trying to feel like I deserved my position and not like I was some redneck imposter, trying to fake like I belonged.

I had only come to terms with being happy with who I was in 2010 and truly only became confident enough to give up a big title in Washington, DC, when I moved to California. Keeping my ego in check is not too difficult. If I ever feel like I might be amazing, one call to my sister will get the ball rolling on embarrassing things from my childhood and I am suddenly back down on earth with the regular people. Family will keep you grounded.

And grounded would have been fine. What he often did wasn't keep me grounded, it was more like shooting me out of the sky, when I was trying to fly. When I would come home from work after a hard day, I would retreat to my room after a cursory 'hello' and a check on his condition/mood. I would stay there until it was time to eat as I simply need quiet to relax; I don't require actual sleep. Even with my bedroom door closed and his door closed, at the other end of the house, I could still hear the TV. When I asked if he could turn it down, he claimed he couldn't hear it. When I asked him to use his hearing aids (that he insisted he did not need although the Audiologist issued to him after an ear test I had to schedule behind his back) he assured me he did not need them. When I tried to explain what I needed, he would get mad and tell me I was trying to act like I was smarter than him, fancier than him, better than him. It was a lose-lose situation and it impacted my work. It got to the point that I would stay late at work just to avoid him; Starbucks was more relaxing, as were most any restaurants. It didn't help that this caused me to spend more money than I should and gain weight I shouldn't.

During this same time, I was involved in a national leadership program called Excellence in Government. It's a cross-agency program with five weeklong learning sessions and a group project. I always want to do well when involved in an activity and I was one of only ten VA employees out of 200 people from across the federal government.

During my last national leadership program in 2008 I was used to being able to relax at home before and after each week. I needed time to think, relax, plan and complete the required research and homework for my project in addition to my already hectic schedule and sometimes stressful job. Travel takes a lot out of you especially flying to the east coast from the west coast as four of the five trips were to DC.

I was not used to being required to take care of someone who preferred, it seemed, to be purposefully dependent on me. I didn't need to feel guilty for traveling out of town. I also didn't need a 72-year-old toddler with constant complaints and questionable requirements; acting out when

I didn't perform to their liking. You can't put an adult in time out. Believe me, I tried.

It was one of the reasons there were few blogs during February and March. Once the detail ended, I was able to talk about something, even if it wasn't The Dad.

Friday, March 29, 2013

Putting the math in fashion since 1984

Last week I was in Portland, Oregon for a leadership conference and as the attire for most days was business casual I decided to wear my colored chinos with appropriately coordinated shirts/sweaters and accessories. As we have previously discussed, I think I'm a cutie-tootie in my ensembles (pronounced ahn-sahm-blahs because I'm like that) and I receive myriad reactions depending on the audience for these outfits. And other than a younger, more attractive homeless contingency, I wasn't sure what to expect from Portland locals.

I was staying at the Heathman Hotel. I will let that sink in. If you are confused as to the reference, then you're fine; I was confused too. If you recognized that name, know that I am judging you and not just a little bit. Apparently, this hotel featured prominently into the confoundingly popular *Fifty Shades of Nasty* book series (or whatever it's called), according to some of my friends who shall remain nameless as they should be, but I assure you are not, properly shamed. Someone asked me if I had read any of the series, of which there are three. I responded, "If the fans of the books call it 'mommy porn', I don't think I have to read it to make an assumption of the level of yuckiness therein." Feel free to disagree. It won't be the first time we've not seen eye-to-eye.

And I said all that to say this, the breakfast breads in the hotel restaurant were so good I was able to stop feeling all 'ookie' and partake each morning. Their croissants were delectable, and the scones were delicious. I told The Dad this story and he asked what a scone was, and I explained it was like a biscuit made with sugar, which he appreciated but it dampened my 'fancy' just a touch. The manager of the restaurant was the nicest lady who remarked on my outfits every morning and decided I needed a free scone for "being so dapper". Since I agreed, I accepted her offer of cinnamon scone with marionberry jam.

On my jaunts around the city that day, I met all and sundry of Portland. Some of them weird like the homeless guy I gave money to for he and his woman to eat at Subway (how does he have somebody, and I don't? At the very least, I have a home).

Also, I had a messenger bag full of $1 coins because the public transportation ticket kiosk wouldn't take debit cards and I only had $20 bills, so I ended up with a ticket for a train ride I didn't want to be on to go to a bowling alley in a sketchy neighborhood and $18 in $1 coins because that's how they roll at the Portland Transit Authority.

Don't get me wrong, I love me some Sacajawea, but I don't need eighteen of her likeness ruining the line of my trousers, which at this point were red. What I mean was they didn't turn red; they started out and remained red throughout the day. It had nothing to do with setting the tone for possible gangland slaying and whatnot, although the neighborhood was a little more CSI than made me comfortable.

The bowling alley had loaded tater tots which more than made up for it the gang-territory feel of the neighborhood. I'm not going to list off what I would eat a tater tot. Suffice it to say, when I see potatoes in 'tot' form, it is *on*, do you hear me?

But getting back to this homeless person, I think I am some sort of magnet for odd people and this was before I embraced the rainbow of chinos. Mr. Subway and his woman saw me later that day and gave me an update on his life (his issues with Social Security which I presume he thought he told me about) and asked for more money. When I reminded him, he had just eaten at Subway in the last two hours and I didn't think it was possible for him to be hungry again, he seemed confused. I don't know, maybe his girlfriend is a heavy eater.

Portland is an awesome city because they are all about their vintage/thrift store clothing choices. And there is a difference between vintage and thrift. Vintage means sometimes ugly stuff from past decades at today's retail prices. Thrift means sometimes ugly stuff from today at past decades' retail prices. And, you know I love me some thrift stores.

There are so many of these stores in downtown Portland, I found one that is solely big and tall vintage, called Fat Fancy. Who knew? The manager and I became fast friends (Hi, Carlie!) and we had a fun conversation about, among other things, rodeos…in a thrift shop…in Oregon.

After leaving Fat Fancy, I got caught in a sudden sleet storm and sought shelter in the nearest Starbucks, of which there is one every six inches. Seriously, there are two across the street from each other. When I entered, I was awarded "Best Pants of the Day" and another free scone. How people equate baked goods with awesome pants is beyond me, but who am I to argue although at this point, *mis pantalones* (that's Spanish) were going to be *el tighto, por favor* (also Spanish), if I kept eating said scones.

I could find the homeless guy and give the scone to him, I suppose. But I'm not going to walk around looking for him since I already went to all the thrift stores. I'm wearing fuchsia chinos (with a gray pea coat and gray suede wingtips); maybe I'll just walk to the center of Portland and let him find me. But, is that really helping him? Give a man a scone and he eats for one meal; give him teal chinos and he eats for two meals, if he's lucky, but boy doesn't he look good doing it. I'm trying to stay humble but being all Ghandi-like while wearing Brooks Brothers is hard work, y'all.

At the very least I should be rewarded with one of those 'secret' government drones taking a photo of my breathtaking approach to men's fashion and giving the Department of Defense new ideas to elevate their uniform options. Khaki and Navy are not exciting colors, y'all. Do you really want people defending your country taking their fashion cues from one of those chain stores? It's called Old Navy for a reason.

We want a New Navy, which could be purple or at least aqua. Am I right? And Olive is not a pop color to anyone except my sister and the Mennonites. At least Amish women embrace color and can't we all learn something from them, other than they can be straight-up trashy during Rumspringa. What? I watched that documentary. And no,

I'm not talking about the ridiculous, fake *Amish Mafia* that The Dad watches.

I have been wearing colored chinos, colored socks and pocket squares for a number of years and it seems the fashion world is slowly following suit. Lately it looks like an Easter parade in most menswear departments nationwide. Am I mad at the Johnny-come-latelies jumping on my bandwagon, which sounds like a trailer you pull behind the band bus? Absolutely not. If we can make the whole world a better-dressed place, I am all for it. Plus, it pays unexpected dividends: better service when shopping, access to the first-class security fast lane at airports without ticket verification ('cause you know my government employee butt is not flying first class). And, as we have just learned, free foodstuffs.

And if I become those within my sphere of influences' frame of reference for awesome, then they will have come into alignment with the thinking I have embraced for far too long to honestly admit. Colored Chinos + Suede Wingtips = Free Scones. I wonder if this is the new math I've been hearing about. No child (or tacky person) left behind, y'all!

Monday, April 22, 2013

Narcoleptic Wildebeests at Church

The Dad loves to drink Kool-Aid (registered trademark) and since he moved in with me I have gotten him used to drinking it sugar-free. I initially tricked him but by the time he figured it out, he had admitted to liking it and would rather break his own nose than admit I got one over on him.

I know, I know, fake sugar does as much harm, etc. Since he is diabetic, I think it's less bad for him, don't you? And if you don't, then you need to keep it to yourself. I must live with this narcoleptic wildebeest, not you.

When I asked him his favorite flavor, he said 'Red'. Full disclosure, what he said was, "If God made something better than red Kool-Aid, he kept it to himself." And if you're Southern, red is a flavor, most especially at Vacation Bible School or VBS.

Those who were raised in the land mass known as God's Country know full well to what I am referring. For those of you who are unfamiliar with this school, let me start by saying I am saddened but not shocked and, bless your poor heathen hearts, I will not blame you for the failings of your family and/or community.

Vacation Bible School is exactly what you think; a school where you learn about the Bible while you are on vacation from regular school. And there are snacks like those butter cookies shaped like flowers you could store on your fingers until you ate them. And Kool-Aid, always red Kool-Aid. It never occurred to any of us there were other options for beverages. Orange Kool-Aid wasn't Kool-Aid, it was Tang. And purple Kool-Aid was and is gross. Just like purple Jolly Ranchers (also trademarked) are gross. If you actually like the purple ones, you need to do some inward reflection. Seriously.

Some of the other unique things about VBS were saying not only the Pledge of Allegiance to the American Flag but also to the Christian Flag and the Bible. I assure you I am not kidding. Also, the older kids got the opportunity to pray out loud for the first time. Let me tell you it is a terrifying activity. You don't know stress like a 12-year-old who is desperate to sound both reverential enough to not be smitten from on high yet blasé enough about it to not be picked last in kick ball during the activity period.

And I used to think I was nervous about praying out loud due to my age. I found it was not the case, at least in my family. My Mother, as we have discussed, was 5'5" of Jesus coming at you in white Keds (registered trademark) practically glowing with love and devotion and sometimes Elmer's Glue, as she was often in charge of arts and crafts. She would pray at the drop of a hat and always with conviction and sometimes in King James English. The Dad, on the other hand, was never at church enough to pray about anything other than enough pork roast for second helpings at the Fifth Sunday dinners on the grounds. The running joke at most of our churches was my mother had "made up" The Dad to have a father for her children as he was typically working on Sundays, as you often must when your labor is of the manual variety.

On one of his irregular visits to church, the good preacher, thinking he was dealing with your average man asked The Dad to close the sermon with a prayer. My siblings and I said very quick prayers begging Jesus not to strike The Dad down should he inadvertently cuss or say something inappropriate as he was wont to do. To our, and the rest of the congregation's surprise and confusion, we heard our mother inhale sharply and suddenly start praying. At the end of her eloquent prayer, everyone wondered, but didn't dare ask, why she had stepped in so quickly, not knowing the sharp inhale was due to The Dad elbowing her to pray as I think he, too, was worried about cussing or worse in the House of the Lord.

When in doubt, send in the pros. Can I get an Amen?

Once my detail ended and my mentor, the Deputy Director, confirmed I had done a great job, I felt I had a strong chance to be selected for the position. I made it to the final three candidates and my interview went well, I thought.

Toward the middle of May, the Director of the facility called me into her office and told me they had selected someone else for the Associate Director's position. I was floored and told her so. I asked for feedback from her and from the interview panel and was told that while my answers were good, they were so long that everyone forgot what I was talking about by the time I was finished. I was not surprised by this. I am verbose on a good day and when you factor in the nervousness of a potentially, life-altering job, the outcome is wordiness beyond all reason. However, I am very skilled at recovering from a setback and figuring out how to move forward. Sure, I was disappointed, but if it was meant to be, it would have happened. I firmly believe that. My faith allows me to accept disappointments as I know God will put me where I need to be, when I need to be and give me a chance to acquire the skills I will need when the time comes.

The Dad had a different take on the situation. When I got home that afternoon and shared what happened, The Dad told me I should tell them to "Kiss (my) Ass!" When I declined to agree that was the right move, he proceeded to tell me that my response was unmanly, and he couldn't believe I was just going to "sit there and take it." When I told him that would solve nothing and possibly even damage my career, he told me, "That's the difference between you and me. You'll just take the punch; I fight back." It made me sad to have no real role model at home and it made me wonder if his temper and this attitude were some of the reason we had to move so often when I was a kid.

I began to wonder how many of the times we had to move were because The Dad got mad and told his boss, like Johnny Paycheck wished, "Take this job and shove it"? It explains the bi-annual trek around the southeast. I had never questioned the moves; you don't question your parents. They were in charge and I had to believe they knew what they were doing, but it all started to make sense. I talked to my sister about it and she agreed it seemed to fit. I appreciate my mother's influence and my faith more than ever as I knew the capacity to curse someone out who denied me what I felt was mine lay within my DNA. Literally, thank you Jesus for helping me stay sane and sensible. I wish I had a father who could give sage advice on how to navigate the business world, but one of federal healthcare is entirely different than, apparently, rig welding.

I appreciated that he was upset about me not getting the promotion, but I was disappointed that I couldn't talk to him about my concerns or anything relating to business, really. If I listened to his advice, it would be a mistake and it was a constant negative buzzing in my ears.

I went back to my job and decided not to apply for any further positions until I was able to improve my interview skills and continue to grow as a leader and a person. I told myself I would eventually get an executive position, I felt confident. It just wasn't my time. I hoped that saying it out loud would help me believe it deep down.

Sunday, May 26, 2013

If your duck doesn't speak Spanish, will it still answer?

Prayer has been in the news a lot lately from Oklahoma to the people on *Duck Dynasty* and I have felt a connection to both. For one-half of third grade, my nomadic family lived in Moore, Oklahoma. Someone recently asked me if ever watched *Duck Dynasty*.

I must admit I had not up to that point, but I caught an episode the last time I was in DC at a conference. As a side note, am I the only one who pictures a duck in a sequined gown with huge shoulder pads when someone mentions the show?

I didn't really know what to expect other than familiarity seeing as how the Robertson family is from where I'm from. West Monroe, Louisiana, is about 75 miles from my birthplace of Lake Providence, Louisiana, and I must admit their family is not unlike mine except the Thornton/Thompson family has more funny stories and less facial hair but about the same amount of camouflage.

Now I am about to tell on myself, but I feel in the interest of full disclosure I must admit I did not attend church this past Sunday. And it wasn't to watch football either. I was tired and various other things which are not good excuses, but I simply did not go.

Luckily God does not have a last nerve. So, my backslidden-but-forgiven-self went to meet my new friend

Julie for brunch. We met at Starbucks when I complimented her gorgeous robin's egg blue purse.

Over brunch we talked about many things, one of them being The Dad's lifelong aversion to church. As we have previously discussed, he has not been the greatest of fans of the church itself. While he professes to believe church and loving Jesus are good things, he won't go so far as to actually participate in word or deed unless the words are "no pancakes (if you don't go)" or the deed is "eating at fifth Sunday dinners on the ground".

While Presbyterians will have coffee and doughnuts before the service, there hasn't been a time in the last two years where I have witnessed a cheese covered casserole and it hurts me to my very core, y'all. Although I do not have to have the promise of food to get me to the church on time, it doesn't hurt to have access to some good groceries every now and again. Can I get an amen?

To be fair, The Dad has attended about three times in the last two years which is quite the feat considering he attended the same number of times in the previous 20 years. The first Sunday he attended with me, I took him to our 9:30 contemporary service, whereupon he accused me of joining a cult as the worshippers had the gall to clap along with the singing and actually seemed to enjoy themselves.

Old guard Southern Baptists are like Anglicans who sweat because they believe in their heart of hearts anyone who shows any emotion in church other than wretched heartache over their sins is secretly aligned with the unclean and raising your hands in worship is akin to speaking in tongues or rolling around on the floor like they do at those "other churches" like Assembly of God or Maranatha Bible church. No offense. Now I don't know what Maranatha means, but from what I gather it is not "to frown while singing". That's what Baptist means, people; you heard it here first.

Speaking of prayer, The Dad needs some right now as, unlike Jesus, I do have a last nerve and he is clog dancing on it. Not only did he wake me up this morning by cooking pinto beans with a hambone at 5 am, but I just discovered he ate my leftover quesadilla for his snack between breakfast and his "official" snack even though he admitted, "wudn't too good, but [I] ate it anyway".

To top it all off he apparently decided he prefers my Garden Salsa Sun Chips to his pork skins and tried to sneak-switch the bags on our respective pantry shelves as if I wouldn't notice I was eating *chicharrones* because even when I'm angry I'm at the very least bi-lingual.

Saturday, June 1, 2013

I'd rather my white trash ghost simply say Boo!

The other night, The Dad hiccupped in such an aggressive and abrupt way, I didn't know what was happening and reached for his inhaler. When he caught his breath, he said, "That hiccup was so big it made tears in my eyes as big as a horse turd." I didn't know what to do other than make a judgmental face. He then asked, "You know what a hiccup is, don't ya?" Before I could answer, he said, "It's a fart that got lost!" and then burst into raucous laughter.

Lately, when he makes any similar statement I have taken to looking to my left as if there is someone there to see me roll my eyes. It's not unlike the TV camera I always thought should have been, but am now extremely happy was not, filming me for the reality show that is my life. The Dad has caught on to this practice and asked who I was looking at. I told him it was the ghost he swears lives in our house.

While I do believe in ghosts only because I have seen one face to face (still not over it DeeDee Smith, thank you very much), I do not believe my father has seen any specters in my home. A recent episode of *Dr. Who* solved the riddle of a ghost by discovering it was a time traveler stuck in a rift in the time/space continuum or somesuch quasi-scientific reason. I realize *Dr. Who* is probably not based on real science, it does not keep me from wishing I could have a closet that's bigger on the inside because my colored chino collection is getting out of control.

I can assure you if there were some supernatural force in my immediate area, the activities in The Dad's bathroom would most certainly cause said force to flee to the relatively safe confines of purgatory or wherever they're supposed to go. Look, I said I believed in them, not that I had a doctorate in paranormal psychology or some other pseudo-science like physics. What? Physics is math parading as science. I took it in both high school and college and still have night terrors. Two pages of calculations just to get the formula before you enter the numbers to get the answer? Madness! Complete madness! Said the Journalism major with an Art minor.

Of course, when I mentioned to my father that I believed in ghosts, he began to talk about death and dying as many older adults are prone to do. You must understand I have recently begun to realize The Dad will possibly be living with me until he passes on from this world. I have already begun to acclimate myself to the very real possibility I will forever be a bachelor because who in their right mind would want to marry someone with a 71-year-old belligerent and flatulent teenager? No, seriously, who? I need names, people. Unlike Niles Crane, I have no interest in The Dad's nursing assistant and not solely because she is late. Every. Single. Day.

As he was hyper-focusing on his demise, I gave him a direct order as if he were an employee. Should he feel himself slipping from this realm, he must muster his last bit of energy and take himself into the yard as to not taint the happy feel of my home because I will never live, again, in a place where someone to my knowledge has died. I love my house and do not want to move. No, I don't think it's selfish.

The downside of his death, *besides* the fact he would be dead, would be, were it possible, he would come back to haunt me. Of this you can be sure. I would have history's first farting, burping ghost who would somehow figure out a way to fry a steak on my stove just to keep it greasy.

Being haunted is not a father-son activity in which I would willingly participate. Although, outside of eating and/ or complaining about stupid people, what activity would appeal to us both is beyond me. From the commotion to my immediate left, one of my father's current activities is scratching his chest with his middle shirt button unfastened, like Napoleon, without the couth or the short man complex. When he finished, he didn't re-button his shirt. When I asked why he was insistent on being unkempt, he said, "What if I have another itch?" I can assure you, the Supreme Court hasn't judged anyone as much as I am judging him right at this very moment.

Seeing my look of mild revulsion, he sat and smiled like a cat eating sawbriars through a picket fence. Yes, that's what he said. I asked him to spell sawbriars to ensure accuracy. Even I, with my fluency in redneck, several dialects of country and a passing familiarity with Mississippi trash, am unfamiliar with this particular phrase. Apparently, sawbriars are a real thing, I googled it, and as you know eating any briar, saw or otherwise, would require one to chew very carefully.

Saturday, June 22, 2013

20 Questions, minus 12

Very recently, I am loath to admit, I was not the shining beacon of Christianity you have come to admire. Those who bore witness did not see Jesus in me, to be sure. It wasn't so much what I said or even that there could have been choreography (I believe some people refer to it as gesturing), there was simply a loosening of my self-imposed limitations for public displays of my unhappiness.

Other than the occasional forced wrangling of a wayward server at a dining establishment, I am usually free of anything bordering on pedestrian behavior. And I'm not talking about persons in crosswalks.

As you may or may not know, I am not a fan of bicycles and more specifically, bicyclists. So much so it sometimes causes me pain. Now I would like to say, before you get all out of sorts, I do not hate bicyclists; it would be un-Christian. I even have some very close friends who are cyclists. However, were I to come across them on their velocipede (because I am apparently British) I would want to get them out of my way. Mind you, I don't want anyone to die; I just want them off my streets.

The main reason is I cannot stand the fact they are selfish. They can't decide if they want to be a car and share the road or something far more criminal and ignore stop signs and traffic lights. At least the motorcyclists who weave in and out of traffic state their obnoxiousness through loud tail pipes and/or ponytails. All you see of those blasted cyclists are skintight clothes and weird little helmets.

For those outfits alone, they should be punished. I can assure you, no one wearing spandex should be allowed to do so. Those who have the body to pull it off don't seem to feel the need, at least in Southern California.

But as I am feeling like a benevolent chronicler, I will give them a free pass as I have other questions to share, dear readers. And some of those would be:

1. Why do I get weird songs stuck in my head when I hear my father whistle? And I don't mean weird as in "did he make that song up?" I mean weird as in "why on earth is he whistling *Little Drummer Boy* in June and why does it make me think of Janet Jackson's *Black Cat*?"

2. Why does my father ask me if I brought any leftover butter beans when I come home after a Friday night Happy Hour, where I go to eat inexpensive food whilst my posse drinks it up? Where does he think I go after work, the VFW Hut or Aunt Maudie's house?

3. Why does he consider all my friends who are not fat or a redneck to be a dork or a nerd? And, yes, I have plenty of non-dorky friends, thank you very much. Well, not *plenty*, but some.

4. Why does he insist on wiping his spills on the counter/stove/table with his hand (not a paper towel or dishrag) and even then, only half-heartedly? Has he decided the only way for me not to be able to remove him from my home is because he is literally stuck to the counter in the kitchen, like the tomato seeds and strawberry juice which typically reside there until I come home from work to do house work? Did I mention I walk to work? Uphill. Both ways.

5. Why does he insist on sharing the murder report from across the bay (Oakland) and pretend it's for our little town, acting as if this sleepy haven of wealthy, older folks is dangerous. It's Menlo Park, for goodness sakes; a bedroom community of San Francisco. Facebook is a mile away, people. The police report in our weekly paper is filled with such crime as random noise disturbances and reports of "suspicious persons", which always ends up being a case of mistaken identity with either a new gardener or the housekeeper's grandchildren.

6. Why does he insist on calling my house, which is on the grounds of the medical center, government housing? I know it is in the literal sense, but you

know what he means. And, no, I don't know why it bothers me so much.

7. Why can't he remember that even though both the woman who cleans our home and the woman who cuts our hair (also in our home) are named Clara but they are not, in fact, the same woman? One is 23 and pregnant; the other is at least 50 and clearly not pregnant or even chubby. He can't seem to tell them apart.

8. On that note, why did "Haircut Clara" say to Lulu, on her first visit to our home, "Do you smell my doggie on my hand?" as she offered her hand in a sign of friendship, like you do when you meet a new dog, and then proceed to tell us her dog had died thirteen years prior? Is he stuffed and mounted in her den, I wonder?

Sunday, July 7, 2013

It's about to get real up in here, y'all

I have been blogging about The Dad living with me for almost two years. I can't believe it's really been that long, but it has. Twenty-one months to be exact. I didn't really know what to expect when he arrived, but I figured it would be blog-worthy, hence the blog.

It has not been a smooth transition, but it also hasn't been as bad as it could have been. While I understand he is still, after 13 years, grieving the loss of my mother, there are personality quirks he possesses which continue to confound me.

In full disclosure, I have admitted some of my own quirks like the all-consuming need to have a house which smells 'pretty' and feels 'fancy'; two phrases to which my father likes to roll his eyes ever so sarcastically. He reminds me of a dramatic teenager. He reminds me of, well, me when I was in my late teens. My early teens were mostly about being loved by all and sundry and I was more obsequious than anything.

My 15 years in federal healthcare has given me insight into what many veterans of his generation think, feel and expect. But it wasn't until recently I even considered his life-long anger may have been undiagnosed PTSD. Post-Traumatic Stress Disorder is something you read about, hear about on TV with those now returning from war and even the subject of a couple of movies, mostly on Lifetime and usually starring Meredith Baxter-no-longer-Birney-now-a-lesbian as the long-suffering wife.

He has been very depressed lately, not finding joy in anything. He has, I feel, PTSD, but refuses to admit anything is wrong. Talking about feelings is unmanly. Feeling unhappy is unmanly, he says. Openly pouting when he doesn't get his way, however, he finds completely acceptable. It's an odd dichotomy.

My mother had a response to me whenever I was self-hating and expressed something negative about myself. She would say, "Don't talk about my son like that."

I don't know why it popped into my head, but the other day The Dad was berating himself for something, he couldn't or wouldn't explain what, but I said, "Don't talk about my Dad like that."

He looked at me all confused and I tried to explain it was one of mother's habits. He smiled for just a second but then went back to angry within the space of a head-turn.

It never occurred to me he might have a legitimate reason to be angry and distrustful. I never really gave much thought to why he is almost agoraphobic and seems scared of the world in general. I always assumed he was just a chip off the old block as his father was someone who was, for the longest time, was my frame of reference for a terrible person. I never really stopped to even think of why he would be so unhappy; that he truly hated himself.

When I asked him why he hated himself, he seemed confused and asked me, "don't everybody hate themselves?" To which I answered, "No, they don't. I don't. And you shouldn't". What I didn't say was, I did until I turned 40 and finally decided I was who I was and if people didn't like me, I was far too old to care. Jesus understands me and that is all I need to know. That Jesus understands my Dad was an idea I never really considered.

Some have asked if I feel I make fun of The Dad in my blog and I initially was defensive, stating I was simply reporting facts, not trying to make fun of him. When in all honesty, there was sometimes an edge to the humor; a need to distance myself from him and who I thought he represented. For so long I didn't want to be from where I was from. I didn't want to be from a family that was often lower-middle class from a financial perspective, depending on the job situation. I didn't want to have so many relatives who lived in trailers, which I still refer to as pre-fabricated housing because it sounds funny and I can then laugh at 'those folks', not realizing I was hurting people who are good people. As if money is any indication of the quality of a person.

I always wanted to be somebody other than who I was. I never saw what was so great about me; what was so special. I never put much thought into whether I was smart or funny or ambitious or loyal or any of those traits I have come to appreciate. I was only focused on what I didn't have, which was money, looks and self-esteem. Truth be told, I wasn't aware of self-esteem enough to know I didn't have any. Like my father, I thought everyone hated themselves.

Growing up gay (and so far in the closet I was almost homophobic) in a Southern Baptist family in Texas and Mississippi wasn't the easiest thing to do, to be sure. But when I told The Dad at the ripe old age of 24, he said he already knew and he didn't care. It was not the reaction I expected and for some reason I never really appreciated how hard it must have been for him. *From what I've been told, he shared this information by standing up at a family reunion and announced to all in attendance I was gay. I wasn't there, but it did save me a lot of letter-writing and phone calls.*

I already wasn't the son he expected as his oldest; his namesake. As an Almost Odis, I spent most of the time since the age of 12, wishing I could be someone else; an Actual Odis. I knew I wasn't and didn't know how to be someone different, but it didn't stop me from praying every night to wake up as the son he wanted. There were many nights I prayed to just not wake up at all. Trying to be someone you're not is difficult in any circumstance and I eventually had to give up and just deal with the reality that I was destined to remain Almost Odis, not even truly understanding what that meant. I just knew Almost Odis's didn't live in the boonies.

I was the plaid koala bear in my family and once I realized I was different, I spent most of my adult life attempting to rewrite my story, to reimagine my narrative, to the point that my nieces and nephews are apparently under the impression I spent my childhood at boarding school and want to show me how to ride a horse or drive a four-wheeler. When I remind them that I knew how to do those things, they seem confused as if a member of the royal family suddenly appeared next to them at the Dollar General, buying generic aspirin and Little Debbie snack cakes.

June is Gay Pride month. I attended the parade and festival in San Francisco with some friends. My surprisingly supportive father asked why I had never attended Pride and I told him, half-jokingly, to attend a Pride event, theoretically one should be proud. Until very recently I was not. I wanted to be gay even less than those members of my family who are still not supportive and those who until this very moment didn't have confirmation. I apologize for springing this on you, although to be fair, how surprised could you be? You've met me before.

From the ages of 12 through 40, I was your typical self-loathing Southern Baptist homosexual the likes of who publish painfully narcissistic coming-of-age memoirs with prodigious efficiency. I won't go into any memoir-y reflections today (you'll have to wait for the publication you know is forthcoming). Suffice it to say, I had spent so much time thinking about my issues I never really gave thought to anyone else's; especially my Dad's.

I realized as much as I expected him to hate me, he didn't. And I never gave him credit for it. Unfairly, I gloss over the fact my mother went to her grave devastated and convinced that I was wrong about my orientation. So desperate for her "sweet, precious boy" to be normal, she tried to find me a girlfriend as she lay dying in the hospital. It took me more than 10 years to find it within myself to feel as if I wasn't a walking disappointment and to think I was worth something. That she never got to see my career successes and happiness has always left a trace of sadness around the edges of my personality.

The last few years, The Dad has been supportive, constantly saying he loves me and didn't care I was gay. And for some reason I didn't care that he didn't care. He had his role, written in my teenaged mind, and I refused to allow him to re-write it. I took all my hurt out on him by keeping a distance, which he didn't know how to bridge. How do you apologize for something like that?

As much as I expected him to toe the line when he moved in, he didn't. He also didn't specifically try to get on my nerves and has been somewhat accepting of the changes I have forced upon him. He eats what I cook, he voluntarily washes dishes and recycles with the fervor of a tree hugger. He even sometimes acquiesces to my request for him to wear something other than his house shoes (slippers to my Yankee friends; scuffs to my friends in Lafayette County, Mississippi) to the Wal-Mart when, truth be told, who cares what he wears? I should just be happy he's still around. What I wouldn't give for one more day with my mother.

I am keenly aware I have a limited number of minutes with him as he approaches his 72nd birthday later this month. Why can't I just enjoy what he wants to do? Why do I have to put so many parameters to our relationship? I know we aren't what the other necessarily wanted in a father/son, but we are what we have. And I am grateful I got his sense of humor and his generosity. I am less thankful I got his fiery temper, short legs and weird feet.

For better or for worse, I am what I am and before someone bursts into song, I will say although I have sometimes begrudgingly cared for him these last two years, I hope it still counts as love.

We've discussed how God doesn't have a last nerve and I hope The Dad doesn't either. If he does, I haven't found it yet.

Thursday, July 11, 2013

Can a bus be fueled by Lincoln Logs?

I should have known something was amiss when the tour bus finally arrived, and I pointed out to my colleagues, "um…the back window is plywood… painted black." Let me back up a little.

I was in DC recently for my Excellence in Government Fellowship's Business Acumen session. One of our benchmarks included leadership lessons learned at the Battle of Gettysburg. To get the full effect, we were to travel there by bus and take a tour guided by a retired government executive who has created a very informative lesson concerning the successes and failures on both sides of the War Between the States.

We were supposed to be at the Partnership for Public Service building on New York Avenue early enough to board the bus and leave by 7:00 am. This required me to cut short my much-needed beauty sleep and forgo the free breakfast at my hotel and be all aggressive with Deonte at Starbucks (he had a nametag) opening the doors at precisely 6:00 am even though he was not finished stocking the baked goods display, causing him to under-sweeten my Trenta Black Iced Tea, four Splenda, no water. As a former food service person, I totally understand why he did it. I ain't mad at him, y'all.

My classmate Cory (from San Antonio) and I shared a cab driven by a man who was unhappy to not be taking us to the *aero puerto* (that's Spanish, although he was not) and dropped us off at 6:30 on the nose as we are not ones to dawdle all up and through here. Cory, too, is from the boonies. Oddly enough we went to high school less than 20 miles from each other in the wilds of East Texas. However, as neither of us had a mode of transport other than our bodies (and you know I wasn't traveling any further than the school bus stop in those days, at least voluntarily), we never met each other until this program. The world is tee-niney, dear readers; tee-niney indeed.

I was ready to get on the bus as snacks were promised and I needed a full stomach to fully realize all the American Spirit that lies within me. At least I hoped to learn something other than I freckle like the dickens when exposed to too much sun. I actually already knew it and it doesn't even have to be the sun; a flashlight or bright lamp does the trick most of the time. I hope freckles are deemed sexy at some point in my lifetime. Dare to dream, right?

Those of my classmates who are from out of state (locals had the option of driving their own cars) had assembled at the appointed time and location and were awaiting the bus(es) when 7 o'clock came and went just like I did around the corner to the Subway (sandwich shop, not public transport) as they now serve breakfast. As the hour changed from 7 to 8 with still no bus, our fearless point of contact, Lindsay, made some phone calls and ascertained the buses were now en route, having been caught in traffic. As the hour slid toward 9, there were more calls and no bus, and the report became the buses had been caught behind a wreck on the interstate. More classmates left, Subway did a fairly brisk breakfast shift that morning, as did the quickie mart in the lobby of the beautiful art deco building at 1100 New York Avenue.

After several comments ranging from "Did they say New York Avenue or an avenue in New York?" and "were they behind a wreck or in a wreck?" the buses finally arrived at the ripe old time of 10:15. Wisely I chose to board the bus that did not appear to be powered by a wood-burning stove and off we went to learn of all things leadershippy from His Lincoln-ness.

After we had been driving for more than an adequate amount of time to have left the District of Columbia city/state limits, we received a phone call from one of the other points of contact. Someone on the wood-burning bus had called her and said their bus was, in fact, driving 30 mph with the flashers on as they were in the throes of a breakdown. When our fearless Lindsay asked our bus driver if he could contact his co-worker driving the breaking-down bus, he replied, "No." So, we texted one of the other passengers and had them call us from the seat behind their bus driver who stated matter-of-factly they were not about to breakdown.

When it was ascertained he did not know what he was talking about, our fearless Lindsay stated, "We must go and get our classmates. No EIG-er left behind", while American flag-clad gymnasts flipped behind her holding sparklers and grown men wept at her selfless Americanism. I may have overstated the last part, but she was impressive to say the least. And she was duly recognized by our fearless coach, Feli. There are many fearless people at the Partnership for Public Service, y'all.

After it was decided we would rescue them, we had to exit to turn around on the car-packed highway to get them. In moments of crisis I am very calm but also downright pedestrian in my grammar. My suggestion to "bust off across the median" was wisely ignored. I did that once while driving a truck. I was asleep at the time. It didn't end well.

Once we re-traced our steps, we found the driver of the wood-burning bus had not been truthful to their whereabouts. We then called the bus and through the magic of GPS found that not only had the bus driver been driving too slow, he had also taken the wrong exit and was in Virginia, not Maryland. Once we got there the bus driver was adamant nothing was wrong with his bus even as there was black smoke running up the back of said bus. As our comrades boarded our bus, he took off in his bus, very quickly I might add, shouting about his intended retirement. Whether he meant to retire that day or later was never fully explained.

Upon our return to the highway, we had driven another twenty minutes or so and I saw the exit for College Park. To those from the DC area, you know this means we were FAR, FAR away from Pennsylvania. I commented that we should just exit at the Ikea and have meatballs for lunch. Although many concurred, we trudged ever onward toward the Burg called Gettys.

We finally arrived and went straight to the buffet which was supposed to be the mid-point of the day. Nothing against the proprietors of General Pickett's Buffet, but what I did not need prior to heading out into the open fields to hear tales of leadership gone awry and poor communication in spite of the talent (on the Southern side) was meatloaf and mashed taters. I didn't want to be walking sleepily, stumbling toward an actual ledge atop Flattop or Tabletop, I forget which one.

Suffice it to say, I did learn a lot about leadership from the battle, but I learned much more from the trip getting there. Some of the lessons I learned from the wood-burning bus besides never get on a conveyance that has wooden parts unless it is the paneled side of an estate wagon are:

1. Never be too afraid to speak up in the face of poor decisions.

2. Never lie about your whereabouts.

3. Never leave your team behind. Everyone is important, especially those with granola bars and water.

4.   Never, under any circumstances, eat meatloaf on a walking tour.

5.   The Subway at 11th and New York Avenue in DC is open for breakfast and there isn't a line.

In the heat comes the unhappiness. August in California is hot like most everywhere else, except San Francisco. Even in August, it's cold there. "Crazy from the heat" is a saying from my childhood in the muggy, humid south. "Angry from the heat" is my updated assessment of The Dad.

When he's hot, nothing can pacify him, not even a tub of chocolate ice cream he always begs me to bring him. During the consumption of said ice cream, he is sedate. Immediately upon the last spoonful he is again angry at both the small portion and removal of the distraction.

When he's angry there's not much to write about as I am trying to entertain and maybe educate. I am not trying to have a written version of a reality show. We may parade crazy at a family reunion, but no one wants to hear the tales of woe attached to caring for an aging parent. At least not the unfunny stories and there seem to be more of those than not lately. I only want to share things worth sharing. I'll save my complaints for myself, my siblings, sometimes over dinner with friends or my accountability partner and my conversations with Jesus.

It is interesting to note, he has come to feel entitled to co-opt my time to run errands for him. For example, there is a regional consultant for my program who has an office on the campus where I live. About once a month or so, I meet with her for part of a day to go over my program and discuss upcoming changes, etc. Whenever I work with her, The Dad feels as if I am not "really working" and constantly calls my cell phone demanding I stop what I am doing and run an errand for him. If I ignore his calls, he will literally call every minute, sometimes 20-25 times in an hour, until I pick up. If I turn off my phone, I will possibly miss a real call from my staff, so that is not an option. When I acquiesce, and say I will run the errand, he will call me every 10 minutes to see if I have completed the errand and demand I bring him whatever he wants home at that moment, giving no regard to my work. When I bring up the fact I am at work, he tells me "talkin' ain't really work."

The most recent example involved a ceramic horse, if you can believe that. There was a vendor in the lobby of the canteen who was selling a variety of Asian-inspired items, one of them being a statue of a riderless horse, enrobed in the finery of the Chinese tradition. The artisan who created it had decided to paint it by dripping various shades of green and blue over the statue, giving little regard to the natural lines of the sculpture or the details that made it special. I gave it no more than a cursory glance as I made my way to the elevators.

During the meeting, I received a flurry of phone calls from The Dad. When I finally answered, he demanded I get $60 out of his savings account and buy the horse statue. I questioned why he wanted it and where he would place it, but he simply said, "Buy it!" I told him I would and told him I would bring it home with me at the end of the day.

After I bought it, he called me at least 15 times demanding to know when I was bringing it home; asking me if I could leave work and bring it "right now"? I decided to take my lunch break and took the horse home. When I brought it inside, he asked me if I liked it. Trying to be diplomatic, I said, "If you like it, that's all that matters."

He pressed me and said, "Do you like it or not?"

Again, I tried to be nice and said, "It doesn't matter what I like, it's your horse statue."

He looked at me, seemingly upset and said, "Answer the question. Do you like it?"

I said, truthfully, "It is not my taste, no."

With that, he told me he had bought it for me and he looked crestfallen and walked out of the room, leaving the horse next to the centerpiece of the dining room table.

Not completely sure how this had played out so oddly, I returned to work.

When I came home that evening, I asked the location of the horse as it no longer adorned the dining room table.

He replied, "Oh, it broke. I stood up to take it to my room, and I dropped it, so I threw it away."

I looked at the floor, realized he couldn't have cleaned it up as he cannot bend over due to this back and realized he had thrown the horse away because I didn't like it. I didn't know what to do and I felt excessively guilty and I really didn't know why.

The Dad has the uncanny ability to incite extreme guilt in others. It is definitely his superpower.

Thursday, August 29, 2013

Would Sherlock Holmes wear colored chinos?

Throughout my early childhood I enjoyed solving mysteries. My first partner in crime was Encyclopedia Brown, a 12-year-old as clever as I considered myself to be. After a few years, I widened my mystery solving circle to include the Hardy Boys, with the books and the short-lived TV show starring Shaun Cassidy, Mr. "Da Doo Ron Ron" himself. *Author's note, he is the son of Mama Partridge, Shirley Jones. His co-star was Parker Stevenson, possessor of the manliest feathered hair in TV history and ex-husband of one of my favorite stars, Kirstie Alley. I love Ms. Alley fat or thin; the same way I feel about Delta Burke, Sara Rue and Oprah.*

The original definition of the word clue was "a ball of thread". Therefore you "unravel" a mystery. A fact those of you who have read my southern mystery *A Gone Pecan* already knew. Those of you, who haven't bothered to buy my book, shame on you. You're the reason I'm destitute! Yes, I said destitute! Well, not really. I just like the ego boost of a book sale. I'm only human, y'all.

Those of you who are familiar with my life know The Dad crochets, so lately I have been on a roll; unraveling threads both literal and figurative. The figurative threads have been in relation to my father's sudden uptick in visits outside our home. Prior to the last few months, he would only leave the house to go to his doctor appointments as I refused to take him anymore; hoping it would help him explore the area where we live. All it did was have him retaliate by refusing to drive me to the airport when I have to travel. But it is a small price to pay to help him alleviate some of his stress about living "not in the South".

When he moved in with me I took over his finances as his financial savvy is on par with my small engine repair skills and, at his request, he must justify his "pocket money" each week. I'll share our most recent conversation.

> The Dad (TD): "I'm gonna need my pocket money for Wensdy. I've gotta go to the fruit market."
>
> Me: "The fruit market?"
>
> TD: You know…the…fairy market? Flea market? Fillin' market?"
>
> Me: "Fillin' market? Like a fillin' station?
>
> TD: Getting irritated, "No! You know that market at the hospital. It starts with an F. Frito market?
>
> Me: With more attitude than was probably warranted, "Do you mean the *farmer's* market?"
>
> TD: Yeah, that's it. Boy you sure are mean early in the mornin'."
>
> Me: "I'll ignore that. How much do you need?"
>
> TD: $20. Then I can get okry, tommy-toes and some snap beans."
>
> Me: "$20? Isn't that a bit much for veggies? How much do they cost?"
>
> TD: Well, it's $2 a pound for okry and I get two pounds. And it's $2 a pound for tommy-toes and I get about 3 pounds and then it's $2 a pound for snap beans and I get about 2 pounds of those. So that's $20, just like last week."
>
> Me: "That's actually less than $15. Where's your change from last week?"

TD: I spent it all. It costs $20."

Me: "So you spent $4 on ok*ra,* $6 on tom*a*toes and $4 on snap beans?"

TD: Yep."

Me: "Six plus four plus four is 14, not 20. So how many cookies did you buy?"

TD: Just one…um…I mean, none."

Me: "Really? So how much fried chicken did you buy?"

TD: Suddenly defensive, "None, Mr. Smart Guy. They didn't *have* fried chicken."

Me: "So you had pizza instead?"

TD: Yes. I mean, No!"

Me: "Uh, huh, let's look at the old blood sugar diary, shall we?"

TD: You should've been a detective, butt hole."

Me: "I agree, but figuring out your spending habits is like playing Trivial Pursuit with Mike Tyson. It doesn't take much effort."

TD: Why don't you go play in the traffic."

Me: "I love you, too, old man."

Tuesday, October 8, 2013

Have catheter, will remove it

The Dad and I celebrated our second anniversary last month. I can't believe it's been two years since he came plowing into my life and home with his noises, smells and various old man *accoutrement*.

It's an unhappy coincidence he was back in the hospital this week, just like this time last year. He has had four different outpatient procedures on his butt, if you must know. And the three re-surgeries (if that is a word) are due to his refusal to believe a doctor would know about post-surgery care. You know, because The Dad has four whole hours of college credit and the MD has a measly 16 years of schooling.

The biggest problem is that The Dad is a man of extremes. He is either not interested or all-in. There is no gray area for this one. He either wants a 32-pound steak or none. He wants a vat of ice cream as big as his recliner or none. He asked if I would bring him some gum as the medicine he takes makes his mouth taste 'funny'. I took him a double pack of Freedent, the gum preferred by denture wearers, and he chewed 32 pieces of gum in less than 12 hours.

When he called and asked for more and I questioned how one would decimate a pack of gum in such a small amount of time, he got mad, called me a "butt" and hung up on me. *Quelle surprise,* you say? Then you haven't been paying attention.

His vacation, which is what we normally call the time when a relative is housed in a state-run facility from which they aren't allowed to leave when the mood strikes them, was spent in the hospital for the past week. They are observing him and trying to figure out the cause of the infection at the surgery site. I personally think they are observing the only patient who removed their catheter with a crochet needle. Yes, you read that correctly.

I don't want to go into the details and I honestly don't believe what he tried to describe. All I know is he had the catheter when he came home and about an hour after I left him in his room, he walked into the den, handed me the catheter and reported he had removed it using his smallest crochet needle. I was too horrified to do anything but stare at the used catheter laying on the arm of my leather sofa.

So, I tattled to his care team about the self-removed catheter as well as his refusal to soak his wound every day for ten minutes. His solution to this advice was to not soak it for five days, then soak it for 60 minutes on the sixth day. He was actually surprised this didn't work.

I reported the behavior to his doctor and nurses so we all know the reasons behind the infection, but the nurses didn't want to believe a patient would ignore doctor's orders and then lie about it, so they're getting to spend some quality time with the "Wildebeest in the Hospital Gown", which is what he looks and sounds like when dozing. They're trying to figure out what the issue might be. I guess 'ornery' isn't a medical diagnosis.

He is unsurprisingly unhappy about being "locked up" and has reverted to creating prison stories concerning their attempts to "starve me" and "poke me to death". Although I will say when I snuck a chicken nugget happy meal past the nurses, he was the happiest boy on the floor, do you hear me? He almost hugged me. Almost. But he caught himself and instead shook my hand with more emotion than I expected seeing as how the nuggets only numbered four, not six.

He doesn't like visitors, he says, but what he really means is he doesn't like to ask anyone to visit. Fortunately, he is housed at the hospital where I work so I can see him more often than normal, although I try to limit my visits as he doesn't want to be awakened when slumbering and the clinical staff get nervous when they see me coming as my previous visits to the wards were when I was Acting Associate Director and we were in the midst of our accreditation review.

I have delivered puzzle books, electronic solitaire, peanuts, mystery novels and contraband Coke Zero. I have regaled him with tales of my birthday weekend to Hearst Castle and Carmel, where he was more impressed with the fact Clint Eastwood lives there than the pictures of William Randolph's gauche interiors or the designer duds I got for 70% off in the bargain basement of J. Alexander Khaki's. *Seriously, Mr. Hearst was Donald Trump before Donald Trump was Donald Trump. Everything was silk damasked, gold inlaid and ivory-carved to within an inch of its life. The roman pool was pretty but ridiculous. I mean, who wants to exit an overly tiled lagoon up a wet marble ladder?*

So, here we are two years later, and he is again in the hospital and if geriatrics tells us anything, he will only get worse. He has improved in his outlook, but it is only noticeable to me. He is still somewhat depressed just perkier about it (thank you, Zoloft). He is still afraid of leaving the house without me, but is still too proud to ask me to go with him; instead he demands. And I pretend I don't notice the false bravado and I don't see evidence of the scared man who is truly without his own home and uneasy about having to depend on the one child he has admitted he didn't treat very well.

As much as I complain, I have missed him this week and not just because I don't like making my own coffee in the morning. I miss someone waiting for me when I get home who is truly glad to see me and to talk, even if for a few minutes, over something as mundane as a funny video or a show about ancient aliens. I never thought I would actually miss the old grouch, but I do and the thought he might one day be gone is something I just can't process right now. I am teary-eyed as I type this and it as surprising to me as it would be to him.

Saturday, November 30, 2013

Black and White isn't just a fashionable color scheme

One of the after effects of a large meal like Thanksgiving is the propensity to discuss issues normally avoided by those not on the edge of a food coma. Tryptophan apparently causes neural mis-firings as well as sleepiness. It usually happens when someone discovers I am from the South, they immediately christen me as the "voice of my people" and begin the volley of questions. I haven't lived in the South for 11 years; apparently my accent is permanent. Of course, I do talk to my sister about every other day and the influence of her East Texas twang may be why figurative magnolias burst forth and surround the words I speak.

The conversational topic was racism. Quite naturally, they meant in the South. As I am used to this specificity, I broadened it to include, if we were forced to delve into the topic, racism everywhere. It seems odd to me there is racism at all. In this day and age, most everybody is bi-racial, even those who don't look like they are. Take me for example. To the untrained eye, I look whiter than most Canadians. In my extreme preppy clothes, I could even be mistaken for someone from Connectic-achusetts. Until I open my mouth, that is. Then people automatically put me on a plantation with Scarlett, Rhett and the lot.

No one would believe that there is Native American blood running through my veins. Right along with the redneck blood, should that ever be considered a race. My father's mother's mother was some sort of Native American, no one can remember, or prove, so no casino money for us. However, if you looked at some of my relatives on the Thompson side you see there is something there that's simply "not white". My Dad's brother, my Uncle JM, may he rest in peace, had the coloring and hair of our Native ancestors. He married my Aunt Barbara, who is Hispanic, so their children are very dark complexioned. I say that to say this, there are very few people who are "all white" so to be uptight about someone's race or nationality is silly. If you want to dislike them for their taste in clothing, music or mode of transport, be my guest.

I also find many non-Southern Americans, including members of the media, haven't updated their opinion about Mississippi since the 1960s. I find it truly sad to think much of the rest of the country still assumes there are lynchings and protests and systematic poor treatment of anyone black. Of course, these are the same people that kept *Two and a Half Men* on the air loooooooong after it stopped being funny, which was halfway through the first episode. If you like that show, I am also sad for you but in a much more judgmental fashion. I'm gonna pray for you, heathen.

What people need to realize is while there might be people in the South who do not like someone because of the color of their skin, it is more likely any actual hatred is related more to the color of their football jersey. Talk about throwing around some prejudice. If you want to see angry Southerners, just visit Facebook on college football Saturdays. It is brutal, y'all.

As I am one of the Southerners who left the South, it has fallen to me to try to explain the realities, having lived in "God's Country" from birth through the age of 32. I have lived in many different locales in the last 11 years including Alaska, Ohio, New England, Maryland, Virginia and the District of Columbia, and I have experienced stupidity and prejudice everywhere.

For example, Native Alaskans don't like anyone not from Alaska, including anyone who lives in Anchorage because "it's NOT Alaska". There's even a town called Unalaska, which is actually in Alaska, which doesn't make sense, but you try telling that to an Inuit. I dare you.

I can personally attest to blatant racism in Cleveland, OH; the tiny enclave of blue in one of the reddest states on the electoral map. You might think the blue is from Lake Erie, but you'd be wrong. It is the last bastion of Midwestern Democrats, mostly African-Americans and gays; I lived in the Theatre District when I lived there. Yes, you read that correctly.

Cleveland, while filled with great restaurants and plentiful shopping, smells like freshly mowed dog poop. Anyone who has ever pushed a lawn mower knows the smell; a subtle mix of heatstroke and indentured servitude. When I lived in Cleveland, there were areas of town I couldn't frequent, including the famed BBQ Place, Hot Sauce Williams. My assistant, Valerie told me she'd have to go get me the rib tip basket, which I allowed her to do but only on special occasions…like Wednesdays.

It was the same for her. She wouldn't have felt welcome should she try to have dinner in Little Italy which could have doubled as a break room for extras from *The Sopranos*, y'all. I was nervous, but the food was good.

I explained to my holiday companions, there are definitely Southerners who are racist, but they typically keep their mouth shut in public. And there are those whose dislike or distrust may run near, but still under, the surface. It's more an aversion to spending time with, rather than hatred of, any particular group of people. Southerners are ultimately too polite to outwardly display any negative emotion, not related to sporting events or alcohol consumption both pro and con.

I don't personally know anyone who is active in the KKK. It's not an actual club, like the Junior League. I mean, those who would have that much hate aren't ones who tend to actually possess event planning skills. They couldn't/ wouldn't have a bake sale or run a thrift shop. These are not the people you turn to when you need energetic assistance to implement an idea. Those who I know who might be racist to the extent they would take action are not actually capable of keeping their focus on anything longer than it takes to smoke a Marlboro Light or polish off a six-pack.

These people are theoretically powerless. They are not typically computer literate. I daresay they are barely literate. The Southerners I know are part of the literate South. The South of Faulkner, Williams, Welty and Grisham. The arts and letters of the south don't spell HATE. What they sometimes spell is not always fit to print but quite likely to amuse while tailgating, sitting in a deer stand or floating down the river. I have done all three with varying degrees of enthusiasm.

I said as much to my guests with my patented look which is a mixture of condescension and pity with a dash of Christian charity. I've been practicing. I did remind them this new generation, the Millenials, seemed poised to be the first post-racial society. They don't seem to be bothered by anything not displayed on their iPads or iPhones and even then, it's mostly met with duck lips and tongue wagging selfies. This latest trend lays squarely on the shoulders of Mr. Achy-Breaky Heart, father of Destiny Hope Cyrus. Yep, I did it. I called out Billy Ray. It's time to assign blame.

I just hope the Millenials remain otherwise occupied with Kimye and skinny jeans and don't ever feel compelled to actually listen to Uncle Bo Jimmy Jack and absorb the hatred he may be spouting in the privacy of his 1966 Chevy truck, up on blocks in the front yard. Lord help us all if someone that backward gets the skills to utilize an iAnything or figures out how Meetup works.

All we can do is pray hard and pass the Fritos, bean dip and everything from the left side of the Hardee's menu. We'll keep 'em so full of greasy protein if they ever get a mind to wreak havoc, the gout will keep them stationary. Gout hurts, y'all.

During this time, I was dipping my toe back into the dating pool that I had chosen to leave behind in 2004. I had come to conclusion based on my fundamentalist upbringing that I had to choose gay or God and I had chosen God.

At my non-denominational church in DC, I completed a Bible study that asked whether I was looking at my relationship with God through the lens of The Dad. It was epiphany that I was giving God the traits of The Dad. I thought God was capricious; sometimes generous, sometimes mean, sometimes supportive, sometimes antagonistic.

Once I realized these behaviors were inaccurately attributed to God, I was able to start unlearning the false narratives I had been taught that He hates anything. Being gay is not a sin, so God didn't hate me just because I existed. With this new realization, I began to research and study and really pursue my relationship with God.

Once I moved to California, I still wasn't ready to date, and I continued my pursuit of God, but by the time I was nearing the end of 2013, I thought I might be ready to see if I wanted to date.

I met a gentleman at a fundraiser for a charity, on whose board I served. Academy of Friends is a great organization which raises money to award grants for other organizations who provide services and support for those with HIV and AIDS.

This gentleman and I went on several dates and I really enjoyed his company. Knowing my sexual orientation had been theoretical to my family, as there had been only one person to meet and that had been in 1996, I wanted to give The Dad a heads-up in case I brought my friend around at some point. I had come out to my family in 1994, but never really broached the subject any further when my mother's response to my statement, "I'm gay" was "No, you're not." I had never really dated anyone, so my orientation was theoretical at best.

I approached the topic one evening after my date and said, "I just want you to know I have been dating a gentleman for a couple of weeks and he may be around at some point in the future."

The Dad responded, "Well, I guess that's alright, as long as you don't hold hands or kiss in front of me."

I said, "Are you giving me conditions for behavior in my own home?"

He said, "I'm the Dad. I make the rules."

I said, "You may be the Dad, but you made the rules when I was a child. I am 42 years old and you are living in my house." I have no plans to start making out with some dude in front of you, I assure you, but if I feel the need, I will. It's not your call."

"Why're you so upset? I said it was okay."

"No, you didn't. You're trying to tell me what I can and cannot do in my own home. I know you're not comfortable with it, so I never bring it up."

"You're gettin' mad over nothin'."

I said, "I don't think I am. You let Shontyl marry white trash without so much as batting an eyelash, but you're telling me I can't hold hands with someone I'm dating because it would make you uncomfortable."

"I can't do nothin' right with you, can I?"

"I tried to bring you into my personal life for just a glimpse, but that was a mistake I won't make again."

We just walked away from each other. Like always, we both felt bad. I gave him chocolate ice cream and he tried to take interest in the documentaries I watch on Netflix. I know I over-reacted, but it was unpleasant to see demonstrated what I was afraid might happen; that he truly wasn't okay with it, that his support was theoretical as my sexual orientation had, until now, been theoretical.

At the same time, I was trying to figure out what I wanted out of life and my career. Not getting the job in May had me second-guessing my career goal of becoming a healthcare executive. Did I really have what it takes to make it? Was I only fooling myself? Am I a great leader or is it that I want to be so badly I've convinced myself I am?

I was also thinking about what I would do with The Dad if I was to move. I have spent my adult life in an apartment. I only had a house in Palo Alto as it was part of the recruitment package for my position in Prosthetics.

As someone who grew up in rented homes, I was nervous to consider actually buying a home myself. It frightened me as my skills in the home cover interior design and cooking. And I knew I would need a house with The Dad and Lulu as many apartments do not allow pets.

All this was weighing on my mind. When you set up the premise of your blog as humorous, you can't depress your readership with your stories of woe or anger or pain. Perhaps if a life lesson is learned, it's one thing, but I didn't want to discuss the atmosphere in my home and truly I didn't really want to live in my home. I started spending a significant amount of time with friends or shopping or any other reason I could find to be out of the house.

This only made me feel guilty and made The Dad more depressed. It wasn't a good situation and I didn't know how to fix it. December was stressful and busy, and I couldn't bring myself to document what was happening. Between my job search, the litany of woe that was The Dad's daily laments, holidays and other associated stresses, I documented nothing other than an increase in the dosage of my Melatonin as my brain refused to turn off and let me sleep. My mind insisted on replaying every day in infinite detail; like the movie *Groundhog Day*, without the humor or maple syrup, but with about the same amount of *Jeopardy!*

When my sister left for home after Christmas, she reminded me she had warned me about The Dad, but more importantly, she chastised me for not writing more. Her exact words were, "I want to laugh and laugh. Write something!"

I promised to figure it out and low and behold an event unfolded.

Sunday, January 5, 2014

Are jumper cables made of licorice?

I realize expecting someone wearing cranberry chinos and a paisley button down, baking *brie en croute* to resolve your automotive dilemma is typically far-fetched but if you know me, you know I've got plenty of tricks up my color-coordinated sleeve.

I'm standing in the kitchen by the oven waiting for my brie to finish so I can drizzle raspberry preserves in preparation for the return of *Downton Abbey*. A fabulous British TV show is an excuse for fancy snacks, *n'est ce pas*? I was removing them from the oven when my father walks in and at the end of a string of profanities asks if Greg was in town. Greg, as you may remember, is one of the few of my friends and/or employees to rate a passing grade from my father. Granted The Dad likes most of my friends but prefers Greg based mostly on the fact he looks as if he is a Hell's Angel on his way to court when he's dressed for work.

Dustin's corner of the federal government is a well-dressed corner, people. I'm making the world more attractive one pocket square at a time. He is one of the nicest people I know but his size and girth are intimidating to say the least.

When I ask why, I am met with an exasperated, "Just find out if he's busy."

When I insist on knowing the reason to bother someone on a Sunday, The Dad says, "My truck won't crank. The batt-rys dead."

My response, "Well I can fix that" was met with a look similar to the one Lulu the dog has when she sees herself in the mirror: confusion followed by amusement.

I ignored the look and stated, "Give me a minute to drizzle the preserves and I'll get your jumper cables". He stared at me and asked what brie is.

My response was "Fancy cheese you don't like so put it down", as he tried to pretend he hadn't just burned his fingers trying to grab a piece before I could stop him.

I realize you may be skeptical of someone who owns as many pairs of colored chinos as I would have, at their disposal, the skills or tools to perform such a task. However, as we have discussed previously, I am a unique animal; one who didn't necessarily enjoy the absorption or demonstration of said knowledge.

A life spent in the boonies with cars of questionable dependability will very quickly familiarize you with the information on how to "jump off" a car, how to push a standard shift truck down a hill to get it going, how to convince someone 'bondo' and 'primer' are color options and prayer can sometimes work as an alternative fuel.

Once he saw I wasn't kidding about the jumper cables or the brie, he followed me outside and I proceeded to take control of the situation, gathering the necessary tools and assigning tasks. Like Vanilla Ice said, "Give me a problem; Yo, I'll solve it."

Yes, I am more than slightly embarrassed how quickly that reference came tip-tap-typing out of my fingers. Let's just pretend it didn't happen, shall we, and get back to the issue at hand. Focus!

When I told him to stop trying to push his truck out of the garage until I moved my car, he groused, "This is 'xactly why I wanted Greg. You're too bossy."

I replied, "I'm trying to fix this with the least amount of dirt and sweat. You're decrepit and I'm over-dressed. Humor the preppy, okay?"

Once we had situated the vehicles, excavated the jumper cables from the deep recesses of his "king cab" (along with contraband Mt. Dew bottles and Wendy's wrappers, which earned him a condescending head shake from me and my mother in heaven, I feel sure) we hooked up the cables, he cranked his truck and it awoke from its slumber. I did a small victory dance…in my head.

As he prepared to move his truck back into the garage, I suggested he go ahead and get gas tonight, so the battery would have time to get a little workout and he wouldn't have to fight traffic in the morning. He is scheduled to blatantly lie to several medical professionals tomorrow about his diet, glucose readings and bowel movements. In layman's terms he is going to the doctor.

When he returned from "gittin' gas", he walked past me to his bedroom.

I followed him and said, "You're welcome."

He laughed and said, "For what?"

"I fixed your truck, old man. While wearing chocolate suede wingtips."

"Hmpf. You think you're sumthin' else, dontcha?"

"Yes, yes I do."

"And why cain't you just say brown 'stead of choc-lit?"

"Chocolate is more descriptive; like saying raspberry instead of pink or eggnog instead of winter white."

"I know you think you're fancy, but it sounds to me like you're just hungry."

Touché, pater, touché.

I knew he was going to lie to the doctor, so I invited myself to come along. I decided to situate myself on his left, just a little bit behind as he cannot fully turn his head in either direction, so he wouldn't be able to see me shake or nod my head, signifying whether he was telling the truth.

His medical team began to ask him questions as follow-ups to his most recent surgery.

Dr., "Mr. Thompson, did you clean your wound like we discussed?"

The Dad, "Yeah."

I shook my head, No.

Dr., "Are you sure, Mr. Thompson? It was supposed to be soaked in the solution for 10 minutes per day for a week."

The Dad, "I know. I did it."

I shook my head again.

The Dad, trying to turn his head to see me, said, "What are you doin' back there?"

I replied, "Nothing. But I don't remember you soaking your wound every day for 10 minutes. You did it once, for about an hour. At least that's what you told me."

The Dad, "Yep. 60 minutes."

Dr., "Mr. Thompson, that is the reason it's not working. You can't add all the times together. You have to do it for 10 minutes each day for the treatment to work."

The Dad, "10 minutes times six is sixty minutes. What's the difference?"

When The Dad said, "Oh, I see. Y'all are gangin' up on me" everyone wordlessly looked at him. He continued, "You need to get out my face. You ain't talkin' down to me."

He stood up and turned to me and said, "You can go on back to work. I don't need you in here with me. I think I know what I do at home more than you do."

I protested, "But you're aren't telling them the truth, Dad. It's the reason you aren't healing like you should. You need to listen to them."

He looked at me and said, "If you're not gonna leave, I am" and he walked out the door.

I couldn't do anything but walk out behind him after thanking his medical team and apologizing for what had just happened.

The wound didn't get any better, I'm sure you are unsurprised to hear.

Monday, January 13, 2014

I did say I wanted everything to be thinner...

I'm sitting at the dining room table, eating breakfast and reading the news on my phone when my father walks up and stands beside me as if he is about to embrace me around the shoulders. I stay very still lest I wake what I am assuming is a sleep-walking redneck.

The Dad has never been one for demonstrations of emotion. I can remember a hug about three times: when I became a Christian, when my mother died and, well I can't remember the other one; I'm giving him the benefit of the doubt. "Men don't hug; men shake hands" is the motto of the Thompson men or so I've been told on numerous occasions.

He's looking down at me and he reaches to place his hand on my head as if he is going to tousle my hair, like on one of those commercials. As I learned in Alaska, when you become aware of a wild animal in your midst, remain very still and commence praying. So, I did. He lifts a few strands of my hair and says, "Boy, your hair sure is thinner since you got skinny!"

A Hallmark moment this is not.

Alas, he is correct. For whatever reason, one side effect of gastric bypass surgery is hair loss; not in clumps, mind you, but thinning. I have always had very thick hair. It wasn't something I liked as it wouldn't 'do right' when I entered the hallowed halls of high school and was desperate for awesome MTV hair. I tried to wrestle those tresses into a semblance of Flock of Seagulls' bangs, but it ended up more like Exploding Nest of Pigeon. Sponsored by AquaNet®, of course. It was just so big and, well, un-pretty, y'all; long before those TLC girls had that song that was so good in that *Glee* mash-up with that other song the sister thought about singing in *Dirty Dancing* but then didn't. Exactly three of you know what I'm talking about; please help the others.

However, my hair is not thinning like other men my age. It's still ample enough to cover my head in all its pumpkin-esque glory. I don't think I'm going to be bald; however, truth be told, my mother's father was careening towards a bald spot when he died in his mid-50s. I've been told bald traits come from the mother's side of the family. Everything else on my body is from The Dad's side: weird feet, short legs, no butt and a complexion the same shade of pink as a canned ham. Maybe I'll be able to keep my hair.

Of course, as I have mentioned, my father has been follicly-blessed similar to such Hair Hall of Famers as Johnny Cash, Conway Twitty and Slim Whitman. His hair used to be orange, then faded to a deep red. Mine is a boring brown he calls chicken doody. Well, my Mother used to call it that. My father's salty tongue referred to it as something I'll leave to the mists of time.

The Dad then proceeded to take his hat off and combs his fingers through his hair and says, "You need to have you a real haircut like mine."

I replied, "They've outlawed bear grease, Dan Tucker, but thanks for the tip."

I will say the hair products these days have gotten to be a bit much. During high school when I was attempting to grow out my bangs, we had things like hair spray or mousse or gel. You had either AquaNet ® or LA Looks ® or Dippity-Doo®. At least it's what they had at The Wal-Mart. Oh, who am I kidding, I coveted those who go to shop at The Wal-Mart. I had to deal with what they had at Hudson's Salvage Center, which is where we shopped when I was in high school in Mississippi. You buy your products, take them home and wipe the mud, dirt or smoke damage from the outside of the bottle and you were just like everybody else on the TV. Darn tootin'!

These days I've moved onto Bumble and Bumble's Sumotech Lo-Gloss Elastic Moulding Compound. It sounds like something that would have earned you honorable mention at a science fair. And it's only $27 for 1.5 ounces. I guess I'm paying for the added 'u' in moulding. From what I remember Dippity-Doo® was $1 for a 5-gallon bucket complete with neon purple application trowel. I could be wrong; my memory is hazy, not unlike an AquaNet® fog.

Saturday, January 25, 2014

Don't watch me, watch the road!

As my readers are among the most informed of the citizenry, you are no doubt familiar with the 10-and-2-rule for hand placement on a steering wheel, while driving. Left hand at 10 o'clock; right hand at 2 o'clock. I recently read where that has now been changed to 9-and-3 because of air bag deployment injuries.

As I try to complete all tasks in the optimal, efficient manner, I specifically watched where I placed my hands when behind the wheel of my snazzy Sonata. My rule, while it works for me, is not as succinct as 10 and 2; mine is left knee and 5. Not an easy thing to yell at someone navigating the Pennsylvania road system for the first time, in the dark. Not that I would do that. At least not again. All apologies to Christopher, my longsuffering best friend.

While my hand placement may not work for everyone, for me, it works quite well. I only need to have one hand on the wheel as I am a very good driver and not in the 'Dustin Hoffman in *Rain Man*' sort of way. I am skilled at navigating our nation's roadways with my right hand at 5 o'clock. I need, do you hear me, NEED to have my left hand free to perform any number of motions from gesturing (both Christian and not) to directing the imaginary orchestra playing through my synced Bluetooth iPhone situation of some sort, per the 11-year-old who sold me my car. The Dad, I've noticed, drives in a similar manner.

Outside of the conducting, there are other moments of necessary choreography such as snaps, claps, nose scratches, hair touch-ups and the like. Now I don't do any actual movements which would take my eyes off the road, no matter what others may say viciously behind my back (Will and Matt and, after last Thursday night, Chandra and Alice). Lies, I tell you!

In these times, it is sadly more common than I would like to see many of my fellow motorists driving while they do all manner of inappropriate things, like the young lady who was semi-successfully navigating Highway 101 beside us as several friends and I made our way into The City for dinner and a show (*Beach Blanket Babylon*). Like other multi-tasking trailblazers, this modern-day Sacajawea was attempting to flat-iron her hair and drive.

Don't get me wrong, her flat-ironing skills were not in question; she was *doing* her hair. Her ability to operate semi-heavy machinery (her Corolla was bigger than a bread box but only just) whilst hair-doing was not as strong. I daresay she is the intended audience for some of those ridiculous instructions you find on items such as "Do not use in the shower" on a blow-dryer or "Not to be eaten while seated on a toilet" which I have had to write on all food containers in my home. And speaking of toilets...

One of the downsides of a life history is a sense of familiarity that breeds not only contempt, but a casualness I find off-putting. Case in point, I was cooking last Saturday and after fending off an overly curious volunteer food taster, I realized my house was quiet; calm before the storm quiet. Having a 72-year old toddler at home, I know the need for oversight, so I wandered toward his bedroom, under the guise of dusting, to uncover the activity to which he was up. To my horror and regret, I found him seated on his throne, as it were. With the door open as wide as the great outdoors, and twice as fragrant. I swallowed all my sarcasm and disgust and said, "I'm just...going to...um... yeah" as I shut the door. Moving very slowly and specifically as to not agitate the molecules in the immediate vicinity, I metaphorically fled back to the kitchen. I would have been more verbose but withholding so much judgment takes a lot of effort, y'all.

Monday, February 3, 2014

What's Spanish for Loud, Annoying Boy?

As we have previously discussed, I have a passing familiarity with several languages, including French, Redneck, Spanish and American Sign. You name a language and odds are I can say 'chicken' and 'bathroom' with relative accuracy.

If you didn't know, during my first two years of high school my mother managed a motel called the Nicholson House in Paris, TX. While it had a storied past, we were told, by 1984 it was a jewel past its prime, like Meg Ryan or a '78 Chrysler Cordoba.

Although I was embarrassed and never admitted to anyone we lived there, it was often fun. We had a swimming pool, Centipede in the game room, a Chinese Buffet for the restaurant and, on weekends, I got to work the switchboard, which was something like Lily Tomlin one-ringy-dingying; there were cords you plugged into the board and then dialed the number for the people. You could even eavesdrop. Of course, I would never do that. I have no interest in secrets, dear reader. The fact the Rivercrest High newspaper staff named me "Most Likely to Tell a Secret" is coincidental at best.

One of the unique traits of this particular establishment was half of the rooms were kitchenettes you could rent by the week or month. This was particularly popular with construction crews who were attempting to gentrify the less fabulous parts of Paris proper.

My sophomore year at Rivercrest High, I was taking beginner's Spanish, but due to a car wreck or something our new teacher, Senora Franklin, had been unavailable and for the first couple of months of school we had a substitute teacher. I got more useable Spanish from Morgan Freeman on The Electric Company. Numbers and colors were mastered; verb tenses, not so much. However, by Homecoming or so, Senora Franklin was no longer *ausente* (which is Spanish for absent). Upon her arrival, in gauchos, knee boots and a side ponytail, we dove head first into conjugation which sounded dirty but wasn't. The first phrase I learned, unsurprisingly, was *'calle te!'*, which means 'shut up'. I learned this the second day of class. Verbosity is my middle name; my last name is not control. All apologies to Janet Jackson.

One evening, my mother and I were sitting in our apartment either reading or watching *Knight Rider,* when we heard a commotion in the parking lot. My father had redesigned six motel rooms into a semblance of an apartment. The best part was five bathrooms; the worst was my parent's closet as well as mine, were turned into a hallway to access the other bedrooms. Off the living room, there was a large balcony overlooking the property, so my mother and I decided to investigate from there. My Uncle Bill (my father's sister's husband) was the night watchman but he was hard of hearing and sometimes asleep.

The sight greeting us was a large tenant of Hispanic origin who was being accosted by one of our more senior residents, Miss Lucille. Her 92 ½ year-old, bottle-of-wine-a-day vision had led her to believe her fellow resident, wearing only khaki shorts and himself inebriated, was nude and she felt compelled to use her umbrella as the device to drive home her stance that this was, in fact, unacceptable.

My mother, ever the problem solver, decided to intervene and I wanted to watch, but like Bette Midler, only from a distance. My siblings were more entranced by David Hasslehoff. In retrospect, anything was better than *Knight Rider*. In context, most things paled in comparison. And don't act like you didn't watch, too. My family did not singlehandedly keep that show in the Top 10 in the ratings.

My mother, upon rebuffing Miss Lucille and redirecting her to her room with the promise of a free egg roll the next day at lunch, attempted to ask the gentleman if he was part of the road crew, managed by a man named Juan.

My mother said, "Do you work with Juan?"

The Man said, "*Que?*"

I interrupted "Moootherrrr. He is oooobviously Hispanic and of course I must interpret."

My mother, "I need someone who knows more than colors and numbers, sweetie, but thank you."

Me, "Mooootherrrr. You know I am almost semi-fluent, right? Riiiight?"

My mother, "Okay, honey. How do I ask him if he works for Juan?"

Me (out loud), "Hmmm. Well *trabajar* means 'to work' so *yo trabajo* would be I work so *tu trabaja* would be you work so it's a question so say (suddenly very loudly) *TU TRABAJA CON JUAN*." Which if shown phonetically and I was being honest probably sounded more like TEW TRAYBAHO COWAN WAWUN.

She looks at me with the look (you know the look) but turns to him and attempts to repeat the phrase and I interrupt her to remind her to trill her Rs, so it's more authentic. Then I try to demonstrate how to trill one's Rs. From the balcony. At top volume. It's a testament to her good nature, I was allowed to reach puberty.

Of course, the entire time The Man was swaying gently and repeating "*Que? Que?*"

Realizing neither of us had a knack for languages, my mother decided to mime "work". All the while, I am screaming "TEW TRAYBAHO COWAN WAWUN!" My mother starts to mime a shoveling motion and he stops swaying to watch her. She keeps repeating, very loudly (it must be genetic), "DO YOU WORK WITH JUAN?" followed by air-shoveling. At one point she pats the ground and, misunderstanding, the man lay down in the parking lot and smiled a triumphant smile.

Fortunately, my screaming quasi-Spanish phrases had roused the aforementioned Juan who came out to collect his employee. Feeling quite proud of my bilinguality, I said, "See? I toooold you I could speak Spanish, moootherrrrr." She replied, "Yes you did, sweetie. Good job."

And I always thought it was my father who was always "working her nerves", as my sister would say.

Tuesday, February 25, 2014

Is Wibbly an Action Verb?

Recently The Dad had a doctor's appointment and during the time he was there, the conversation turned to his exercise regimen, or lack thereof. The doctor asked if he used the treadmill we have in the den. The Dad has used it on occasion. I have used it on a regular basis. Well, not in the traditional definition of regular. Let's just say it's more often than Halley's Comet, but just barely.

Quite naturally, the next question was, "How fast do you walk?" The Dad replied, quite proudly, "Two miles an hour!" When his doctor laughed, The Dad was somewhat embarrassed but mercifully didn't say anything. When he was telling me the story, he admitted, "I really only walk one mile an hour; I said two just trying to look better." I laughed but realized laziness must be genetic.

It's ironic I moved to one of the most active, exercise-y locations in America and pretty much stopped exercising, other than walking and even then, typically in conjunction with shopping; thrift, outlet or otherwise. I don't run, even when chased. I have gained 10 pounds in the last year simply through being sedentary and I know it's not healthy but for some reason it doesn't seem to matter.

Did you know all you have to do is eat 100 extra calories a day to gain 1 pound a month? It's true; rude, but true. I could exercise, but it's more mature than I care to be at this juncture. And I'm not so much worried about a few pounds; I am worried about being woefully out of shape. Unless you count wibbly as a shape; although wibbly connotes movement. It sounds as if it is a kinetic fat; a fat of motion. My fat is inert. I don't mean that I don't move. I mean my fat doesn't move when I do. I may be out of shape, but this is the skinniest I have been since I was wrenched from my mother's womb in the wilds of Northeast Louisiana. I didn't want to come out; I had felt the humidity and was having none of it. But Christian folks just don't talk about these things, so I'll stop.

As you know, by the 75% off candy at Walgreen's, Valentine's Day is in the very recent past. Love was in the air and boy could you smell it. Coupled with the plane tickets I have recently purchased for trips to Massachusetts and Scotland for the weddings of two close friends, this has me thinking about love and other four-letter words. If that tasted bitter, don't blame me; that's just your Starbucks Extra Dark Roast, salted with the tears of singles. And I'm not talking about the terrible Matt Dillon movie.

I'm kidding, of course, but just barely. It's not so much I'm unhappy single. I am very happy most of the time. It's just I wonder if there really is someone out there for everybody and if so, why is my person *ausente*. Is it because I'm bi-lingual?

And my reaction is usually one of awe at how so many people have found their forever person. Forever love requires a level of vulnerability I'm unsure I can handle. If you're agreeing to be with someone for better or for worse, does it include them seeing you without your Spanx? I don't even want to see me without my Spanx. I don't think anyone's preference is to be eternally saddled with a partner who, when undressed, looks like an uncooked turkey and/or a Shar Pei puppy.

I'm not being self-deprecating; I'm simply being more honest than I probably should considering at least 51 people are going to read this. Smell that? That is bitterness, y'all.

Everyone, except The Dad, knows Sunday night is the Academy Awards. I serve on the Board of Directors for Academy of Friends (Academyoffriends.org) and we are hosting an Oscar-related Gala in San Francisco. Our Gala theme is 'Return to the Emerald City', celebrating the 75th anniversary of *The Wizard of Oz*. Our Gala color is emerald green. The fact we have a designated color is proof positive I have found the right place to volunteer. Can I get a 90's-era 'what, what'?

I have known about this Gala since I attended last year, and I thought I might have a date for this year's event. And although I have had a couple of sorta-kinda-not-really-dates in 2014, I am currently bereft of escort. However, there is an upside. As Production Chair, I will spend much of the evening in my fabulous tux and a Janet Jackson *Rhythm Nation* headset zipping about ensuring nothing is awry. And it suits me fine.

I have always been more comfortable in any given situation when I have a purpose. And maybe, just maybe my forever love will be there. But I'm not going to go looking; that would simply reek of desperation. I'm going to stand near the entrance, in the spotlight, wearing my new silver reflective loafers from the clearance section of Cole Haan and let him find me. I figure, if he can handle those silver shoes, he can handle the rest.

Wednesday, March 5, 2014

Would the Village People Steal Snacks?

Exercise is universally acknowledged as dangerous; at least in my house. However, I was never aware consuming low-calorie snacks could cause pain and suffering outside of the unpleasant results of eating sugar-free cookies. The snack in question was a 90-calorie bag of Naked Popcorn. Naked in the sense of no artificial flavors; had there been a more scandalous connotation it should have been titled Nekkid Popcorn. There's difference, at least according to Lewis Grizzard.

I have a drawer in my desk at work which holds my snacks. I keep it filled with healthy snacks for all manner of emergencies like late nights, the 2:00 pm energy boost or bribes, depending on the situation. Prior to yesterday, the only danger with this system was the drawer (bottom left) if not closed firmly will sometimes slide open again, like the bedroom window of an unrepentant teen after curfew. I've hit this drawer with my chair and my leg but never with the full force of my body in motion.

I was sitting in my office, talking to my management trainee James and we were discussing some of the ins and outs of leadership and managing people. It should come as no surprise I was telling a story and a good story always needs a snack. I had just retrieved a bag of popcorn from the drawer and opened it, while closing the drawer with my foot, which I felt was the most efficient use of time and energy, just like those dudes from Toyota. I'm *living* the lean journey, people. After a minute or so, I rose to demonstrate something appropriately leadershippy, not realizing the desk drawer hadn't really closed, like those mattress stores that are "Going out of Business" for the better part of a decade.

As you probably know, the desk is inanimate and stationary, and my body isn't, so it should come as no surprise when I encountered the drawer, I tripped over the drawer, slicing my leg, but fortuitously not my suit pants, and fell.

While trying to catch myself, I only propelled my rather large head into the wall, landing with a thud, followed by an interjection that would most certainly not have been exclaimed in the *Schoolhouse Rocks* tune.

You remember interjections show excitement (Wow) or emotion (Hey)? My interjection had several more letters and was followed by an appropriate number of exclamation points.

One of the measures of success, I feel, is the size of one's office. This hadn't occurred to me until I looked up, all prostrate, rumpled and embarrassed, to see at least a baker's dozen people crowded around me. There was the aforementioned James, our student worker, two of our clinicians, one of my managers, two nurses, a cop, a cowboy, a construction worker and an Indian. I could be wrong about the last three; I was woozy from the blow to my head.

I was picked up from the pool of blood on the floor, mostly from the leg; not so much from the head. They rushed me to the emergency room (it's convenient to work in a hospital), triaged me, interviewed me and took me to a room where I examined and then photographed my open wound. James, great guy that he is, accompanied me to the ER and we sort of just stared at the wound. No matter what sort of guy you are, you are drawn by morbid curiosity to gross things.

Cut to a fantastic medical team treating the wound, not laughing directly in my face when I explained how it happened and sewing me back together with 17 stitches in my right shin. You know I'm going to try to be #1 in anything I do. Simply fall? That is sooooo not me. I will fall with prejudice. I will have an open wound, with possible infection. I will not take painkillers. Ok, maybe my head got hit a little too hard. I'm strong-hearted (per the book of baby names), but not foolish. Pain pills, please.

When I got home The Dad had graciously fixed dinner (Pork Chops, Home Fries and Fried Cabbage; the last two items containing at least a pound of bacon between them) and I ate like I hadn't had my afternoon snack or dinner, which I hadn't. Can I tell you I needed some comfort food? It was sooooo gooooood, I cleaned my plate, which is something I haven't done since 2008.

The Dad was so pleased he didn't even make fun of me for falling; at least not to my face. I wonder what he'll say at breakfast? But a more important point to ponder, what happened to my popcorn?

Tuesday, April 15, 2014

Surely Doris Day Knew

Rock Hudson died the day I turned 15. Seeing as how I really didn't know who he was, it didn't make that much of an impression at first. What I came to find, via *The Enquirer* at the 7-11 next door to the motel my mother managed, was he was an old movie star and he had died of AIDS. This being a time before we bought our first VCR out of the trunk of some guy's car at the Paris, Texas Wal-Mart, I was not familiar with his movies I would later come to love, like *Pillow Talk* or *That Touch of Mink*. As far as I was concerned, he was simply an old-looking dude who kissed Linda Evans in the barn on *Dynasty* and she had FREAKED OUT when he died. And not just because of the hay he left in her hair.

Living just to the left of the buckle of the Bible Belt, I didn't have much information about AIDS other than it was bad, it had killed him, and he got it because he was gay. Thanks to the Reagan White House and the rest of the country's seemingly mutual agreement to not educate people about this disease, I thought you could get AIDS just by being gay; like black people and Sickle Cell Anemia. What did I know? I was newly 15 and encased in a family so far inside our Southern Baptist bubble that to this day, my parents have never actually had "the talk" with me.

I suffered in silence terrified I would get AIDS and die based solely on the fact that I knew I was gay, but in title only. I hadn't kissed or even held hands with anyone. My family is Southern Baptist; conservative but not as uptight as those Duggar people from *19 Kids and Counting*. The most daring thing I did in 1985 was watch 14 of the 17 hours of LiveAid, including both of Phil Collins' performances. Remember, he sang in London and then flew across the Atlantic and sang in Philadelphia? On the same day? Partying like a rock star, receding hairline and all, y'all. Kanye wishes he had that much swagger.

Quite honestly, I never knew, and could not find, much information about AIDS until I did a research paper in my Senior Honors English class in 1988. I asked my teacher to "assign" me homosexuality for my topic so I could find out something about it, me; whatever, I didn't care. In an era before the internet, our only research option was the local library. And can you guess how many books there were on homosexuality in the Tylertown High School Library? Exactly zero, unless you count Encyclopedia Brittanica, which I did.

I was *forced* to do this "stupid paper, on this crazy topic by that darn Miss Boyd; what's *her* problem" and finally realized I really wasn't the only oddball in the world; just the only oddball in Mississippi. And God bless her ahead-of-the-curve thinking, she gave me a 96 instead of 100 because "you spent too much time focusing on equating homosexuality with AIDS and that's not accurate". I will forever be thankful for Nola Faye Boyd, God rest her beautiful soul. I wonder if she knew she was the first person I came out to, unofficially or not?

The reason this is even on my mind was an article in *Vanity Fair* magazine about the remake of Larry Kramer's *The Normal Heart*. The author asked why this piece? Why now? And as a member of the Board of Directors of Academy of Friends and living about 26 feet from San Francisco, I can tell you the average person simply doesn't think the AIDS is a real threat anymore. They seem to think drugs and treatments have essentially solved the problem of HIV and AIDS, and that's not accurate.

My organization raises money to award grants to groups who provide services or education for those living with HIV/

AIDS in the Bay Area and this year's beneficiaries are doing wonderful work: PAWS (Pets Are Wonderful Support), Project Open Hand (meals for the critically ill), Shanti (HIV/AIDS support and counseling), LGBTQ Connection (Napa Valley Youth Program), Maitri (residential end of life care) and Clinica Esperanza (HIV/AIDS services for the Latino Community). And I'm glad I can do my part to support a community I've never fully embraced. Outside of the way I dress, I've never been very good at being gay and never been overtly interested or supportive of gays in general.

I've been reading Philip Yancey's book *What's So Amazing About Grace* and I've realized I haven't offered much grace to my fellow LGBTQers and I am not proud of it. At various points in my life, I was, for all practical purposes, a homophobic homosexual. I was taught to hate gays and since I was gay, I was taught to hate myself; at home, at church, at school, at work. And as someone who tried to do everything to the best of my ability, I was hating on an Olympic level, y'all.

"Love the sinner, hate the sin" is a phrase used by some self-professed Christians professing to "not *hate any*body". And I believe it's true. The opposite of love isn't hate; it is indifference. The Church has been, at best, indifferent toward the LGBTQ community. I'd like to believe they have love for all, but I wonder if some say the beginning of that phrase solely to allow them to say the ending. Why can't we just say, "Love the sinner" and then actually do it; we're all sinners. As a Christian I try to do that and many of my friends and family do, too. Not all Christians are hateful; at least true Christians.

Let's just all agree to try to love each other in this broken world, okay? I'll be the first one to try.

Sunday, June 8, 2014

My own Phenomenal Woman

Maya Angelou recently passed away and in her honor, many have been quoting from her poem, "Phenomenal Woman". This got me to thinking about my mother who has been gone for 14 years. For the first couple of years I simply did not celebrate Mother's Day because it hurt too much. A few years ago, someone said those whose mothers have gone should use the day to celebrate their legacy. And I did but I never shared. I know it's late, and she wouldn't like it one bit, but I thought I'd offer a list of the things my mother taught me through both word and deed.

1. **Show love every day.** Every time she would see me, she'd say, "Hi, guy!" and then give me a hug or a peck on the cheek. Even if she had just hugged me 10 minutes before.

2. **Be kind to yourself.** Whenever I would get mad at myself for making a mistake or call myself a name, she'd always tell me, "Don't you talk about my child like that!"

3. **Never downplay someone's feelings.** Once, when I was having a very dramatic response to something in seventh grade (because everything is dramatic in

junior high) and had decided, and then apparently announced, I would run away, she listened and quite seriously asked "Where would you find the love you have here?" Having no answer, and quite frankly no concrete plans, I stayed.

4. **Always learn.** She stopped at every roadside marker to see what historical significance it held. My brother and sister were none too keen on learning new things in the wilds of America, but I was always game.

5. **Try new things.** One of the added bonuses of these side trips was any time we explored an area, we got to explore the food. Her favorite phrase was, "Let's get a little snack".

6. **Enjoy the now.** On road trips, I would sit in the middle of the back seat and lean my elbows on the console and she and I would talk the entire trip, whether it was 13 minutes to town or 13 hours to my grandmother's. My brother and sister usually slept, but I was up and I was chatty.

7. **Find a hobby you love**. She loved to read and passed that love onto her children. It was a common sight to find all five of my family sitting and reading at home.

8. **Make time for yourself**. She would give anything for those she loved, and I always wondered how she kept giving and giving without tiring. But I

distinctly remember when she needed to be by herself, she made it happen. There was more than one occasion growing up where my siblings and I would find ourselves ushered toward the door with the admonition to "go play", hearing the door lock behind us. When we protested the heat, or wondered what to do if we became thirsty, she'd point at the water hose and blow us a kiss. We became adept at creating games, some as simple as the "it's your fault we're out here" game. I always lost.

9. **Don't wait to be asked; offer your help**. We never had much money but what we had she tithed and shared. Her mini-van was the unofficial youth and children's church bus for Mesa Baptist and free taxi for many others. She was never put off by someone's appearance, reputation or circumstances. She simply loved.

10. **Work for what you want**. In 4th grade I wanted a calculator. Yes, I know I was a nerd from way back. She told me I needed to earn the money, so I took over her Amway route for a week. She told me to make sure I told my customers why I was trying to earn money. It worked. I earned enough money for the calculator in one day.

11. **Support should be felt, not just heard.** Even though I was chubby most of my life, my mother never made me feel bad about it. She would point out healthy choices on the menu at restaurants and

taught me to eat as healthy as possible in the South, but she never shamed me.

12. **Be proud of yourself**. No matter our financial situation, our house was always well-decorated and spotless, and we were always appropriately dressed; ironed and starched, if necessary. She taught us "You are who you are, regardless of your circumstances. Always be proud."

13. **Don't be late**. The only time you shouldn't arrive early is to a dinner party, unless you are assisting the hostess. She usually was assisting.

14. **Take time for God**. She started each morning with a cup of coffee and her Bible. She knew she needed God every day.

15. **Those who can should**. She taught me to pay it forward and help those you can with whatever you have. That's why I started the Thompson Scholarship for Student Leaders at Southwest Mississippi Community College in her honor. If anyone would like to donate, please contact the Office of Institutional Advancement, 1100 College Drive, Summit, MS 39666.

My mother was a fierce protector, prayer warrior, child advocate, creator of macramé things and lover of God, books, coffee and chocolate, in that order. Every time I watch *Steel Magnolias*, Sally Field's character, M'Lynn, reminds me of my mother, Catherine Waynette Thornton Thompson.

Sometimes it makes me smile and laugh, sometimes it hurts my heart, but it always makes me miss her and gives me the hope to carry on her legacy, often with mixed results. But every day I try because if you're still here, you've still got work to do.

The one thing The Dad has never recovered from is the death of my mother. He went from someone so closed off it seemed he had no feelings to someone who cried regularly, almost overnight. I say overnight when truth be told I hadn't had much interaction with him outside of holiday meals and the occasional "talk to your father" hand-off during my mother's weekly phone calls.

On their first anniversary, about three months after she died, I called to see how he was and to give he and I a chance to reminisce about the happy memories. He couldn't handle the conversation and was upset at me for reminding him she was gone and that it was their anniversary. He couldn't deal with it.

Here we are 14 years later, and the hurt seems to be fresh; the feelings right at the surface. It takes little to make him cry. When he does cry, he gets mad at himself for crying and lashes out at whomever is there; me, if I am around, himself if I am not. When he lashes out it is to cause pain because he says things he cannot possibly believe.

He once told me his hurt is far worse as her husband than ours, as her children, could be. He's mad at God for taking her away from him. He sees her death as some form of punishment, for what sin he will not say. When I question his thinking, he looks at me, startled at even the idea that he may be wrong.

When I ask him why he thinks God works like that, he can't say. He spent 30 years sitting, living, eating, talking to and sleeping beside one of the strongest Christians and he doesn't seem to have learned anything about the character of Christ. Did he listen when she prayed out loud?

I question him to help him heal; he feels it is disrespectful. When I counter with "You know what Waynette would say…" he quickly changes the subject and I acquiesce as you can't perform therapy on family members if they are unwilling, especially if you aren't a therapist.

He won't talk to anyone at the VA. He started talking to a psychologist and was actually starting to improve, in my opinion, when he told me a story one night, as usual, apropos of nothing. He asked if I had ever heard of soldiers (in Vietnam) who collected the ears of Vietnamese they had killed during the night. Having worked at the VA for 16 years, I had and answered affirmatively.

He continued his story stating he had done that on numerous occasions. Not knowing what to say, I simply sat there, surprised, not only by what he was saying but also by the fact he was saying anything. He had never revealed anything about his service other than he was in the Army at the same time as Elvis and had enjoyed Germany, right alongside him. He had also shared that his parents had spent all the money he had sent home to save to buy a car when he finished his military time. His lifelong generosity explained in a one-comment remembrance. When I asked him why they spent his money, he said when he asked them they stated, "We needed it." Giving is his way of showing love and I now knew why.

My silence concerned him, and he asked, "Are you ashamed of me for doing that?"

I said, "No. You were doing a job you were trained to do. It was a different time in a difficult situation. There's no need to be ashamed."

He looked at me, surprised, and said, "You don't hate me?"

Just as surprised, I said, "Why would I hate you? You were doing what you thought was the right thing at the time. Of course, I don't hate you."

He just sat and looked at me, seemingly unable to comprehend what I was saying, but he said nothing else.

I stood and hugged him, saying, "I love you, Old Man" and quickly left the room, having breached protocol.

About a week or so later, he announced he was stopping his visits to the "shrink". When I asked why and mentioned he had been making great progress and seemed to be less unhappy and depressed, he replied, "She makes me remember stuff I want to forget. I don't care how pretty she is. I cain't go no more."

When he stopped, he began to regress quickly. He had dredged up many memories and he didn't know how to deal with it and did not want my, or anyone else's, assistance. Trying to help only made it worse as he reminded me I had started "all this" or he accused me of "looking down on (him), like you're better'n me."

One question he always asked, and I never answered was, "Why'd God take your mama and not me?" There is no answer; I don't know. No one knows. My mother died of complications from sarcoidosis, a lung condition, even though she never smoked. Ironically, The Dad smoked for almost 60 years and has emphysema and has had eight (by his count) heart attacks, but is still chugging (slowly) along.

My sister and my mother's sisters have never forgiven him for not quitting smoking when my mother was so ill and couldn't breathe. He got upset when he stopped smoking several years later, and no one congratulated him.

It was one of the requirements I placed before he moved in. I'm glad he stopped when he did, but it begs the question, if he loved her as much as he says he did, and does, why didn't he stop then? Why now? It's the main reason my sister does not communicate with him outside of holidays. I can't really blame her. I just don't bring it up.

It's a conversation that goes unspoken each time he decides to ask why my sister doesn't call except on his birthday and Father's Day or any holiday when she is not visiting me. He complains incessantly that no one calls him on the phone; however, as soon as someone does he immediately gets antsy and tries to figure out how to hang up as quickly as possible. He doesn't really want to talk, he just wants to be remembered.

My refrain for the longest time was, "If you want someone to call you, don't spend the entire time when they do call, complaining about the fact they never call. It's literally the reason they don't call and it's inaccurate because they called you. Surely you know this?"

It's never what he wants to hear. He wants deference and a respect for his position as The Dad. It's how we always behaved growing up; I assume it was how my mother was with him. I don't remember.

Now that I often feel like the parent, it has shifted the dynamic of our relationship and I am still determined to honor my father as much as I can, but it can be difficult. I guess I've never stopped trying to earn his acceptance, even when I, mostly, have it. Old habits die hard.

I want him to have a good life in his later years. Life has not been fair to him. He grew up in poverty with selfish parents and worked himself into the ground to provide for us. He was absolutely screwed over by Chevron when he hurt his back offshore and when he got his settlement check. He was also underpaid by worker's compensation while he was waiting for the trial and the settlement. His monthly Social Security check is lower than it should be based on his earnings, or at least this is his monthly refrain. He remains bitter and obsessed with money. Absolutely obsessed with it as he equates money with self-worth.

I agree with his lament that he shouldn't have to rely on family for his housing in his old age but what you can't change, you must stand but he seems content to wallow in self-pity. If you wonder from which parent I inherited my flair for drama, it is The Dad for sure. "Life's a bitch and then you die" is his favorite saying. He repeats it almost daily, sometimes hourly and it's hard to take the repetition and complete lack of interest in how this affects those around him.

If I try to focus on the good, he'll improve his attitude somewhat but typically it's only changed for the length of that particular conversation, or during a really great meal. Otherwise he seems to thrive on anger and woe, in equal measure.

But the reality is, no matter what happens to you, you should get over it and move on. You can't expect life to always be fair. If I let everything bad that's happened to me keep me down in the dumps, I would never have a good day. But he chooses to stay in the same head space and to wallow and it's not up to me to fix him. I tried.

A job as stressful as mine requires a time to recharge, refresh and reboot, especially if you are an extroverted introvert like me. I seem to be extroverted and can perform with a moment's notice, but in true introvert fashion, people tire me, and I have to recharge, or I am not functional. It became impossible to do so at home and it kept me on edge.

When I applied for, and was a finalist for, Assistant Medical Center Director at the San Diego VA, I struggled with what to say to him. I knew I couldn't tackle an executive position with so much negativity at home. Home should be your haven, your place to unwind and my home was in no way a good environment.

I knew what I had to do but I didn't want to be mean. I was at a loss.

When I went to my final interview in San Diego, I thought it went well. They called my references; it seemed like a done deal. I knew I had to talk to him. My mentor received a phone call and told me he thought the job was mine. I was about to have my life changed and I needed to make sure it was successful.

I asked him to leave. I didn't come out and say those words. What I said was, "If I get this position in San Diego, I am moving there alone."

He looked at me and said, "So, you're kicking me out?"

I said, "I am not kicking you out. I am simply letting you know that I cannot take on the responsibilities of an executive position with nowhere to recharge. I need a stress-free home life and I do not have that."

"I stress you out? How?"

"We have been over this, many times in the last three years. You are negative, you are depressed, you refuse to get help. I need to be able to come home and unwind and I can't because you won't let me."

"You never said that to me."

"I have been saying it almost daily since you got here. I cook for you every day to try to help you get healthier as it will make you feel better. I try to keep your blood sugar down because high blood sugar makes you tired, makes your neuropathy worse, impacts your vision. I tricked you into seeing a shrink because you can get better, but you don't want to."

"So, you're making me homeless?"

"No."

"Yes, you are."

"I didn't say you had to leave tomorrow. I haven't even gotten the job yet. I just wanted you to know what I was planning so you could figure out where you want to live."

"Well I hope you don't get the job."

"What? Thanks a lot."

"If you don't get it I don't have to leave."

"I'm going to get one eventually. Don't you think I have the potential to be an executive?"

"I don't see why you want me to leave. I can just stay here with you."

"That is not an option. You can go to Alabama with Aunt Louise or back to Louisiana with Aunt Gladys. You have plenty of time. Even if they call me tomorrow, I wouldn't move until probably September. It's the government; things don't always move quickly."

"Oh, no. If you're kicking me out, I'll leave first thing."

"You don't have to do that. Don't overreact."

"I'm not overreacting. My son is kicking me out of his house and making me homeless."

"Don't do this. Don't leave mad. You have plenty of time. There is no hurry. We will figure this out."

He just looked at me and walked away. By the time I came home the following afternoon after work, he had his truck packed and he left. His parting words to me were, "I can't believe I'm homeless. But you did it to me, so I'll get out of your hair and go back to Gladys's. I hope you get what you want out of life."

"Thank you. You know I love you, right? Call me when you get there so I'll know you're safe."

He looked at me sideways and smiled a quick smile and said, "Bye, butt wipe."

"I love you, too, Old Man."

Thursday, June 19, 2014

He is departing, with recliner and dog

Unlike Diana Vreeland, I was unable to arrange to be born in Paris. I was born in Lake Providence, Louisiana, literally on the banks of the Mississippi River; a fitting start to a gypsy life lived on the periphery. And when I say gypsy, I mean in relation to constant movement as opposed to the wearing of head scarves and bangle jewelry. Just like in Cher's memorable hit, there are additionally both tramps and thieves in my extended family. The original words said,

"Gypsies and white trash" and I've got some of them too. I'm not saying who; I'm just saying.

We moved on the average of once every 18 months throughout my formative years, but always in the same general vicinity. I call it Ark-La-Homa-Tex-Ippi. Y'all would call it the boonies; some of my readers call it home. In my leadership video on YouTube ("Funniest Leadership Speech Ever"), I define the boonies as "a place so far outside the city limits even animals question your presence". And it's true. The animal that is me questioned, mostly to myself, the constant movement. Whether we were running from or toward something, we were making good time.

From birth through high school graduation at 17, my family lived in 19 houses in 10 towns in five states. Combining college and graduate school, I spent seven years at three schools, all mercifully in Mississippi. If you're doing the math, I had two junior years and that is a whole different story. I will tell you my Native American name was "pick-a-major-already".

Since I began working for the Department of Veterans Affairs, I have lived in 15 houses in 12 cities in 11 states. All of them decorated to within an inch of their lives. That's a lot of throw pillows.

And I wonder is wanderlust innate or learned? My mother lived in the same house from the age of two until she married, and The Dad's family stayed in the same general vicinity most of his life. It seems we were the inaugural gypsies. My siblings and I have mirrored this behavior to a degree, but with cuter outfits.

My sister has moved several times, but nothing outside of the norm. My brother is in the Air Force, so he and his family move often, but it was a requirement of his commitment. I have moved many times to get where I wanted to be in my career. Fortunately, I have nothing living in my house except me; no pets, no plants, no children, no spouse. In that order.

I recently asked The Dad why we moved so much, and he insisted it was always for a better job and I have no reason to think he's hiding something, although moving with a gooseneck trailer in the middle of the night, from Oklahoma to Louisiana, bears questioning. We only did it once to my recollection, so I guess I believe him. About that, I mean. I don't believe him about many things, however, because he has only a passing familiarity with the truth.

It's not so much he tells lies on a consistent basis; it's more he's told the same lies so often he really doesn't remember they're untrue. And I understand it to a point. I used to lie so much about my family's financial situations, I forget when I now tell the truth people don't believe me.

And the only reason I'm even talking about this is The Dad is moving on again. He is returning to Louisiana to live with his sister, the sainted Aunt Gladys, she of the peanut butter cake fame. He has decided there is "too much town" out here in the land of the heathen and he wants to go back where they have trees and things.

The fact "town never stops" from San Francisco to San Jose bothers him. I did drive him out to where the trees and cows live but the fact that it took 45 minutes and I wouldn't let him get a hot dog at the Sonic by the Tractor Supply Store, did not bolster my case. I argued the fact there was both a Sonic and a Tractor Supply Store, but he countered with "fine, we can live in this parking lot, then." So, you see I had no choice.

I am unaccustomed to living in a parking lot and have no desire to get outside of my comfort zone by being, well, outside. If I could get one of these tech nerds out here to figure a way to get me to work, shopping and church through a series of air-conditioned tubes, I'd be good to go.

Just as I've been unleashed into the blogosphere, I am unleashing The Dad on metropolitan Shreveport/Bossier City. He'll live at the end of a red dirt road, off a gravel road, off the main road in Bethany, Louisiana (which I am assured is on the map), but he must enter the city limits for doctor's appointments at the VA and the occasional trip to the casino buffets or Piccadilly.

So, gird your loins, folks, he's a-coming…with recliner and dog.

What I shared in the blog was true; he constantly complained about "town doesn't stop" but he never said he wanted to leave. At that point, I really didn't know what else to do. I felt I was making the best decision for me and my career.

I felt I had honored my father as a good son should, but I also felt I needed to focus on me, so I could have the life I wanted and had worked so hard to achieve and the one I know my mother and he wanted for me. I had finally gotten past feeling like I was being selfish when I focused on my well-being; not giving everything I had to other people.

I did not get the position in San Diego; however, I was selected as Assistant Healthcare System Director in Long Beach, California, and started the position on January 25,

2015. I do not regret the decision I made, although I do regret causing The Dad any pain. We were back on our normal speaking terms within two weeks of his returning to Louisiana. I guess a good biscuit with red-eye gravy and a homemade peanut butter cake (my Aunt Gladys's signature dishes) can soothe even the most injured of feelings.

*Author's Note: While I was editing the book,
I had a post-Dad moment of insight.*

Monday, September 4, 2017

An Open Apology to The Dad

Throughout my childhood and even into adulthood, there were preferences The Dad had that I found annoying or ridiculous. It sometimes seemed he was trying his best to be difficult with the specificity of his demands. Requests such as extra ice in his tea, pockets on all his shirts, the eternal search for biscuits "as good as your mama's" and irrational cravings for Zagnut candy bars, which I didn't even realize they still manufactured.

Now that I am sneaking up on 47 like I'm a ninja, I understand what he was talking about. Over the last year, I have noticed that I order extra ice in my tea because it's usually not cold enough. Iced tea should mean just that; iced. I have never ordered lukewarm tea. I don't think anyone has other than Amy Farrah Fowler in her inaugural appearance in *Big Bang Theory*, and, if memory serves, she asked for "tepid water". God doesn't even like lukewarm things, like that Bible verse tells us so our preference is, at least, religious in nature.

I also celebrate when I find French-cuff dress shirts or polos with a pocket. Now, I don't store crochet needles, reading glasses and false teeth in my shirt pocket like The Dad does, but I do like to have a place to put my phone or writing implement when I need to use both hands. You'd be surprised how often you need to use both hands. At least I was surprised. I also place my glasses there when I am outside and forced to wear my prescription sunglasses because my pupils are too large and my eye color too light according to my eye doctor. I don't want to be "blind when (you're) old, Dustin" so I adhere to her suggestion of sunglasses when outdoors. I really do wish someone would hurry up and invent tinted, air-conditioned tubes for transporting people to and from important places like the bakery or TJ Maxx.

The Dad also distrusts automatic withdrawals for bill payment and depositing checks via cell phone. I'm okay with automatic withdrawals as I have only been burned once in 20 years with a double-charge, but I do not like the depositing check via phone. I received a large check recently and went to the bank to deposit it in person. The teller asked if the ATM wasn't working. When I told her it was fine, I just felt more secure depositing it in person, she looked at me with that mixture of condescension and pity, not unlike the look you give people who can't operate a revolving door. I wanted to protest her attitude but realized that would only confirm my "old man-ness" to her and I was already behind schedule for my trip to Starbucks and the thrift store, because it was Saturday and that's what I do on Saturdays.

I will never find a biscuit as delicious as my mother's but I, too, find myself ordering them when available and enjoying the treat much less than I should because they don't measure up. I should simply be happy I found a biscuit in the land of the gluten-free, vegan hippie bakers.

I don't crave Zagnuts, but I do crave Oh, Henry candy bars and they are just as difficult to locate, although I have found a cute little boutique candy store which sells both and I treat us to one every three or four months. Mine, I start eating on the way home; his I mail in his 'happy box' as soon as I have procured four or five books I think he might like to justify mailing something other than a candy bar. A happy box from Uncle Dusty is one of the perks of being related to me. Constant reading and word puzzles is what has kept him sharp and ornery, so it's good for him but not so great for the dynamic duo of my brother and sister-in-law, who have been housing him for the last year. Their crowns will be large in Heaven, which I hope is a comfort to them.

The last thing I noticed is something which might surprise people. My father and I are both introverts. I am an extroverted introvert; he is simply an introvert. I have no problem talking to people but as I've gotten older, it tires me much more quickly and I find myself, like him, with the overwhelming desire to be left alone (except my boyfriend Ben and/or my sister) but still privy to all information concerning available activities or outings should I decide I want to participate. It's an odd thing to try to explain. Suffice it to say, I get it now.

So, I apologize, Old Man. I thought you were just old and crazy when I was younger. Now I realize you were simply requesting things you felt made sense because they made sense to you. Now that I am older, I am right there with you; closer to becoming an Actual Odis than I care to ponder, much less admit. To say you are crazy would be to acknowledge I have crazy tendencies and we are not getting into that discussion right now. An Almost Odis, I shall remain, if for no other reason than my wardrobe.

I know The Dad's golden years are not what he imagined and not just in relation to my mother's death. He has every right to be angry that he has much less than he should to show for years of back-breaking work. He is retired, unwillingly, due to his injuries and the many times he has been treated poorly by everyone from his selfish parents to a faceless bureaucracy has kept his anger real, his wounds fresh.

As we are a family of meager means, I have nothing in the way of inheritance coming should The Dad not outlive me. However, from him I have inherited intangible things worth more than money: a fiery, but mostly controlled, Irish temper, which fuels my passion; the mindset of generosity; artistic ability; the clear, high singing voice of a good ol' gospel tenor; a flair for the dramatic and the ability to make people laugh. Whether I have learned from his example or seen him as a cautionary tale to be heeded, he has irreparably impacted my life and his life is inextricably linked with mine. Regardless of my level of Odis, I am who I am because of him and the woman he has loved for more than 50 years.

I still call him every weekend. Sometimes he's complaining, sometimes he's laughing with a joke or a story to tell, but I relish the fact he is there for me to call and I can hear him say, one more time, "Joe's Pool Hall, Eight Ball speaking."